D0437326

The

Good Jobs
Strategy

How the Smartest Companies
Invest in Employees to Lower
Costs and Boost Profits

ZEYNEP TON

MIT SLOAN SCHOOL OF MANAGEMENT

New Harvest
Houghton Mifflin Harcourt
BOSTON   NEW YORK

For information about permission to reproduce selections from this book,
write to Permissions, Houghton Mifflin Harcourt Publishing Company,
215 Park Avenue South, New York, New York 10003.

www.hmhco.com

Library of Congress Cataloging-in-Publication Data
Ton, Zeynep.
The good jobs strategy : how the smartest companies invest in employees to lower costs and
boost profits / Zeynep Ton, MIT Sloan School of Management.
pages cm
ISBN 978-0-544-11444-9 (hardback)
1. Job creation — United States. 2. Manpower policy — United States.
3. Quality of work life — United States. I. Title.
HD5724.T63 2014
658.3'01 — dc23   2013032234

Book design by Brian Moore
Figures by Mapping Specialists Ltd

Printed in the United States of America
DOC 10 9 8 7 6 5 4 3

The names and identifying characteristics of some of the individuals featured
throughout this book have been changed to protect their privacy.

To my husband, Carlos, and to my children,
Ali, Hakan, Ela, and Kerem

Contents

Introduction

THERE ARE DIFFERENT ways to make money, I tell my MBA students on the first day of the class I teach on operations for service industries. You can certainly succeed at the expense of your employees by offering bad jobs — jobs that pay low wages, provide scant benefits and erratic work schedules, and are designed in a way that makes it hard for employees to perform well or find meaning and dignity in their work. You can even succeed at the expense of your customers; for example, by offering shoddy service. People may not enjoy buying from you, but plenty of them will do it anyway if you keep prices low enough.

In service industries, succeeding at the expense of employees and at the expense of customers often go together. If employees can't do their work properly, they can't provide good customer service. That's why our experiences with restaurants, airlines, hotels, hospitals, call centers, and retail stores are often disappointing, frustrating, and needlessly time-consuming.

Many people in the business world assume that bad jobs are necessary to keep costs down and prices low. But I give this approach a name — the *bad jobs strategy* — to emphasize that it is not a necessity, it is a choice.

There are companies in business today that have made a different choice, which I call the *good jobs strategy*. These companies provide jobs with decent pay, decent benefits, and stable work schedules. But more than that, these companies design jobs so that their employees can perform well and find meaning and dignity in their work. These companies — despite spending much more on labor than their competitors do in order to have a well-paid, well-trained, well-motivated workforce — enjoy great success. Some are even spending all that extra money on labor *while competing to offer the lowest prices* — and they pull it off with excellent profits and growth.

At this point in the class, I tell my students that if they end up founding or leading a business, they will be able to choose *how* that business makes money. They can choose a "low cost at any cost" approach, but they cannot say they had no other choice. And finally, I tell them that if instead they choose the good jobs strategy, they had better take a lot of operations courses — like the one they're in — because operations is what makes the good jobs strategy possible.

They laugh, but they soon discover that I am not kidding. And that is what *The Good Jobs Strategy* is about — how companies can use operations to deliver good jobs to employees, strong returns to investors, and low prices and good service to customers all at the same time.

The good jobs strategy is not just a book title, it is a concrete strategy. It combines investment in people — much more investment than normal — with a set of operational decisions related to (a) how many products and services a company will offer, (b) the balance of job standardization and employee empowerment, (c) the allocation of work among employees, and (d) staffing levels and how employees will engage in continuous improvement. I did not invent this strategy. It is not the product of academic speculation. I observed it in a group of highly successful companies. I wanted to know how these companies managed to do very well and keep their prices low without making life miserable for employees and frustrating for customers.

This book tells what I found. Chapter 1 describes what the bad jobs strategy and the good jobs strategy look like when you're working in them and highlights the possibility and benefits of pursuing the good jobs strategy even in low-cost retail. Chapter 2 explains why operations and investment in people are the key ingredients of the good jobs strategy. Chapter 3 shows how poor operations is more of an Achilles' heel than most retailers realize and is a natural result of trying too hard to control labor costs. This chapter introduces what I call the "vicious cycle of retail." In chapter 4, we meet the four "model retailers" that are the core of this book — companies that follow the good jobs strategy, offering good jobs, low prices, and excellent customer service, and generating great financial results all at the same time. Rather than being stuck in the vicious cycle, these companies are benefiting from what I call the "virtuous cycle of retail."

Chapters 5 through 8 are the practical heart of the book. They discuss in detail the four operational choices that transform the investment in people into high performance. In addition to the benefits just listed — good jobs, low prices, good service, and strong financial performance — two further strategic benefits of the good jobs strategy are shown in chapter 9. In chapter 10, we look at how companies can stick with the good jobs strategy even when circumstances are pushing them hard the other way.

Although the strategy I will describe has been very successful, it is neither quick nor easy. In fact, it is complex and has to be carried out carefully, forcefully, continuously, and in the face of many obstacles. In return, it not only allows for better day-to-day and year-to-year performance, but it also allows companies to seize strategic opportunities by adapting to changing circumstances more quickly than other companies can manage.

The good jobs strategy can be seen at work in a variety of contexts, but in this book I focus on low-cost retail for three reasons. First, retail is where millions of people work. Walmart, the eight-hundred-pound gorilla of low-cost retail, is the world's largest private employer, with more than 1.3 million employees in the United States alone. Second, low-cost retail jobs are notorious for their low pay, minimal benefits, unstable schedules, and lack of meaning and dignity — the epitome of "bad jobs" as I define the term. Third, of the people who believe that offering good jobs is possible, most do not believe it is possible to do so in such industries as low-cost retail. If the good jobs strategy is possible in low-cost retail, then it is possible pretty much anywhere.

Although the context of this book is retail, the good jobs strategy allows many other types of companies to use operations to provide good jobs for employees, high quality of goods and services at low prices for customers, and strong financial returns for investors. The examples include airlines, restaurants, hotels, call centers, distribution centers, and manufacturers.

I wrote this book for managers, executives, and entrepreneurs who want to offer good jobs but don't think they can because controlling costs is so important to their business. You will see that offering good jobs can in fact reduce costs and increase profits as long as it is combined with operational excellence. If you want to offer good jobs and low prices at the same time, operational excellence is not optional, it is mandatory.

I also wrote this book for people who believe that offering good jobs may be good for individuals and for society, but that business decisions should be made solely to maximize profits. You will see that the companies that follow the good jobs strategy don't do it just to be altruistic. They have found it to be the best and most sustainable way to provide superior returns to their investors in the long term.

The good jobs strategy is a long-term investment in your employees with the expectation that those well-paid, well-trained, well-motivated employees will generate even more than they cost. What makes them worth more than they cost is operational excellence. The companies examined closely in this book have all found this strategy to work. Many more companies should join them.

CHAPTER 1

An Unnecessary Sacrifice

GROWING UP IN Turkey, I envisioned the United States as a place where anyone who worked hard could do well. For ten years, my experience in the States showed me how right I was. My hard work took me from an undergraduate volleyball scholarship to a professorship in operations, a good job that paid me well and gave me a chance to feel pride in my work.

When I began conducting research on retail stores — and, more important, *in* retail stores — I was in for a shock. I began to meet people — a lot of people — who worked every bit as hard as I ever had, but were not making it. Their work life did not give them dignity or satisfaction, much less enough money to make ends meet or enough stability to have a sane family life. They had bad jobs.

The people I met through my research were not just people who were unwilling to look for a better job or who wouldn't be able to handle one even if they got it. Nor were they just high school dropouts. In fact, more than a third of working adults with bad jobs have at least some college education or have a degree.[1]

Why do these people accept bad jobs? Many of them have been laid off or have had to close their own businesses. They can't find anything better, because there simply aren't enough good jobs to go around.

Take Janet, for example. She had her own small video rental business, but it wasn't making enough money. In 2005, she had to close it down. Luckily — or so it seemed — she became a sales associate in the electronics section of a large retail chain. Even better, it was a full-time job. Her job included making sure everything in her section was properly shelved and priced correctly. Her starting wage was only $8.20 per hour. While Janet's managers recognized her hard work and promoted her several times, her raises were miniscule.

By 2012, Janet was a customer service manager in charge of dozens of employees at the front end of the store, including cart pushers, cashiers, greeters, and employees working in the money centers, in which customers could cash checks, make wire transfers, and buy prepaid debit cards. She was also responsible for solving customer service problems at the checkout, such as pricing errors or credit cards that didn't go through. On top of all that, she frequently had to solve equipment problems — or at least try to. "Like the other day," she said, "the money order machine went down at the money center. I had to crawl around on the floor and get on tech support from National Cash Register and sit there and tinker with the money order machine. Unplugging the cable and plugging it back in as he was directing me from the phone until I got the money order machine back up and working."

Janet is a problem solver who manages dozens of employees and lots of different equipment, yet after all her merit-based raises she still earns only $11.60 per hour. Supposedly she works full-time, but in fact she's often scheduled for fewer than forty hours a week, so she never really knows how much money she will make.

Nor does she know *when* she'll be working. Every week, her hours are scheduled on different days and at different times. One day she could be scheduled from 2:00 p.m. to 11:00 p.m. and the next from 10:30 a.m. to 7:00 p.m. Some days her work ends around 9:00 p.m., yet she's scheduled to arrive at 5:00 a.m. the next morning, leaving her only eight hours to drive home, eat dinner, try to sleep, get ready for work the next morning, and then drive in. "My life is always in turmoil because you can't sleep," she said. "You can't just go to sleep on cue." Sometimes she reports to work without having slept at all.

Janet is in her fifties, and both her work — with all its lifting and crawling — and her schedule can be tough on her health. She has health insurance that covers her and her son, but she can't afford to get sick. Even though her insurance premium is only $70 per month, her deductible is a whopping $3,500. That's a fortune for someone whose yearly income is around $22,000. The last time she had an infection in a lymph gland, the bill came to $998, which had to be paid out of pocket. She's now paying it off at $20 a month. Her doctor recommended a simple surgery, but she can't afford it; that would have to be out of pocket, too. Plus, missing work for the surgery would get her written up. Sick days at this retail chain — even hospitalized sick days — do not count as excused absences.

And so, after seven years and several promotions, Janet can still barely make ends meet. "I need a second job, but the way they schedule me, every time I get a second job, I can't hold on to it."

Despite all this, Janet maintains her strong work ethic. She tries to do a good job and serve her customers well. But even there, she often fails and feels helpless. Complaining about the long lines at the cash registers at her store, she said, "Customers are angry at the under-poverty-level workers standing there in front of them ringing them up, at the under-poverty-level customer service manager . . . They stay in line so long that their ice is melting. Many of them walk off and leave full baskets." It's Janet's job to manage those checkout lines, but she can't make them any shorter because she doesn't have enough cashiers. Other workers in the store are trained to run a cash register, and Janet can page them if the lines get too long. But that doesn't mean they'll come. Sometimes they ignore the page, and Janet knows why. They're under pressure to finish their own shelving tasks. If they help her — that is, if they come and help the customers — they'll fall behind in their own work and end up in trouble.

The Bad Jobs Problem

Retail, where Janet works, is an industry with a lot of bad jobs. In 2011, the median hourly wage for the nearly 15 million retail workers in the

United States was $10.88, 34 percent lower than the median wage for all U.S. workers. Salespeople and cashiers, who made up most of the retail worker population and were the two largest occupations in the United States, made even less: $10.10 and $9.05, respectively. So a typical salesperson working forty hours a week would make $21,008 a year, below the poverty threshold for a family of four.[2] And, as we saw with Janet, there is no guarantee that a so-called full-time employee is working a forty-hour week, since most retailers consider anyone working more than thirty hours a full-timer.

For the part-timers who make up around 40 percent of the retail workforce, the situation is even worse. Their hourly wages are about 35 percent lower than those of their full-time coworkers,[3] they often do not receive health benefits, and they are scheduled too few hours to earn a living.

The pay in retail is so low that many employees rely on public assistance. In 2004, researchers estimated that Walmart employees in California were receiving over $85 million in public assistance annually.[4] A 2013 study by the Democratic staff of the U.S. House Committee on Education and the Workforce estimated that an average Walmart employee in Wisconsin received $3,015 to $5,815 in public assistance annually.[5] These are people with real jobs.

In addition, as we saw with Janet, millions of retail employees have irregular and often unpredictable work schedules. Retail chains try to match staffing levels to customer traffic as precisely as they can, so they schedule their employees only a week or two in advance. Even those schedules can change during the week, depending on customer traffic.[6] Employees are often asked to work short shifts (three to four hours) and to be on call.[7] Changing shifts on such short notice can make it difficult, if not impossible, for workers to meet family commitments, to hold second jobs, and to arrange for child care. It can also wreak havoc on increasingly fragile family budgets — how can you budget when you never know what your income is going to be? Of course, this practice also makes it difficult for employees to go to school or to hunt for a job — so much for the bad job being a steppingstone to a better one. And forget about establishing family routines, taking your children to visit their grandparents, or spending a Saturday or Sunday at the beach.

Apart from all this, retail employees are rarely given the necessary training, the proper equipment, or enough time to do their jobs well. Their jobs are designed in a way that almost guarantees they will fail. And like Janet and her cashiers, fail they do.

You might think most retail employees are high school or college kids who are not fully supporting themselves or families. In fact, most people who work in retail are like Janet. This *is* their livelihood. This is how they support their families. In 2011, the median age of U.S. retail workers was thirty-eight, only slightly lower than the median age of all U.S. workers, which was forty-two. Only 23 percent of retail workers were between the ages of sixteen and twenty-four. Women make up slightly more than half the retail workforce;[8] many of them are the sole or primary source of income for their families. And, according to the Bureau of Labor Statistics, nearly 30 percent of part-timers would rather work full-time; they just can't find the work.

This is not just an American phenomenon. The *Independent,* a British newspaper, reported that in the United Kingdom only one in seven people working at supermarkets earned a living wage in 2012.[9] Nor is it only a retail phenomenon. Almost a quarter of all American working adults between the ages of twenty-five and sixty-four have jobs that do not pay enough to support a family.[10] You encounter these people whenever you eat out at a restaurant, stay in a hotel, pick up your children from day care, or visit someone in a nursing home. You talk to them when you have to call about an insurance claim or discover why your Internet connection went dead.

And bad jobs are not going away. For many people, they are what the future holds in store. The Bureau of Labor Statistics estimates that most of the occupations with the largest employment growth during the next seven years will be low-wage occupations such as cashier, restaurant worker, customer service representative, and day care worker. According to the Economic Policy Institute, nearly 30 percent of all U.S. workers by 2020 are expected to hold jobs that pay below-poverty-level wages.

A Logical Trade-off?

If you're concerned but relieved because it's not your problem — not so fast! The prevalence and growth of bad jobs is not just a problem for the workers and their families, or for taxpayers who are unhappy about subsidizing companies whose employees require public assistance. Bad jobs are a serious business issue.

We learned decades ago that capable and committed employees are crucial for delivering good performance in all operating environments — from factories to service businesses such as hotels, restaurants, hospitals, and retail stores. In their book *The Service Profit Chain* James Heskett, W. Earl Sasser Jr., and Leonard Schlesinger argue that satisfied employees provide good customer service, which then drives customer loyalty, which, in turn, drives sales and profits.

So how can it be that a lot of companies offer such bad jobs? Wouldn't they want to make their employees more satisfied in order to bolster sales and profits?

Here's why they don't. It is widely believed in the business world that investment in employees is a great idea when companies sell differentiated products or compete on the basis of service. Four Seasons Hotels can afford to provide good jobs because customers are willing to pay high prices for the beautiful decor, attractive amenities, and excellent customer service. Similarly, the Container Store, a successful chain selling storage and organization products — from clothes hangers to shoe racks to cutlery trays — can afford to provide good jobs because customers are willing to pay a premium for the selection of products and the knowledgeable salespeople who help them organize their homes or offices. But in industries such as low-cost retail, where companies sell standardized products and customers are (supposedly) willing to sacrifice good service for low prices, the link between satisfied employees, good service, and good profits (supposedly) breaks down.

In the world of low-cost retail, where the profit margins are razor-thin, what matters most to management is keeping expenses as low as possible. Since labor is such a big expense and personal service isn't really what keeps customers happy, these companies seek to keep labor costs as low as possible. Hence the belief that offering good jobs is a luxury that low-cost retailers cannot afford. This is the argument for bad jobs in retail, and similar arguments can be found in other service industries.

It can be a persuasive argument, especially when you hear it from a company that has been a success story for fifty years and is now the world's largest. Walmart is both famous and infamous for its determination and ability to keep labor costs to a minimum. Store managers at Walmart are under constant pressure to reduce labor costs. The pressure is so high that they often staff their stores with too few employees to get everything done. Some managers even resort to unethical practices such as paying their employees for fewer hours than they actually work. In December 2008, the company said it would pay at least $352 million to settle lawsuits claiming that employees worked off the clock.[11]

Walmart's choice to operate this way forces the whole industry in the same direction. Competitors often react to Walmart defensively by reducing their own costs, which — as they see it — means reducing labor costs. Two independent studies found that when a new Walmart opens in an area, retail wages in that area fall.[12]

When Walmart executives are asked about the bad jobs they provide, they often give an answer that goes something like this: "We need to run a really *efficient* operation because customers come to us for *low prices*." And it's not only Walmart executives who suggest that bad jobs are necessary for low prices. People who follow Walmart closely — analysts, journalists, academics, and even critics — often acknowledge that improving jobs would mean either that Walmart would make less money or that customers would have to pay more.

But they are wrong. The assumed trade-off between low prices and good jobs is a fallacy. There is, in fact, a good jobs strategy, even in low-cost retail, that combines high investment in employees with a set of operational decisions that deliver value to employees, customers, and investors.

A Great Job *Where?*

Patty began working at QuikTrip, a large retail chain, when she was nineteen years old, right out of high school. Her starting wage was low, like Janet's. She had planned to work there while attending a technical college, but after two years, she realized that QuikTrip was "more than just a job." It was a great career. So she stayed. And like Janet, Patty got several promotions. But unlike Janet, Patty has a *good job*.

Remember that, after seven years and several promotions, Janet was still making only about $22,000 a year. After seven years with QuikTrip, Patty was making almost triple that. And when I interviewed her in October 2010, she was making more than $70,000 a year. Patty also has affordable healthcare, enjoys a stable schedule, and finds dignity and satisfaction in her work. "I've always loved people," she said, "and that's what this company is in business for. Helping people and giving them great service."

Patty's job allows her to have a fulfilling life. "You were asking what makes me excited about going to work every day," she said. "It's knowing that you're going to be able to attend your kids' activities at school. You're going to be able to take care of your kids, and knowing that the company that you work for is growing each day. And you don't have to worry about, Am I going to get laid off tomorrow? or, Where's the next meal coming from? There is no other company that will pay you your regular wage, a customer service bonus, a profit bonus, and even an attendance bonus. You go to work, you do your job, you're excited, and you know everything's pretty much taken care of. QuikTrip has never let me down."

From Patty's description of her job, you would think she is a saleswoman at a high-end department store helping customers find designer clothes while a pianist plays in the background. Or perhaps she is a manager at a medical supply store helping people find the right wheelchair or a coffee cup they can hold with a hand weakened by a stroke. You would think that QuikTrip must compete on personalized customer service, not on low prices and a fast checkout line. How else could they pay Patty so well? How else could they give her so much leeway for her family life?

But QuikTrip is a large chain of convenience stores with gas stations. Yes, one of those places we often associate with dark interiors and strange smells. Patty's work involves managing about fourteen employees as well as working the cash register, changing the coffee filters, putting product on the shelves, and cleaning the bathrooms. But that's not how Patty and the dozens of other QuikTrip employees I met see their jobs. They see themselves doing something worthwhile, doing it well, and getting paid and treated well for it.

QuikTrip has appeared on *Fortune* magazine's list of the top one hundred companies to work for for eleven straight years. Think about that — a convenience store chain that sells gasoline and merchandise at lower prices than other convenience stores is consistently voted one of the best places to work.

It's not just the employees who love QuikTrip. Customers love it, too. Ask anyone who lives in Tulsa or Atlanta or any city that has QuikTrip stores and they will tell you that QuikTrip has low prices *and* excellent customer service. What does customer service look like in this setting? Patty is friendly and knows all the regular customers, but she doesn't spend much time chatting and helping them choose the right donut. Instead, she focuses on putting the right product onto the right shelf at the right time with the right price tag. She and her crew are vigilant about keeping the store clean, including the bathrooms — *especially* the bathrooms. They make sure everyone has a quick trip through the checkout line. Those are the elements of customer service that distinguish QuikTrip. And the customers keep coming back. That's why the company's sales per square foot are 50 percent higher than the industry average and its gas sales are twice the industry average.

But if QuikTrip is providing lower prices and paying higher wages than its competitors, is it making as much money as it should? Absolutely. QuikTrip's profit per store is more than double the industry average for convenience stores and 89 percent higher than the top quartile in the industry. Its labor productivity is 50 percent higher than the top quartile in the industry and the company turns its inventory three times before it has to pay its suppliers.* Needless to say, QuikTrip's investors are very happy.

QuikTrip's model works for everyone involved — employees, customers, and investors — and that is not coincidence or luck. Patty's success is not a byproduct of QuikTrip's success; QuikTrip's success is a byproduct of Patty's. QuikTrip's employees don't get treated well because its profits happen to be up. QuikTrip's profits are up because it puts its employees at the center of its business. They are the creators of that success — not its lucky or occasional beneficiaries — and they are treated accordingly. That's what the company says, that's what its policies and procedures convey, and that's how its employees feel. Rather than seeing its labor force as an expense to be controlled, QuikTrip sees its people as an engine of sales, service, profit, and growth. The better that engine is humming and the more it can be fueled, the better the company will do.

QuikTrip Is Not Alone

QuikTrip is not the only company that delivers value to employees, customers, and investors all at the same time. Other companies in retail and beyond — including Southwest Airlines, UPS, Toyota, Zappos, the Wegmans supermarket chain, and Shouldice Hospital in Canada — do the same. Later chapters will mention these companies, but our main focus will be on four retailers that exemplify the good jobs strategy: Costco, a wholesale-club chain with more than 580 stores and $76 billion in sales; Mercadona, the largest supermarket chain in Spain, with more than 1,400 stores and €19 billion in sales; QuikTrip, with more than 600 convenience stores and over $8 billion in sales; and Trader Joe's, an American supermarket chain with more than 340

---

* Inventory turnover is measured as the cost of goods sold divided by average inventory. It is a measure of how quickly a company converts its inventory into cash (by selling it). If a store's inventory turnover is twelve times, that means that an average product stays on the shelf for about a month; it is "turned over" twelve times a year. If inventory turnover were fifty-two times, that would mean an average product stays on the shelf for only a week. Of course, one expects very different turnover in a grocery store than in a jewelry store.

stores and $8 billion in sales. Throughout the book, I will refer to these four as "model retailers."

These four model retailers operate in a variety of businesses — supermarket, convenience, and wholesale club. They differ in many aspects, including ownership, size, products, and customers. None of them is currently led by the person who founded it. But all four offer employees good jobs while providing customers low prices. At the same time, they deliver great service. And yes, they all make plenty of money, satisfying investors with growth and returns. When you look at the metrics that matter in the retail industry — such as sales per square foot, labor productivity, inventory turns, and shrink* — these firms all outperform their major competitors and perform better (often much better) than the average in their industries.

For QuikTrip — and for the other model retailers — giving Patty and her coworkers good jobs rather than bad jobs is a strategic decision. The founders and subsequent leaders of these companies believed that they would be more successful operating in this way than in the usual way for their industries. They were right.

I've Heard All the Excuses

If companies can be highly successful financially while offering good jobs, why don't we see more of them doing it? Why is the bad jobs problem so prevalent?

Excuse #1: Public companies can't do it.

When companies invest in wages, benefits, training, or staffing levels, the costs of those investments are direct, short term, and easy to measure, while the benefits are indirect, long term, and hard to measure. Investors often do not have a good understanding of the long-term benefits and push companies to cut labor costs for the short-term benefits. Hence people often argue, "We are a public

---

* "Shrink" is a retail industry measure for a decrease in stock through theft, damage, or error rather than through sales. It is never a good thing.

company and public companies can't do this because of short-term pressures."

Well, Costco is a public company. And yes, it faces short-term pressures. In fact, when it announced lower-than-expected earnings in August 2003, many blamed the company's generous employee benefits. The Deutsche Bank analyst Bill Dreher told *BusinessWeek,* "At Costco, it's better to be an employee or a customer than a shareholder." And Wall Street responded. Costco's share price plunged 19 percent in one day. But Costco doesn't care about the short term as much as it cares about the long term. And here's the benefit its shareholders received over the ten years from June 2003 to June 2013:

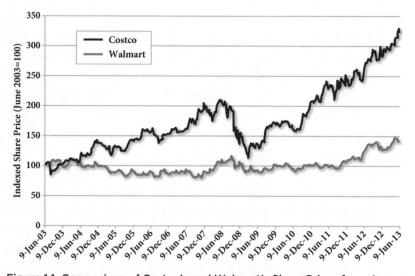

Figure 1.1. Comparison of Costco's and Walmart's Share Prices from June 2003 to June 2013[13]

Costco is not the only public company that has been able to resist Wall Street's short-term pressures. When Howard Schultz, the founder of Starbucks, returned as CEO in 2008, he faced pressure to cut health-care benefits. As he told the story:

> Within this past year I got a call from one of our institutional share-holders. He said, "You've never had more cover to cut health care

than you do now. No one will criticize you." And I just said, "I could cut $300 million out of a lot of things, but do you want to kill the company, and kill the trust in what this company stands for? There is no way I will do it, and if that is what you want us to do, you should sell your stock." What I stand for is not just to make money; it's to preserve the integrity of what we have built for 39 years — to look in the mirror and feel like I've done something that has meaning and relevancy and is something people are going to respect. You have to be willing to fight for what you believe in."[14]

Excuse #2: You have to be born this way.

"We don't operate this way and it's impossible to change." People think a model company has to be "born this way." Only an enlightened founder can create one of these businesses. But one of the model retailers, Mercadona, was not born that way at all. It drastically changed its strategy in response to competition. It started investing in employees and restructured its operations, believing it would be much more likely to succeed by offering good jobs.

Perhaps the best example of a dramatic change in corporate culture is the transformation of a General Motors plant in Fremont, California, after Toyota took over its management. The Fremont plant had closed in 1982, hardly trailing clouds of glory. The plant was not delivering value to employees, customers, or investors. It was notorious for strikes, sickouts, high absenteeism, low productivity, and poor quality. In 1984, Toyota and GM created a joint venture, called New United Motors Manufacturing Incorporated (NUMMI), that would produce a subcompact car at the plant. Within two years of Toyota's taking over operations, the NUMMI plant had become the most productive auto assembly plant in the United States, its labor productivity almost equaling that of a comparable Toyota plant in Japan. And this was, to a large extent, the same workforce and the same union that had performed so poorly before.[15]

Granted, an auto plant is not a supermarket or a convenience store. But the idea that a well-established company or facility can't change its stripes is simply not true.

Excuse #3: Big companies can't do this.

"We are too big and we can't put employees at the center of our success because we just can't find enough hardworking people. Investment in people is not 'scalable.'" Costco employed more than 140,000 people in 2011. Mercadona is Spain's largest supermarket chain. And then there's Home Depot, a company that, for a while, invested unusually heavily in its employees, of whom there were more than 200,000 in 1999. At the same time, Home Depot offered low prices and good customer service. Big companies can do it if they want to badly enough.

Excuse #4: Those model companies must have idiosyncratic qualities that we don't have.

People think that the companies implementing a good jobs strategy must have idiosyncratic qualities. They say, "Costco is a wholesale club. Its customers pay to be members, so their business model is different than, say, Walmart's and they can afford to pay their employees more." But Sam's Club, a division of Walmart, is a wholesale club too, yet it isn't a model retailer.

The common explanation for Trader Joe's is that it's the private-label products they sell. In QuikTrip's case, people point out that the company originated in Tulsa, Oklahoma: "People are just nicer there." And as for Mercadona, "Labor laws in Spain are different." As if those same laws do not apply to Mercadona's competitors, who do not offer good jobs.

None of these is a legitimate excuse. Every company has its own idiosyncrasies. If it were Walmart that provided such good jobs, no doubt someone would offer up the opposite of excuse #3: "Well, Walmart is unique. It's so big, it can do whatever it wants."

The real reason we don't see many retailers offering good jobs while also offering low prices, good customer service, and great financial performance is that doing so isn't easy. You have to get many things right to achieve the good jobs strategy. Even retailers that want to do right by employees, customers, and investors may not know what it takes to get there. Others may simply conclude that it is too difficult. As we all know, excellence is much harder to achieve than mediocrity.

The Good Jobs Strategy

The first ingredient of the good jobs strategy — the ingredient that most companies don't realize will make so many good things possible — is remarkably unglamorous by most people's standards. It is simply operations — all those factory-like activities that have to take place to deliver a product or service. Of course, all companies know that their operations are important, but many tend to think of operations in too limited a way — just a matter of making things or getting things from here to there.

Model retailers have much more in mind. They design and manage their operations in a way that makes their employees more productive, reduces the costs of doing business, and puts employees at the center of the company's success. The way model retailers design and manage their operations turns out to be the means by which well-paid, well-trained employees create even more wealth than they cost.

Model retailers do this by making four operational choices, which are not the typical ones in their industries, but which allow them to deliver value to employees, customers, and investors all at the same time:

1. *Offer less.* Whereas most retailers try to offer their customers a wide range of products, promotions, and hours, model retailers offer fewer products and no promotions. Some are open fewer hours than their competitors are, and some do not even accept most major credit cards. Offering less reduces their costs significantly, yet it can increase customer satisfaction.

2. *Standardize and empower.* Whereas most retailers take decision rights away from store employees and have them execute plans made higher up, model retailers combine standardization with empowerment. This combination allows them to be highly efficient and, at the same time, adaptive to customers' needs.

3. *Cross-train.* Whereas most retailers manage variability in cus-

tomer traffic by changing the number of employees and hence creating unpredictable work schedules, model retailers cross-train their employees. Instead of constantly changing the quantity of employees, they change what employees do depending on customer traffic. Cross-training ensures that employees are continually busy and that customers always get good service.

4. *Operate with slack.* Whereas most retailers try to cut costs by understaffing their stores, model retailers err on the side of overstaffing their stores — they deliberately build slack into their staffing. Operating with slack improves customer service and — believe it or not — *reduces* costs by allowing employees to be involved in continuous improvement.

Model retailers make all four choices in tandem, not just some of them. It's a package deal.

The second ingredient of the good jobs strategy is investment in employees. Model retailers invest heavily in their employees. They view their workforce as a valuable asset to be enhanced, not as a big, scary expense to be kept under tight control. In these companies, the employees are seen as the key to the company's success — not only in word but in deed. One could say that the company puts itself in its employees' hands, then does its best to make sure those hands are strong, skilled, and caring. This is not a matter of happy talk, PR, and employee-of-the-month awards. This is concrete policy, manifested not only in wages and benefits but also in recruitment, training, scheduling, equipment, in-store operations, head count, and promotion.

Investment in employees includes setting and enforcing high standards for employee performance. Patty's work has to be right up to the mark in a number of ways; her boss and even her coworkers are watching. If you are used to thinking of labor as a cost — a burden — you probably don't realize how much of a motivation high standards can be. One QuikTrip employee told me that what separates QuikTrip from other retailers for whom she has worked is not only the pay but also the fact that performance expectations are high. A lot is expected of her, and she loves being held accountable for her work.

• • •

These two ingredients are highly dependent on each other.[16] The four operational choices make the high investment in employees possible by reducing business costs and increasing labor productivity. At the same time, it is the high investment in skillful and motivated employees that makes these operational choices work well. So, in a way, when Walmart executives insist that improving jobs would mean either lower profits or higher prices, they could be right. If all QuikTrip did were to pay Patty a higher salary and give her more training and better benefits than Store 24 or 7-Eleven would do, it would simply be putting itself at a dangerous competitive disadvantage with those other companies. It is the combination of investment in employees with operational choices that produces excellence and permits retailers such as QuikTrip to break the low prices/good jobs trade-off.

The good jobs strategy—the combination of operations and investment in employees—allows companies to make more money than their competitors do, to create jobs that give dignity and respect to their employees, and to provide low prices and excellent service to customers. There is nothing idiosyncratic about the companies that have adopted this strategy. In a wide range of industries, ranging from retail to auto manufacturing to airlines to hotels and restaurants, they are the companies that have figured out what needs to be done operationally to make this approach work, and they are doing it.

CHAPTER 2

Great Operations Need Great People

T HE RISE AND subsequent stumble of Home Depot, once one of the great success stories in retail, is a case study in the importance of investment in people, both for customer service and for financial performance. But it is also a case study in the importance of good design in operations. Making a retail store, or any service environment, hum requires not only employees who are capable, knowledgeable, motivated, and sufficient in number, but also close attention to the design of operations — what those employees do all day and how they do it. The good jobs strategy is a blend of investment in people and in operational design.

Home Depot's Early Years

The home improvement industry veterans Bernie Marcus and Arthur Blank founded Home Depot in 1979 to provide do-it-yourself customers as well as contractors with one place where they could find everything they needed — not only the tools and supplies, but also, for the do-it-yourselfers, plenty of advice on how to use them.

The stores Marcus and Blank opened were larger than a football field and not pretty. They looked like warehouses. But the prices were low and the service was great. Stores offered a wide range of products, and the sales associates were knowledgeable and willing to do whatever it took to help you, even if that meant explaining that you didn't actually need what you came to buy. Marvin Ellison, Home Depot's executive vice president of U.S. stores in 2012, described his experience at a Home Depot store during the company's early years, when he was still working for Target and came into Home Depot as a customer looking to replace a bad faucet.[1]

> I took my old faucet with me to make sure I got the right size and color. An associate approached me and asked, "Can I help you?" I told him what I was looking for and he asked what was wrong with the faucet I had. I told him it was leaking and showed him where and he said, "You don't need a new faucet." Next thing I knew he opened up a box, took out a part, put it on my faucet and said, "Here you go." When I asked how much I owed he said, "Nothing, just come back and see me next time." From a retail perspective I'm sitting there thinking, this guy created shrink; he has to take a markdown, I'm going through all the negative things in my head. But to him it was, "you don't owe me anything but next time you need anything for your home, remember me and come back and see me again." Not only did I do that, but I told the story over and over and over again. I'm still telling it 20 years later.

Home Depot became a huge success. Customers were driving two hours to go to its stores and, once they experienced the service and great prices, they kept going back. Home Depot became the fastest-growing retailer in the world. It was the youngest retailer to hit $30 billion, $40 billion, and $50 billion in sales, and it was profitable. Wall Street loved the combination of fast growth and profitability. Carol Tomé, Home Depot's chief financial officer in 2012, said, "By 1999, basically, we could do no wrong, everything we touched seemed to turn to gold. We'd go into a shareholder meeting and people would applaud and cry because we created so much wealth, not only for our associates but for so many people. It was an incredible time."[2]

How Did Home Depot Do It?

Home Depot offered good merchandise at low prices and put employees at the center of its success. As Arthur Blank put it, "The person the customer is going to interact with, the person who is going to build the image of this company with the customer, is always going to be a sales associate." He thought associates were the spinal cord of Home Depot.[3] And so, Home Depot hired former plumbers, electricians, and other craftspeople who really knew their stuff — and invested in them. The company gave its associates training in merchandising, product knowledge, and customer service, and it employed them full-time. The company's inverted-pyramid organizational model explicitly put the CEO and corporate support group at the bottom and employees and customers at the top.

Home Depot also gave the stores a startling amount of autonomy. Store managers made their own assortment,* advertising, hiring, and compensation decisions. Such decentralization helped store managers and associates take ownership of their stores and understand their importance for Home Depot's success.

Here, then, was a case in which the necessity of trading off good jobs for low prices was revealed to be false. Home Depot's customers and investors were experiencing a potent combination of low prices *and* employees with good jobs. Employees with good jobs were both willing and able to provide great service. But it wasn't sustainable, because Home Depot wasn't designing and managing its operations with much discipline. Instead of instituting standard operating procedures, the company relied on people doing things their own way. The executives even took pride in the chaotic operating environment they had promoted. Arthur Blank said, "We teach our associates to be messy. We don't have time in the stores for a 'place for everything and everything in its place.' There are too many customers to wait on, and product is being unpacked, shelved, and sold too fast for that. Besides, we know that home improvement is messy by definition."[4]

Apart from lack of discipline in the stores, there was a lack of disci-

---

* In retail, a store's "assortment" is simply the mix of products it carries.

pline in how stores communicated with headquarters, how the company selected its products, and how the company communicated with suppliers. In 2000, bills and invoices were still processed by hand, and headquarters communicated to 1,134 stores via fax because there was no companywide e-mail. In 2008, two senior IT executives newly hired from Walmart concluded that Home Depot's IT systems were about where Walmart's had been in 1991.[5]

Declining Performance

After some two decades of breathtaking success, this lack of discipline, systems, and centralization began to tell. There were still many stories of Home Depot associates who went out of their way to help customers, even if it meant buying the product the customer wanted at a competitor's store and driving it to the customer's home. Yet the company's executives were noticing a decline in customer satisfaction.

It is no surprise that reliance on individual initiative rather than on operational discipline led to inconsistencies in customer service. If you don't have discipline in how you order 35,000 products, there will be many times when stores don't receive the right products. If you manage 35,000 products in 110,000-square-foot stores without any standard operating procedures, of course customers — and even employees — will have a hard time finding what is there.

Why Operations Matter in Service

The predicament that Home Depot found itself in is a classic example of a service company that did not fully appreciate the role of operations in making customers and investors happy. In any service environment, customer satisfaction and financial performance depend on two factors: managing operations and managing customer interactions.

Operations are all those factory-like activities that a business has to carry out in order to provide whatever it is that it sells. In manufacturing, operations involves getting parts and materials, assembling them, testing them, and so on. In service industries, the meaning of operations varies. In a retail store, for example, operations involves things like having the right product in the right place, having a fast checkout, and having a clean store. In a hotel, it involves fast check-in, clean rooms, and all the necessary products being present in the bathrooms. Operations in a restaurant means managing food inventory, clearing each table before the next customers get to it, having clean silverware, and making sure all the meals for one table arrive together. In short, service operations involve all those things that take place behind the scenes to create a seamless service experience.

In some service environments, managing operations is actually a lot more important than managing customer interactions. Remember that the way Patty made her QuikTrip customers happy was largely through accurate shelving, thorough cleaning, and quick check-out — in other words, operations. Many companies miss this point. So do customers. When a restaurant's kitchen operations are sloppy, it's the server who gets blamed for the long wait or the wrong dish or the one person who's still waiting while all the others are halfway through their meals.

One retailer I worked with had a system for scoring a store manager's performance. Twenty percent of the score had to do with the store's customer interactions. "Mystery shoppers" — undercover evaluators hired by retailers — would come into the store, acting as ordinary shoppers, and score it for how the employees greeted customers, made eye contact, and answered questions. But those factors, important as they may seem, had no effect on the store's profits. What mattered for profits was operations — measures such as how well the shelves were organized and labeled, the percentage of items that were supposed to be on display but stayed in the back room, and the percentage of poorly selling or obsolete goods that were supposed to be returned to the distribution center but remained in the stores. But those measures were given only about a 10 percent weight in a store manager's score. This retailer wasn't paying enough attention to what actually mattered for its own profits.

It's not that customers do not like to be smiled at or treated nicely. But kindness or friendliness won't make up for operational incompetence. It is hard for a grocery store to make you happy if it repeatedly doesn't have what you came in for, or if the checkout line is often long and slow, or if you get home and find that the eggs you just bought have already expired. It is hard for an airline to make you happy if it loses your bags. It is hard for your dry cleaner to make you happy if you can't wear your favorite suit to an important interview because they didn't get it cleaned on time.

In addition, if certain businesses such as Home Depot try to operate without operational discipline, they can become unsafe for employees and for customers. Think about some of the products that Home Depot carries — heavy objects such as tiles, roofing shingles, doors, lumber, and bags of cement. If there are no standards in how products will be received, shelved, or put into storage, accidents are likely. Indeed, by the 1990s, Home Depot was having a disturbing number of accidents, some of which resulted in employee deaths.[6]

Bringing Discipline

In October 2000, Home Depot missed its quarterly earnings target by approximately 10 percent, and its stock price dropped 28 percent in one day as a result. Meanwhile, Home Depot's competitor, Lowe's, was paying attention and stealing market share. Marc Powers, Home Depot's senior vice president of operations in 2012, said, "We had a competitor that came in that we should have crushed, but because we were so disorganized it grew and started to put pressure on us because it could execute, had all the infrastructure, had the foundation, and was out-executing us."[7]

Home Depot had to bring more discipline to the way it designed and managed its operations throughout the whole chain. In 2000, the company's board brought in a new CEO, Robert Nardelli, from General Electric, a company known for operational discipline.

Nardelli went right to work trying to make Home Depot more disciplined and efficient, and, in some respects, he succeeded. He brought discipline to merchandise planning and purchasing by centralizing both and investing in systems. Previously, Home Depot would make deals with vendors — for example, a discount in return for prominent displays in the stores — but the company's culture was such that store managers did not have to comply and often didn't. Because Nardelli's centralized purchasing and merchandise planning made compliance more important, Home Depot standardized store processes and measured employees' compliance with those standards. The firm also started recruiting junior military officers, who were passionate about process discipline. In 2006, around 13 percent of Home Depot's 345,000 employees had military experience, a much higher percentage than at other retail firms.[8] To improve employees' productivity, Home Depot invested in inventory-management and checkout technologies.

Nardelli also brought discipline to the corporate office's communication with stores. An internal TV channel, Home Depot TV (HDTV), piped in messages from the headquarters to the stores. Every Monday night, executive vice presidents for marketing and merchandising delivered the store staff's "marching orders for the week" through a twenty-five-minute live program called "The Same Page."[9] At other times, HDTV ran segments reminding staff of key messages and policies.

Finally, Nardelli overhauled the performance evaluation process for store managers, assessing them on thirty metrics. Store managers would be evaluated on how well they carried out cost-cutting measures as well as on their stores' sales and profitability.

All this discipline paid off in some ways. During Nardelli's six-year tenure, gross margins increased from 29.9 percent in 2000 to 33.5 percent in 2005. During the same period, net profit margins increased from 5.6 percent to 7.2 percent.

Cutting Investment in Employees

But while Nardelli strengthened what had been weak, he also weakened what had been strong. The culture of cost-cutting was soon felt at the local level, where store employees, who were once at the center of Home Depot's success and at the top of Home Depot's inverted pyramid, became a cost to be minimized.

The first blow to Home Depot's traditional investment in its people was a change in the composition of the workforce, starting with the imposition of "flexibility." Having veteran plumbers and electricians at the stores had been a big part of Home Depot's excellent customer service, but full-time employees like that were not "flexible." They couldn't just be sent home — or told not to come in at all — whenever store traffic happened to be slow. So Home Depot started increasing the percentage of part-time employees, who were generally not as experienced and knowledgeable in home improvement as the full-timers were.

Home Depot also cut investment in labor by decreasing the quantity of employees at the stores. The number of employees per store decreased from 200 in 2000 to 170 in 2006.

....

PART-TIME LABOR

Part-time doesn't always mean bad. Service companies need part-timers to manage extreme variability in traffic, and there are a lot of people, such as students and people who need a second job to get by, who can work only part-time. Part-time work can be good for employees and companies. But when hiring part-timers is done solely for cost-cutting purposes or as a way to avoid paying benefits, companies end up with less-capable and less-motivated employees. From the employee's point of view, predictable part-time work is one thing, but when you never know from week to week or even from day to day how many hours you will have and when, other things in life are made difficult or impossible.

....

Customer Service Problems

If you shopped at Home Depot during the early 2000s, chances are you sometimes left the store frustrated. A lot of customers — and even analysts covering Home Depot — complained about trying to get help from "kids" who didn't know anything about home improvement. Customers complained that when they went into the store, they couldn't find anyone to help them, and when they wanted to pay and leave, the checkout lines were too long because there weren't enough cashiers. There were also plenty of complaints about not being able to find the right product or discovering that it had the wrong price on it. In part, such hassles were the byproduct of not having enough employees on the job or not having employees who were sufficiently well paid, trained, and motivated to do a great job.

Customer satisfaction declined so much during Nardelli's tenure that, by 2005, Home Depot was ranked lower than Kmart, a retailer notorious for bad customer service, in the American Customer Satisfaction Index. Of course, that level of dissatisfaction started showing up in financial metrics. Although the company's sales doubled during Nardelli's tenure, some of that increase came from Home Depot Supply, a new wholesale building supplies business that grew to $12 billion in 2006, largely by acquisitions. In its core business, Home Depot started losing significant market share to Lowe's. This was reflected in the retailer's same-store sales growth, a measurement of how much individual stores grow during a year rather than how much a chain as a whole grows. Same-store sales growth is a strong indicator of retailer performance. Home Depot saw this measure slow down and, in 2002 and 2006, even become negative. While Home Depot's stock hardly moved during Nardelli's tenure, Lowe's stock price tripled.

Operational Designs Don't Execute Themselves

Nardelli saw what many fail to see in service operations — the need for well-designed and disciplined operations that result in a good service experience for customers. But what he failed to see was the importance of the human component in operational execution. Even the best-designed operating system does not guarantee good outcomes if that design is not carried out every day by competent, motivated employees.

Put another way, good service rests on a foundation of good operations. But good operations rest on a foundation of skilled and motivated employees. The quality of employees is, of course, a matter of whom you hire, but even more so, it's a matter of how you invest in them. Looked at in reverse, if you decide to go cheap on labor, you're going to undermine service, not only directly, but indirectly through operations. And the extent of that indirect degradation is often much greater and more damaging than many service companies realize.

A Tale of Two Auto Plants

Research on many different industries has consistently found that operational performance depends not just on operational design but on people. Stores or factories with pretty much the same system — the same procedures and rules — nevertheless perform very differently. At one retail chain I studied, for example, all the stores had similar layouts and the same process design, used the same IT systems, and offered the same employee incentives. And yet the performance of the best store and the worst differed by a factor of forty-three. Stores that had higher employee turnover, less training, and more workload for employees performed worse.

When I taught operations management at Harvard Business School, I — like many others — held up Toyota as a best-practice example of a production system that delivered excellent quality.[10] I always told my students how difficult it is to copy Toyota, but frequently a student who worked at some other auto manufacturer would object: "We have the exact same system at Acme Auto." But there was a reason Acme Auto didn't perform as well as Toyota.

The Toyota Production System is founded on standardization. As Steven Spear and Kent Bowen describe in their groundbreaking *Harvard Business Review* article, "Decoding the DNA of the Toyota Production System," Toyota standardizes each task, communication, and process (a process is a sequence of tasks), and even standardizes the process of process improvement. It uses a lot of tools to help workers on the assembly line do all this.[11]

One of the tools for process improvement is the *andon* cord, a rope strung above the assembly line. Work is so standardized that workers know exactly what to expect each time they perform a task. If a worker sees any deviation from that expectation, he or she pulls the *andon* cord, whereupon some music starts to play, alerting the team leader that there is a problem. Team leaders immediately come over to investigate the problem and try to solve it. They do not try to solve just the immediate problem — whatever defect the worker spotted — but the problem that caused the problem: What caused that defect and how did it get this far down the assembly line?

When you visit a Toyota factory, you see that workers and managers always adhere to the standards. The culture of discipline is immediately obvious. For me, it started with the little things the managers did as they showed our group of professors around. When we left the conference room, they erased the boards and put the chairs back where they belonged. The conference room looked as clean when we left as it had been when we walked in. When we toured the factory, the managers adhered to all the rules — staying within safety lines, wearing eye protection, and so on. As we strolled the factory floor, the *andon* music played so frequently that it almost felt like background music. In fact, I'm hearing it in my head as I write this.

Acme Auto indeed had the same system, right down to the *andon* cord. In fact, when a different group of professors, including myself, met with Acme mangers, they were holding a copy of the Toyota case study we taught in our classes and telling us they used the same system. But when we left the conference room, they didn't erase the board and put the chairs back. When we were walking around the factory, it was okay for them or for us to break the rules a little. We didn't stay inside the line designated for visitors.

And when I watched the workers, I saw that they, too, were breaking little rules. I watched one worker whose job included inspecting each car's left back-door frame and then putting the rubber trim between the frame and the window. Eventually a car came down the line with a small dent right where he was supposed to put the rubber trim. But instead of pulling the *andon* cord, he hammered out the dent with a mallet and off it went to the next station. That car was probably okay, but whatever problem had caused the dent was still in the system. We saw another worker encounter a problem with his welding equipment. He didn't pull the *andon* cord; he jumped up onto the equipment and did something to get it working again. It was impressive — rather heroic — but clearly dangerous and only a short-term fix, not a real solution to the underlying problem. It is no wonder, then, that this plant did not produce cars of Toyota's quality. Management had adopted the

Toyota system on paper, but it had not invested enough — whether in salary or training or just attention to and insistence on discipline — to build a workforce that could execute the Toyota Production System minute by minute, day by day.

Great performance, whether in customer service or the quality of manufacturing, requires operational excellence. Operational excellence requires a great operational design *and* great people to carry it out. Neither can make up for the lack of the other.

We Have Seen This Before

We've seen the importance of great people for operational excellence in the manufacturing sector before. Remember the U.S. manufacturing crisis in the 1970s and 1980s? Just as today's retail workers are now, factory workers then were often unmotivated and poorly trained. The prevailing attitude toward them was best captured by Henry Ford's remark several decades earlier: "Why, when I only want to hire a pair of hands, do I get a whole person?" The result was a plague of inefficiencies and quality problems. Cornerstone American industries began losing out to foreign companies that took a different view of labor.[12]

Researchers who studied manufacturing performance — from steel minimills[13] to auto assembly plants[14] — found that human resource practices that improve employees' skills and motivation contribute to higher performance. They also showed that human resource practices such as job rotation, performance-based compensation, and training work best when they are practiced together and when they are used in combination with specific manufacturing principles such as low inventory and repair buffers. That is, operational excellence requires both a good operational design and great people.

We have also seen the importance of great people for operational excellence in the service sector. Researchers have documented the positive link between good human resource practices, such as those mentioned previously, and performance (for example, service quality and labor productivity) in a wide range of service settings, from call centers[15] to airlines[16] to banks[17] to hospitals.[18]

How Much Do Employees Matter in Low-Cost Retail?

You may be thinking that manufacturing environments and the service settings listed here are highly complex operating environments that would require great people. You may also think that although Home Depot is a retailer, it is also a special case. Employees not only have to put the right product on the right shelf, they also need to know about thousands of products — ranging from little screws to large air conditioners — and how to use them. They also need to be able to interact well with customers, many of whom come to the store expecting help with their projects, not just their purchases.

But does service — and its interactions with operations — matter as much in low-cost retail, where there is not much customer interaction? Does the nature of work in that environment really require much investment in people? Can't we standardize every task in such detail and make it so easy that it doesn't matter who performs it? Can it be made "employee-proof"? Pulling all that off is not as simple as it seems.

Let's take a careful look at a familiar low-cost retail setting — a supermarket. A typical supermarket carries close to 40,000 products, runs hundreds of promotions a week, and serves about 2,500 customers a day. The work-flow diagram in Figure 2.1 shows some (not even all) of what supermarket employees do. Each rectangle in the diagram represents a physical action, the inverted triangles represent the storage of products, and the diamonds represent decisions employees need to make. The lighter rectangles represent the actions carried out just before a product leaves the store, either as a sale or as waste.

Each day, the store receives deliveries from manufacturers and distribution centers. These deliveries typically come on pallets, which usually hold sixty to eighty cases of an item, but sometimes a lot more. Store employees process the new shipments and open the pallets. Some of the cases unloaded from the pallets remain in the back room — the store's own storage area; employees take other cases to the selling floor — the part of the store where the customers shop.

But sometimes there isn't room on the selling floor for all the products in a particular case. Now what? Employees shelve the units that fit on the selling floor and take the extra units back to a storage area. Much of this happens at night when there aren't many customers or the store is closed. And this work is physically demanding. Some products such as beverages are heavy and not easy to move. Some, like eggs, are fragile and require extra attention.

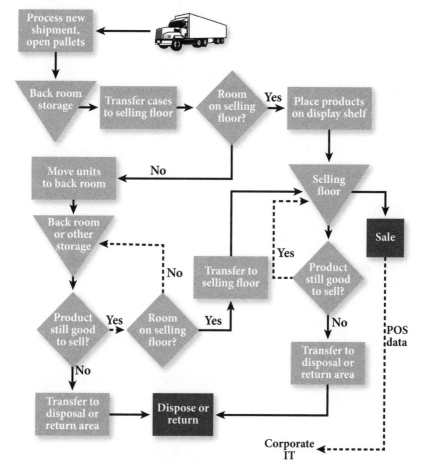

Figure 2.1. Work-Flow Diagram for Store Operations in a Typical Supermarket

During the day, as products on the selling floor are sold, employees are supposed to bring those extra units from the storage areas to the selling floor. Notice that the employee who placed the extra units in the storage areas is not the same employee who replenishes from the storage during the day. So if the night employee put something in the wrong place in the back room — possibly from carelessness, possibly from not knowing better, or possibly because the correct place was blocked off by other pallets — the replenishment process can be difficult. Most back rooms are small and do not have a designated space for every product, so it's not necessarily clear what the "right" place to put something is.

Of course, in a typical supermarket, many products can be damaged and the perishable products can expire. But these are not tracked by IT systems, so store employees are supposed to keep an eye out and bring the expired or damaged products to a disposal or return area.

As you can see, there is a lot of moving stuff around. And we haven't even mentioned promotions. For most products, it's the employees who create the promotional displays. Have you noticed how frequently the prices of things change? It is the store employees who change the prices on the shelves and on the products.

Amid all this activity, employees are required to make a lot of judgment calls. It may not be obvious to retail executives, but even in a highly centralized environment, such as the one Nardelli tried to create at Home Depot, store employees still have a lot of decisions to make. If you are a supermarket employee shelving a case of toothpaste and all but two of the tubes fit on the shelf, should you take the two extras back to storage or would it be better to squeeze them onto the shelf, even if it doesn't look so good? If a tomato looks just a little soft, should you take it to the back room now or wait until it looks worse? Maybe it will be just fine for a customer who wants to make tomato sauce. If you notice that a shelf has ten cans of black beans and there is room for twenty more, should you bring twenty from storage right now or wait until the shelf has close to no cans left? If black beans and red kidney beans are supposed to be shelved right next to each other and there are not enough red kidney beans in the store but plenty of black beans, would it be okay to use the shelf space dedicated to red kidney beans for the black beans? Or should the space allocated to red kidney beans stay empty, which of course means that some black kidney beans will have to go to storage?

It is hard, if not impossible, to make such work so simple and so standardized that anyone can do it without exercising judgment. Things happen in real time at retail stores and employees have to learn how to react.

Meanwhile, customers are coming up to you with questions. Should you spend time answering them if doing so keeps you from restocking a popular product? Should you go looking for something a customer can't find if that keeps you from setting up this week's promotion? As one Walmart employee told me:

> You can only do as much as you can. So . . . you're shelving stationery . . . and a customer comes and asks you a question. They say, "Oh, where is Pantene shampoo?" . . . I answer their question to the best of my ability. Of course, it is true that it does create sort of an adversarial relationship between the employee and the customer, in that you can't help but feel, "Oh, well, this person is asking me this frivolous question, but I'm being held accountable to meet this time frame and I have to get this work done." So instead of properly taking the customer to where they could find the product . . . I just point, "It's over in that corner of the store. Take a right down that aisle." That's not proper customer service and it's not striving for excellence, as Walmart claims to want to do. But you can only do what you can.

Every day, each store employee has to make decisions like these. Is she motivated or unmotivated? Does she understand the consequences of her choices or not? Does she even have time to do the right thing? Does she see the possibility of any reward for doing a good job or not? Does she identify with the store and want to do right by it, or does she feel her employer is ripping her off and deserves to be ripped off in return? The answers to these questions determine whether customers find what they're looking for and buy it or give up and buy it somewhere else.

Complexity Is Winning

For over sixty years, retail stores have become bigger and more complex. In 1949, a typical supermarket offered around 3,750 different items. By 1971, that number had more than doubled to around 8,000, and in 2012, it was close to 40,000. Retail checkout operators have to learn ever more new processes — how to handle loyalty cards, age restrictions, returns, coupons, and so on. One UK retailer found that its checkout operators had to know a lot more processes than bank clerks did, yet received much less than bank clerks' pay.

If I had to choose one phrase to describe how retailers tend to manage this complex operating environment, I would quote one of the employees I interviewed: "mismanaged chaos."

Some retailers are simply operating the way Home Depot used to do, without good systems or standard operating procedures for store processes. I have seen retail chains rely on their employees to use their common sense, to remember how things are done and when to do them. I have seen retail chains where access to storage areas was blocked and the employees had a hard time just getting in. I have seen retail chains where the storage areas were so disorganized and clogged with boxes that no one could find anything. I have seen retail chains where the planogram — a map of the store showing where products are supposed to be — doesn't even match the actual layout of the store.

But even retailers with standard operating procedures, good systems, and good store design end up operating in "mismanaged chaos" because of their lack of investment in employees. Employees deviate from the procedures because they do not have the skills or the motivation to follow a particular procedure or because they don't have the time to follow it or because it conflicts with something else they are supposed to do.

While complexity has increased, retailers have been investing less and less in their employees. This is evident not only in retail workers' wages, but also in how their wages compare with those of an average worker. In 1948, an average U.S. retail worker earned 91 percent of what an average U.S. worker earned, but in 2011, an average retail worker earned only 65 percent of what an average worker earned.[19] In 2011, while the average wage for all occupations in the United States was $21.74/hour and the median was $16.57, the average for the 4.3 million retail salespersons was $12.08/hour and the median was $10.10. For the 3.3 million retail cashiers, the average was $9.73/hour and the median was $9.05.[20] Training is abysmal. Most retailers provide only a few hours of orientation, which usually consists of watching videos, before new hires are thrown onto the selling floor.

Companies are not only investing less in the quality of labor — that is, how well workers are paid, trained, and motivated — but also in the quantity of workers. Surveys of store managers indicate that while workload at their stores has been increasing, their payroll budgets have not been. Increasingly, stores are trying to do more with fewer people. As one employee I interviewed recalled:

> You [used to have] sales floor associates that help[ed] do the freight. Now you have very few sales floor associates and department managers are not only responsible for more than one department, but they're responsible for all the department manager work plus the freight. . . . They're doing the job of four to six people and no increase in their pay.

When I teach executive education classes, executives and managers from a wide range of industries are keenly aware that complexity in their operating environment has been increasing while their labor investment is staying flat or even declining. You may have noticed it in your own business. But complexity outrunning investment in people is still an underappreciated problem in many settings, including retail. Even those who know it is happening often don't realize how much it is undermining their businesses.

The Price We Pay As Customers

The experience of low-cost shopping has become a hassle. More and more, it seems that you can't find what you want, things aren't where an employee tells you they are, and even the employee trying to help you can't find what you're looking for, although he's sure it's in the store somewhere. If you make it to the checkout line with what you came there to buy, you might have a long wait and you might find out the price is different from what it says on the tag.

These things happen so frequently that we customers think bad service is the price we have to pay for the low price of the goods or services. But, as U.S. manufacturers have learned, it is not the "true" price; it is more like a tax on low prices that are achieved by keeping labor costs to a minimum. That is, it's a tax on trying to manage a complex operating environment with employees who are not sufficiently trained, not sufficiently motivated, or just too few in number. Like all taxes, it is a choice, not a necessity. And while a tax is sometimes a useful choice, this choice by retailers is not.

CHAPTER 3

The Penalties of Going Cheap on Retail Labor

ARLY IN MY doctoral program, I joined a group of researchers from Harvard and Wharton who were developing new algorithms to improve retail supply chains. During a conference attended by executives from more than thirty retail chains, the CEO of a large office supplies retailer expressed some frustration with our research approach. While we were busy developing better algorithms for forecasting demand and for planning inventory and assortment, customers were coming into his stores and walking out without buying what they wanted because, even though the requested items were in the store, they were in the wrong place and no one could find them. He called these instances "phantom stockouts," and other executives in the room said they had the same problem. No one, however, knew how big a problem it really was.

Intrigued by the question, the CEO of Borders, now bankrupt but at the time a large and successful book retailer, agreed to let us study phantom stockouts in his company. That's how I began to learn the extent to which the retail industry tends to go cheap on labor and what a steep (and largely unrecognized) price the industry has been paying for that decision — not to mention the burden it places on employees.

The Real Cost of Going Cheap on Labor

As I began studying store operations, I constantly heard from store employees that they simply did not have enough time to do everything they were supposed to do because their stores were understaffed. Often their managers agreed. I decided to test the problem of understaffing empirically.

At a theoretical level, the relationship between the amount of labor a store employs and the store's profits is an inverted U (see Figure 3.1). When there is too little labor, tasks don't get done and customers are not served or cannot find what they're looking for, because it has been misshelved or is still in storage. The company loses sales — that is, it doesn't sell as much as it could have. As the level of labor increases, the situation improves. But while the marginal cost of each additional unit of labor stays the same, the marginal benefit of each additional dollar spent on labor decreases.

Presumably, retailers would want to maximize profits by choosing staffing levels at the peak of the inverted U-curve — the point at which the marginal cost of labor equals the marginal benefit of labor (L^* in the Figure 3.1). If retailers operate to the right of L^*, they are overstaffed; that is, they are wasting money on more labor than they need. If they operate to the left of L^*, they are understaffed; that is, they are

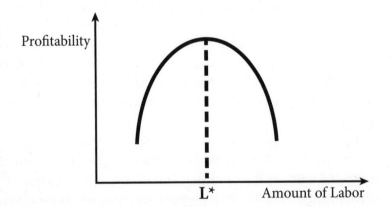

Figure 3.1. The Relationship Between the Amount of Labor and Profitability

cheating themselves, making less money than they could be making if they were to spend more on labor.

It seemed clear that many stores were understaffed in the ordinary sense, that employees couldn't get all their assigned work done. But were they understaffed in the economic sense — that they were making less money than they could have been making with more staff? To find out, I collected four years of data from over 250 Borders bookstores between 1999 and 2002 and examined what happened to a store's profitability when that store increased or decreased its labor spending from one year to the next. If increasing labor spending increased a store's profitability, it must be that the store had been operating to the left of the optimal point, L^*. That is, it had been understaffed and was now properly staffed, or least *less* understaffed. If increasing labor spending decreased a store's profitability, it must be that the store had been operating to the right of L^*. That is, it had already been properly staffed and was now overstaffed, or it had been overstaffed and was now even more overstaffed.

There is one potential problem with an analysis like this. Even if we see that periods with higher profitability correspond to periods with more labor spending, how do we know if more labor spending is really the cause of that increase in profitability? Perhaps those store managers were accurately predicting higher sales and hence higher profitability and were simply increasing their labor in order to handle the expected increase in workload. To eliminate this possibility, I collected data on what the planned payroll spending was based on sales projections — that is, what the payroll was expected to be for the next year given how much the store was expected to sell during that year — and controlled for that. I also controlled for several other factors including competition, composition of employees, employee turnover, and product variety.

I found that increasing the amount spent on payroll in a store resulted in higher profit margins, meaning that these stores had been operating to the left of optimal; there was more money to be made by increasing staffing. Put another way, by controlling their labor costs to the extent that they were in the name of profitability, they had actually been undermining profitability.

Marshall Fisher of Wharton and his colleagues Jayanth Krishnan and Serguei Netessine collected data from another retailer and found a similar result. After analyzing seventeen months of data from more than five hundred stores, they found that increasing payroll by $1 in a store could result in an increase in that store's sales of $4 to $28. This retailer earned gross margins of about 40 percent, so even with a $4 sales lift, the incremental profit of $1.60 ($4 × 40 percent) exceeds the additional $1 payroll expense.[1]

Other companies have come to this same conclusion themselves. At Tesco, a UK-based retailer with close to three thousand stores in that country alone, the number of full-time-equivalent employees per square foot decreased from 6.77 in 2006 to 5.47 in 2011, almost a 20 percent drop. In February 2012, Tesco's CEO publicly admitted to understaffing and announced that the company would hire eight thousand more people in the UK. Presumably, Tesco's management had decided that it was on the wrong side of the inverted U-curve and that hiring more people would bring in more money than it cost.

What Really Goes Wrong

The problem with understaffing is not simply that there aren't enough bodies to do the work. Even when there are enough bodies to do the work, that doesn't mean the work will be done as well as it should be. There are many effects of failing to invest enough in one's employees, including — but by no means limited to — phantom stockouts; promotions that are executed incorrectly or not executed at all; data corruption that undermines inventory and strategic planning; and loss of products due to theft, spoilage, and faulty paperwork.

Misplaced Products and Phantom Stockouts

Most people don't have strong feelings about supply chains. But for me, a supply chain can be awe-inspiring as it brings products to markets halfway around the world; guides them through various ports, customs, and transportation links; and finally delivers them to retail stores on time — still cheap enough for the average consumer to buy.

It's almost heartbreaking, then, to see all that effort and ingenuity wasted when the product ends up somewhere in the store where neither the customer who wants it nor the employee trying to help can find it. And this happens all the time.

At Borders, we found that one in six customers who approached a salesperson for help experienced a phantom stockout. Another retailer conducted a systematic analysis of stockouts. After auditing fifty products at ten stores, it found that 60 percent of the stockouts were phantom stockouts. According to Grocery Manufacturers of America, close to a quarter of all stockouts in consumer products retailing are phantom stockouts.[2]

Even companies that have made substantial investment in their supply chains to get the right product to the right store at the right time suffer from misplaced products and phantom stockouts. Mark, a former Walmart employee whom I interviewed, said he was shocked when he started working there. He was a seasoned retail employee, having spent six years at Target and having worked at a few other chains, too. He said, "You hear that Walmart is supposed to be great at this stuff, but the store where I worked was so disorganized. And people just didn't care. Not even the managers."

Walmart customers agree. When Bloomberg ran an article in April 2013 highlighting how understaffing caused empty shelves at Walmart stores, more than a thousand customers felt passionately enough to write to the reporter to tell their stories.[3] When *Consumer Reports* rated the best and worst supermarkets in America, Walmart was ranked second to last.[4] Why were customers so unhappy with the company? Being out of stock of routinely purchased items was one of the top reasons.

But how could a huge, experienced, and supposedly efficient company like Walmart run out of products so frequently? Many times those items are just sitting in back rooms. A product that has made it all the way from China to Topeka can get stuck in a back room because there aren't enough employees to bring it the last ten yards to the selling floor, or because the employee who was supposed to bring it forgot or chose not to do so for whatever reason. Misplaced products were one of the reasons that Walmart took the lead in implementing technologies attempting to reduce this problem (see the sidebar on RFID on page 44).

In some retail chains, misplaced products don't just lead to stock-outs — sometimes they lead to products' being sold for substantially lower prices than they should be. When customers take something off the shelf, they rarely look at the price on the product label. Instead, they look at the price on the shelf. Say a customer thinks that the olive oil she is buying costs $5 a bottle, because that's what the shelf tag says, but the olive oil that an employee put on that shelf by mistake actually costs $8. If the cashier rings up $8 and the customer points out that it said $5 on the shelf, the store often ends up selling that $8 bottle of olive oil for $5, swallowing the cost of its own error. Swallowing that error doesn't cost the store just the $3; it also costs the store in wasted time, as a manager had to talk to the customer and the cashier, trying to figure out what happened and what to do about it. If the customer doesn't notice the discrepancy until she gets home, the outcome can be even worse, because she may lose trust in the retailer and decide not to come back.

Why are products misplaced in the first place? Stores with high employee turnover, less training, and greater workload experience this problem more often.[5] And it's easy to see why. An inexperienced employee isn't going to be familiar enough with thousands of different products to replenish them from the back room correctly. I asked one interviewee who worked in the stationery department of a Walmart store, "How can you even put the stuff in the wrong place? Isn't it obvious where paper goes and where pencils go and where pens go?" She replied, "Well, not really, because you have to consider — let's just talk about the pens and pencils for a minute — there's an entire wall of those. There's probably hundreds of them right there on the wall. And you cannot possibly know the location of every single pen or pencil, especially if they've been changing the [layout]. It's not as easy as it sounds like it would be."

Back rooms are often so messy that it takes an experienced employee to find products there. And sometimes employees simply don't have the time to replenish from the back room. I have visited stores in which employees made up their own ad hoc storage locations — for example, hiding extra product underneath display tables or behind other products on the shelves — because they just did not have enough time to take things back to storage. Some of the store managers I spoke with even knew about this, but they understood why the employees did it.

Lost sales and reduced margins are not the only consequences of phantom stockouts. Here's what happened to a customer at a large office supplies store — and then, in turn, what happened to the retailer as a consequence.

This customer wanted to buy ten small leather-bound notebooks. The store he visited had only one, which he purchased, but the store manager checked the computer system and found that a nearby store in the same chain had six in stock. The customer drove to that store, but neither he nor the store employee he asked could find the notebooks. According to the system, however, another store had nine of them. The customer was not interested in visiting yet another store before confirming that it really had the notebooks, and in any case, it was now too late for him to make another trip. When he got home, he called the store that supposedly had nine of the notebooks, but the employee with whom he spoke couldn't find them anywhere. By now, this customer had wasted a lot of time and still didn't have what he wanted.

The notebooks cost $16 each. Assuming that there really were ten of them somewhere in all those stores, the chain had lost $144 in sales. It may also have lost that customer for good after such an exasperating experience. Then there is the cost in labor productivity. One store manager and two store employees wasted time looking for those notebooks, accomplishing nothing. Finally, there is the effect on the retailer's centralized merchandise planning system. The forecasting system thinks the product is in the store but sees no sales for it. So the system assumes that there is no demand for that notebook and therefore will not send more units to the store.

In-Store Implementation Sharegroup (ISI Sharegroup), an industry collaboration of manufacturers and retailers, estimates that execution problems such as these cost consumer products retailers 1 percent of their sales.[6] This is a big number: Consumer products retailers often have profit margins lower than 5 percent, so every sale counts. At Borders, we estimated that profits would have been 25 percent higher had there been no phantom stockouts. Those were only estimates of

lost sales; we didn't even try to take into account lost labor productivity, lost customer goodwill, and the effect on merchandise planning
systems.

SOLVING EXECUTION PROBLEMS WITH TECHNOLOGY

Retailers now are more aware than ever of how much poor operational execution is costing them, and several companies are
working on a technology they think will help — radio-frequency
identification (RFID).

The vision is that each product in the store will have an RFID
tag, which when prompted by an RFID reader broadcasts its
information via a radio signal. This technology has several advantages over bar codes. With ordinary bar codes, each product
needs to be scanned — one by one — with a scanner that has to
be held close to the product and pointed right at the code. RFID
doesn't require a line of sight between the tag and the reader.
The reader could be three feet away from the tag — or around the
corner — and still read it. And the reader can read multiple tags at
the same time. If all products are tagged, and there are enough
readers at the store, store systems will know where each product
is and which products need to be moved. RFID tags could also
make shopping more pleasant for the shoppers. Imagine going
through checkout and a reader scanning everything in your shopping cart all at once. What a great time-saver, both for the shoppers and for the store.

But because RFID tags, even the least sophisticated ones, are
expensive — running around five cents per tag in 2012 — retailers
such as Walmart have tried the technology largely at the case
level, that is, putting an RFID tag on a case of candy bars but
not on each individual candy bar. Pilot studies at Walmart have
shown that implementing RFID on the case level does help improve store execution; at twelve stores where 4,554 unique products were tagged at the case level, RFID contributed to a 21 percent reduction in stockouts.[7]

However, when I visited Metro Group of Germany in 2005 — one of the world's largest retailers and, along with Walmart, one of the leaders in promoting RFID technology for retail at the time—I found that most of the savings resulting from using RFID at the case level could actually have been realized just by using ordinary bar codes on each case and having employees scan the case each time it moves within the store. Yet most retailers don't do this.

Given the economics of the technology, implementing RFID at the case level just does not make any sense. It is through tagging each individual product—each tube of toothpaste, each box of paper clips, each bottle of Coke—that RFID could really make a huge difference for store execution and for shoppers. But that is still too expensive for most products. In addition, the standard RFID tags do not work as well with products that contain metals or liquids.

Even if RFID tags were implemented at the individual product level, operational excellence would still depend on employees exercising good judgment. RFID would provide better information and would replace some human labor, but it wouldn't be able to move the products around and make all those small but important decisions about what to put where so that customers can find what they need.

So far, then, RFID—like factory automation in the 1980s—is proving to be an expensive solution to people and process problems that have much better and simpler solutions. Moreover, researchers have already documented—in industries ranging from auto manufacturing to healthcare—that purely technological innovations often do not work so well. It is the integration of technology and work systems that generates significant improvements.[8]

....

Promotion Compliance

In-store promotions are deeply affected by a company's lack of investment in its people. Every year, manufacturers and retailers spend millions of dollars planning promotions. They agree on when certain products will be on sale and how they will be displayed. But what is agreed upon or planned is often not what is executed at stores, either because there aren't enough people to set up the promotions or because employees do not have the training or the experience to do it correctly.

This is where companies such as McCurrach come in. McCurrach is a UK-based company that represents brands such as PepsiCo, Unilever, and Nestlé. McCurrach has over a thousand territory managers, each of whom represents a specific brand and visits about twenty to twenty-five stores. What do these territory managers do? Every week, they go to the stores of retail chains such as Tesco and Sainsbury's and check whether the agreement between the manufacturer and the retailer is being carried out correctly. You would think that store employees and managers would not like to be inspected all the time. But it's quite the opposite. When I visited stores with some of McCurrach's territory managers, I was surprised to see that store managers actually welcomed them, because they helped to solve the store's merchandising problems and to increase sales.

There is only one reason why McCurrach exists: poor operational execution at stores. McCurrach's CEO, Neil McNicol, told me that 50 percent of in-store promotions in retail are either not carried out in time or not carried out at all. ISI Sharegroup makes the same estimate. AMR Research's survey of one hundred people in charge of merchandising from a range of retail chains found that only 37 percent of them were confident in the ability of store operations to execute merchandise and promotional strategies. According to the survey, only 59 percent of the merchandisers felt that merchandise and promotional instructions and initiatives were executed by stores in the intended fashion.[9]

Data Quality

We all have read about the cool stuff retailers do with their sales and inventory data. Apparently Target can figure out that a woman is pregnant even before she tells her friends. Walmart is known for the vast amount of data it captures and its ability to make decisions based on those data. But how accurate are their sales and inventory data?

In many cases, this question depends on our overworked, under-trained, and poorly motivated employee. A former Target cashier told me that she was under a lot of pressure to ring up sales as quickly as possible. To keep up with this pressure, she used the quantity keys to ring up different items that happened to have the same price. Let's say a customer bought ten bottles of Gatorade, but in two flavors. She would scan the first one and then hit the quantity key for ten. And right there she caused inventory data inaccuracy. Now the inventory system thought that the store had sold ten lime-flavored Gatorades and no cherry-flavored Gatorades, when in fact it had sold five of each. Did the cashier know that Target was actually using the data she keyed in (or miskeyed) to determine not only what the customer had to pay right at that moment, but also which type of Gatorade sells more and what to order in the future? Not likely. She received only eight hours of training when she was hired.

Nicole DeHoratius of the University of Chicago investigated the extent of data inaccuracy at retail stores and found that even sophisti-cated retailers have very inaccurate inventory data. One example was "Gamma Corporation" (not its real name), a retailer with hundreds of stores and over $10 billion in sales. DeHoratius examined inventory data for nearly 370,000 products at thirty-seven Gamma stores and found that the system had the right information for only 35 percent of those products. For the remaining 65 percent, the average discrepancy between what the system thought was in inventory and what actually was in inventory was nearly five units, or 36 percent of the average target stocking quantity (the number of units the retailer intended to stock). And interestingly, almost all the products that were out of stock at the store at the time of the physical audit appeared as being in stock in the system. In other words, the system thought the store had those products in stock but, in fact, the store was out of them.[10]

In one instance, management at Gamma received a letter of com-plaint from a regular customer, noting that a specific product he sought was persistently out of stock, even after he had brought the stockout to the attention of the store manager. After researching the problem, management discovered that, although the product was out of stock as the customer said, inventory records showed forty-two units on hand in that store. Since that was considered sufficient inventory to meet demand, the automatic replenishment system saw no reason to send additional inventory to the store.[11]

What's more, sales records naturally indicated that although Gamma stores typically sold one unit of this product per week, this particular store had not sold a single unit in the past seven weeks. (Of course not. They didn't have any to sell.) The demand forecast was then automatically updated to reflect this low level of sales. Not only had customers been unable to find the product on the shelf for the last seven weeks, but even after restocking, customers who wanted it in the future would be more likely to be frustrated because the store would be sent fewer of that item on account of the (purely fictitious) low demand. Finally, it is important to note that the product may have remained out of stock until the next physical audit or cycle count had this customer not written to Gamma. The inventory software would have gone on presuming there were forty-two units in the store and that nobody was buying that product at that store anymore.

Gamma, I might add, uses electronic point-of-sale scanning for all its sales. Things are usually worse at supermarkets, where employees have to enter the price look-up (PLU) code manually for those products that do not have bar codes. One supermarket chain executive told us that every year, on average, his chain sold — according to the system data — 25 percent more medium-red tomatoes than the total amount shipped to their stores. Store employees were mistakenly entering the PLU code for medium-red tomatoes when customers were buying other types of tomato.

Shrink

Every year, retailers lose around 1.5 percent of sales to what is evocatively (or ironically) known in the industry as "shrink," that is, loss from employee or customer theft, paperwork errors, or product damage.

When companies do not invest in their employees, those employees may be more likely to steal. A study of the convenience store industry by Clara Xiaoling Chen of the University of Illinois and Tatiana Sandino of Harvard Business School found—after controlling for employee characteristics, a store's socioeconomic environment, and other factors—that the store's relative wages (defined as the employees' wages relative to the wages of other stores' employees performing similar jobs in the same region and sector) were negatively associated with employee theft. In other words, the lower paid that a store's employees were as a whole, the more employee theft there was.

The link between higher wages and less theft has several explanations. For one thing, better-paid employees are more likely to want to keep their jobs. For another, they are more likely to want to do right by their employer since they are compensated fairly. It could also be that the firms that do offer higher wages are also the firms that have invested more in recruiting and may be better able to attract honest employees.[12]

Oddly enough, when companies do not invest in their employees, customers are also more likely to steal. Store employees I interviewed told me that shoplifters typically target stores during understaffed hours.

The Vicious Cycle

We have seen how operational problems exacerbated by low investment in employees decrease sales and, at times, increase costs. This is even worse than it sounds. It would be bad enough if retailers were simply chugging along with lower financial performance than if they were to do things differently. When it comes down to it, every company's performance could be better if it did a better job of one thing or another. But the situation here isn't necessarily as stable as that. Rather, low investment in employees has the potential to set up a vicious *downward* cycle.

At most retail chains, payroll budgets are determined as a percentage of sales. For each month or week, store managers are given a target for payroll as a percentage of sales. So when sales drop, store managers will do whatever they can to bring their labor budgets down in proportion. They will schedule fewer hours or shift the mix of employees toward more part-timers.

This is not the logical response it may seem. It's more like a negative feedback loop, reacting in a way that reinforces whatever caused the reaction in the first place. A given store's sales can go up and down for all kinds of reasons. But one consistent reason for going down might well be that customers are responding to the low quality of service. If so, they are probably responding — though they wouldn't know it — to a sinking level of operational execution. They're finding it more of a nuisance to shop *here* and maybe less of a nuisance to shop *there*.

As we have seen, if customers are responding to poor operational execution, they are indirectly responding, at least in part, to a retailer's low investment in its employees. Add it up, the result is management responding to the customer-displeasing effects of low investment in employees with even lower investment in employees.

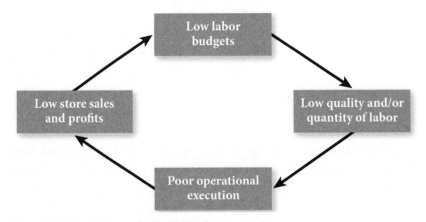

Figure 3.2. The Vicious Cycle of Retail

Then what happens? Even lower investment in employees contributes to even lower operational performance, which contributes to even lower financial performance. As shown in Figure 3.2, this is the vicious cycle set in motion by accepting the low prices/good jobs trade-off.

Why Does Retail Go Cheap on Labor?

Isn't the vicious cycle inevitable if retailers operate a highly complex environment with employees who are not well trained or well motivated or are just too few in number? Why, then, do retailers continue to underinvest in both the quality and quantity of labor?

Philosophy: Labor As an Expense to Be Minimized

When Marshall Fisher of Wharton described the results of his and his colleagues' study — namely, that retailers could make more money by increasing staffing levels — the CEO of a retail chain responded, "I spend my days saying no to a long line of people suggesting ways to spend money, including adding store staff. I don't need a couple of Ivy League professors with their fancy statistical analysis giving them more ammunition!"[13]

This response pretty much captures how most retailers view store labor — as a cost-driver, not a profit-driver. And labor is not just any cost. After the cost of goods sold, labor is the largest cost for most retailers. Perhaps more important, labor is the largest controllable cost. In a pinch, retailers cannot quickly cut other large expenses such as the cost of the products they sell or their real estate costs, but they can quickly and fairly easily reduce what they spend on training, benefits (by changing their mix of part-time and full-time employees), or the total number of employee hours.

Seeing labor as a cost to be minimized is so common that some retailers even do self-destructive things to minimize costs. In March 2007, Circuit City — at the time, the world's second-largest electronics retailer — fired 3,400 of its most experienced and hence highly paid hourly workers (who were reportedly making 51 cents more per hour than the market average) and hired replacements willing to work for less. This was a signal of the vicious cycle Circuit City was already in.

Meanwhile, Circuit City's largest competitor, Best Buy, was paying attention and investing more in store employees. By 2007, Best Buy had earned a reputation for having higher staffing levels and delivering better customer service than Circuit City, and that showed in its financial performance. In the first quarter of 2007, Best Buy's profits increased by 18 percent compared with the first quarter in 2006, and the company started stealing more and more sales from Circuit City. Circuit City's same-store sales kept declining until the company went out of business in 2009.

But here's the thing: While Best Buy was delivering better service and better financial performance than its competitor, Wall Street analysts were criticizing the company for not paying enough attention to controlling its costs. That's how high the pressure to cut labor costs can be for publicly owned retailers even when they are performing well.

The pressure is even higher for retailers that are no longer in their phase of rapid growth and are therefore eager to keep looking good to investors. One way to show earnings growth when sales growth slows down is to cut costs. Home Depot, Borders, and Tesco have all gone that route. However, earnings growth achieved by reducing labor costs is often short-lived because of the toll these reductions take on operations, labor productivity, and customer service.

The pressure to reduce payroll expenses can go beyond self-destructive to criminal. Store managers at several large chains, including Walmart, have been widely reported to have had their employees illegally work off the clock, paying them for fewer hours than they actually worked.

Performance Management

All this pressure to underinvest in people comes down on the store managers in the way they are evaluated by their own bosses. An important criterion is often how well the store managers meet their monthly, weekly, or even daily targets for payroll as a percentage of sales.

The idea is for the managers to get the most sales possible out of their staff. But store managers don't have too much control over sales. They are often not the ones making decisions on merchandise mix, layout, price, or promotions; the corporate staff decides all that. They also have no control over the weather, which is a significant driver of sales. What the store managers do have a fair amount of control over is payroll. When sales decrease, managers immediately reduce staffing levels, often with very short notice. That way they can make their short-term targets for payroll as a percentage of sales.

The criminal behavior sometimes observed — forcing employees to work unpaid hours and so on — can also be attributed to how companies assess store managers' performance. Although store managers are constantly measured on payroll expenses, they are seldom monitored for labor practices.[14]

Failure to Weigh Long-Term Harm Against Short-Term Gain

Store managers may make their targets, but at what cost? We've already had a glimpse of what that kind of pressure means for employees — erratic scheduling and an unpredictable income, not to mention more tasks than they can reasonably accomplish. But the retailers themselves pay a stiff price in phantom stockouts, promotion noncompliance, data corruption, and shrink. Unfortunately, while the financial benefits of cutting employee costs are direct, immediate, and easy to measure, these less-desirable effects are indirect, longer-term, and more difficult to measure. The carrot is in plain sight, but the stick is invisible and doesn't hurt that much until well after you've been hit.

Failure to Recognize Any Other Way

A fourth reason that retailers underinvest in labor is that they are stuck in mediocrity and think that the current model is the only way to operate. Many retailers who make the low prices/good jobs trade-off are leaving a lot of money on the table, yet they are still in business and doing fine. They have endless problems managing that trade-off, but that's just the way business is, right? They don't think the trade-off itself is a mistake. Walmart, for example, is now so big that its ability to leverage its scale and hence offer low prices can compensate for its bad service. Customers still go to Walmart for low prices. In some locations, Walmart has driven many retailers out of business, so customers don't even have a lot of alternatives. And people still want to work there because they can't find any other job.

However, retailers aren't necessarily "getting away with it" as well as they think. Many don't realize the price they are paying for the low prices/good jobs trade-off.

There Is a Better Way

The current practice of low-cost retail — or what I call the bad jobs strategy — is stressful for management. It fosters an endless trench warfare mentality of keeping labor costs as low as possible while dealing with all the operational and service problems created by doing that. The vicious cycle set in motion by the low investment in employees is also aggravating for customers and can prove disappointing for investors. But it can be downright brutal for millions of employees.

The bad jobs strategy, even in low-cost retail, is not necessary. It is a choice, and there are other, better choices.

CHAPTER 4

Model Retailers: Who Knew It Could Be This Good?

THE BEST-KNOWN SPANISH retailer in the world must be the fast-fashion retailer Zara. Even if you are not a typical Zara customer — young, price-conscious, and up-to-date with the latest in fashion — you have most likely heard of them.

Zara's business model and the responsive supply chain that supports it have been the topic of business school case studies all over the world. While most fashion retailers take months to make new products, Zara's supply chain is so fast that it can design and deliver new products to its stores in a few days. Zara's speed, along with its ability to collect information on what's selling and what's popular, helps the company produce products that its customers want, *when* they want them. For example, when Madonna was on tour in Spain, teenage girls turned up at her final show wearing the very outfit she had worn for her first show — purchased from Zara, of course.[1]

I was intrigued by Zara and went to Spain to study the company. But I wanted to look at it from a different angle. I wanted to find out how Zara managed its store operations to deliver the right product to the right customer at the right time in its approximately 1,500 stores in more than seventy countries.

Zara's human resource director told me that when it came to human resource management and store operations, the model company she looked to was Mercadona. Unless you have been to Spain, I'll bet you have never heard of Mercadona. I hadn't either, so I had to ask the HR director what Mercadona was. Her answer took me by surprise: It's a supermarket chain. Really? Super-cool Zara models itself after a supermarket chain? I set out to explore.

Mercadona

I visited my first Mercadona store in Ciempozuelos, a small town south of Madrid. The store was under an apartment building, so even though Mercadona is the biggest supermarket chain in Spain, this store felt very much like a neighborhood grocery store. Most people would find the interior of the store quite ordinary. They might even find it unappealing because of its low ceilings and old fixtures. But for an operations professor, this store was amazing. The shelves were neatly stocked. Product locations were intuitive for the customer and for the employees, with good signage. Price tags were placed in the center of each product's display so it was easy for customers to see how much each product cost. Two checkout areas, each with five cash registers, helped reduce congestion during busy periods.

The store was neat and clean — not just the selling area, but also the bathrooms, the employee locker rooms, and the back room. Even the small storage area for cleaning materials was tidy, with all the cleansers, brooms, and so forth labeled and hung in their proper places.

Being at this Mercadona store was like being at a Toyota factory. Things were really humming. Employees knew exactly what they were supposed to do and when they were supposed to do it. They were given the right resources, including enough time to perform their jobs well. They didn't seem to be in a rush. In return, they were *expected* to do a good job, both in the sense that it was expected of them and in the sense that their managers were quite confident in their ability to get the job done.

Before my store visits, I spent some time with Nichan Bakkalian, the head of processes at Mercadona, who told me how process improvement works there. For example, he told me that they had just begun implementing a new way to display vegetables used for stew. Previously, those vegetables had been sold just where you would expect — in the produce section. But then an employee suggested that it would be better if there were a package of stew vegetables near the meat section so that the "bosses" — Mercadona's word for customers — could get all the ingredients for a stew quickly.

When Mercadona gets a suggestion like that from an employee, it first tests the idea at one store to quantify its effect on various performance measures such as number of transactions, kilos of product sold, or reduction in kilos of waste generated. If there is an improvement in performance, then they test it in an area, such as southern Madrid. If the performance improvement is still there and if higher management supports the innovation, then Mercadona rolls it out across the entire chain. At the time I visited, the whole chain had just rolled out the new placement offering stew vegetables near the stew meat.

My immediate response to Nichan was, "Let's see how many of the stores we visit this week have actually implemented this plan." He gave me a strange look and explained — assuming I had missed the point — that the plan was to do this in all stores. "Yes, of course," I said, "that's the plan. But let's see how well it's executed." Remember, I was used to an average of 50 percent execution. But Nichan anticipated 100 percent execution. That's what Mercadona expects and that's pretty much what it gets.

I visited seven Mercadona stores that week and they all had the stew vegetables stocked near the stew meat — with the right signage.

If the retailers that trade in good jobs for lower prices and operate in a vicious cycle are in a "mismanaged chaos," Mercadona stores are quite the opposite. They are highly disciplined in the way they are organized, in how store processes are defined, and in the high expectations to which employees are held. There is discipline in the way trucks deliver products to the stores, the way maintenance personnel do maintenance work, the way cleaners clean the stores, and the way managers manage the stores.

For example, I asked each store manager what his or her typical day was like. They all gave me the same answer. They begin each day by going around the store and saying hello to all their employees. This gives them a chance to gauge people's feelings. Then they check the computer for the previous day's financial performance. Then they visit each section of the store and have a talk with the section specialist about the previous day's sales, what had to be thrown away, what was out of stock, and the specialist's objectives for the new day. And so on.

Contrary to appearances, Mercadona employees are not robots performing mindless tasks. As we will see in chapters 6 and 8, Mercadona's discipline is implemented in a way that frees and empowers employees. Processes are efficient enough that store employees can carry out all their standardized work and still have time to find out what's on their customers' minds and to initiate improvements — even chainwide improvements. Putting the vegetables near the meat was a suggestion from a very "disciplined" employee.

Where does that discipline come from?

Mercadona Wasn't Born This Way

Until 1993, Mercadona was a pretty ordinary supermarket chain. Its labor practices were less than ideal, its store operations were not well designed, and its stores suffered from operational problems just like the ones we saw in the previous chapter. Like other supermarkets, Mercadona also offered a lot of products and many promotions.

But the family-owned chain started facing major challenges. Large international retailers, such as France's Carrefour chain of so-called hypermarkets, started taking market share away from Mercadona and putting pressure on the company to be more efficient. In order to stay in business, Mercadona had to change.

At the time, Juan Roig was president and CEO, having taken control of Mercadona from his family in 1981. Roig was an avid reader. He was deeply influenced by Stephen Covey's book *The 7 Habits of Highly Effective People*, which helped him develop strong values that he wanted to instill in his life and business. Indeed, Roig had a dream of creating a company "whose objective was not only to generate profits, but also to take care of customers and employees and to demonstrate that if you give opportunities and training to people, you get real leaders."[2] For Roig, the competitive crisis he now faced was a perfect opportunity to change Mercadona into just that kind of company.

Roig made a strategic switch from high-low pricing with promotions to "always low prices," and he promoted a culture of continuous improvement by implementing what was internally called the Total Quality Model (TQM). For him, the key to continuous improvement was staying true to nine principles:

1. *Everyone is reliable.* This means that the company can rely on people to perform a task. If they can't perform it, the company will examine what circumstances impede them and what it can do to overcome those obstacles.

2. *Anything that does not provide value to customers is not done.* The company will constantly look for opportunities to reduce waste in its products and processes.

3. *Every company is an assembly line.* The assembly line at Mercadona goes all the way from raw materials for the products sold at the stores to the checkout. Mercadona will do whatever it takes to make the entire assembly line work better.

4. *Have a scientific mind.* Mercadona's process improvement and product improvement involve generating hypotheses, conducting experiments, collecting data, reviewing the results, and then implementing change.

5. *Do it right the first time — zero defects.* Mercadona does not define acceptable defect rates. As we saw with the stew-vegetable rollout, the company expects 100 percent execution 100 percent of the time.

6. *Everything can be improved.* Mercadona encourages each product and process to be continuously improved.

7. *The company has to prescribe.* Mercadona does not view itself as a retailer that offers all products to customers; rather, it has a responsibility to choose the best products for its customers. Store employees who become experts in an area such as fish, vegetables, or cosmetics use their knowledge to recommend the highest-quality, most affordable, or safest products to customers.

8. *Abide by the law.* Mercadona conducts its business in compliance with the law.
9. *Convince, don't defeat.* Mercadona understands that policies cannot be implemented successfully by forcing an idea or task onto others. One must explain the reasoning behind the policy, convincing one's colleagues rather than defeating them. Gaining consensus is preferable to winning the argument.

Investment in Employees

Because continuous improvement requires a lot of involvement from employees, Mercadona also had to change the way it managed employees. The company started giving them more stable work schedules (and therefore a more stable income), more training, more benefits, and more opportunities for advancement. Employees, in turn, took greater pride in and ownership of their jobs.

An equally important change was that Mercadona constantly communicated with employees and started letting its employees know how much it appreciated them. The company officially made its employees number two on its list of priorities, right after the customers, but conspicuously *before* the investors. Marcos Barberán, Mercadona's human resource director for central Spain, told me: "Employees are not treated merely as hands, but as complete human beings, with hearts and brains. They don't just work at Mercadona, they have different roles in their lives, they have families, hobbies; they are part of society." I can hardly tell you how refreshing it was to hear this from a high-level manager of a low-cost retail chain.

Mercadona pays higher salaries than its competitors do. In 2012, the salary for a new full-time employee was €14,693, almost double the minimum wage in Spain.[3] That salary would increase by 11 percent during the first four years, so a full-time employee who had been there for four years would make €20,094. After the fourth year, the salary increased in line with inflation. The salary for assistant directors started at €21,180 and went up to €32,152 by their fifth year; store managers started at €42,362 and earned €64,309 by their fifth year.

In addition to salary, all Mercadona employees, from the cleaner to the CEO, received an annual bonus if their individual and local goals were met and if the company met its overall targets. The bonus was two months' salary for employees who had been with Mercadona four or more years and one month's salary for those who had been there less than four years. In a typical year when company targets were met, about 95 percent of the employees qualified for the bonus because they had met their individual and local goals. If the company targets were not met, no one — neither the cleaner nor the CEO — would receive any bonus.[4]

In 2012, all 74,000 employees at Mercadona had permanent contracts. Approximately 85 percent of Mercadona's store employees work full-time. Unlike the full-time employees at other low-cost retailers — who can actually get as few as thirty hours a week and whose schedules change all the time — full-time employees at Mercadona are salaried employees with stable schedules. They typically work 6.6 hours a day for six days a week. There are four main schedules: 7:00 a.m.–2:00 p.m., 8:00 a.m.–3:00 p.m., 2:00 p.m.–9:00 p.m., and 3:00 p.m.–10:00 p.m. Store employees alternate each week between a morning shift and an afternoon shift and know their schedules one month in advance. Employees also receive thirty days of vacation a year, maternity leave, and day care benefits.

Apart from all these benefits, Mercadona employees can see clearly how much they matter for the company, and they are given the resources and training to be able to do their jobs well. Mercadona invests approximately €5,000 for every new store employee in a four-week training course. During the first week, new employees learn TQM. Then, for three weeks, they attend a program called "from parents to children," in which the region's most experienced area specialists personally tutor the new employees in their assigned areas. The specialist is not paid to do this but takes great pride in it and is rewarded with a day off on the last Friday or Saturday of the course — *if* he or she has trained the new recruit well enough to run the assigned area alone.

Mercadona also offers training on new products and processes and in other areas such as leadership, information technology, and English. Store coordinators attend a four-month training course in TQM, leadership, the assembly line, and the company's human resources administration software. In 2012, Mercadona spent more than €44 million on employee training.[5]

Mercadona's employees are so satisfied that once they start working at the company, they seldom leave. When Marcos told me that Mercadona's employee turnover was 3.4 percent, I didn't believe him. I thought perhaps he was using a different definition of employee turnover. But he was indeed measuring turnover just as others do — the number of employees who left divided by the average number of employees during that year. Still skeptical about such a low number, I asked all the people I talked to in the seven stores I visited how long they had been working there. I heard ten years, fifteen years, twenty years, twenty-five years.

The Virtuous Cycle of Retailing

In the vicious cycle of retailing, lower investment in employees leads to worse operational performance, which leads (both directly and indirectly) to lower financial performance, which leads to lower investment in employees. With Mercadona, we see the virtuous cycle of retailing. Investment in employees contributes to operational excellence. This results in high sales and profits, which allows for greater investment in employees.

Mercadona's sales per square foot and labor productivity are much higher than its competitors (for example, its sales per square foot is about 50 percent higher than that of Carrefour). Not only is Mercadona's store performance high compared with that of its competitors, but it keeps improving. Sales per employee went up steadily from €109,474 in 1995 to €257,797 in 2012. And this is not a numerical trick managed by understaffing the stores. In fact, as we will see in chapter 8, Mercadona errs on the side of having too many people rather than too few.

Because the virtuous cycle is a cycle, it doesn't simply stop with higher sales and profits. When sales and profits are up, Mercadona can further invest in its employees. And it does. By 1999, all employees at Mercadona had become permanent. In 2000, Mercadona opened its first nursery school for employees' children. In 2003, it started closing its stores on Sundays. "People have a family life," Marcos explained. In 2005, Mercadona added an extra month of maternity leave.

Figure 4.1. The Virtuous Cycle of Retailing

In 2007, Mercadona opened a fully automated distribution center — not because it was cheaper to operate the distribution center that way, but because lifting heavy cases over and over was unhealthy for the employees. The director of the distribution center, José Miguel Meneses, explained: "Its construction was based on one premise: Don't make a person do what a machine can do. The only effort we want from our employees is for them to give us their skills and their knowledge."

Keep in mind that all the things Mercadona does for its employees are an investment. They are not gifts, not disbursements, not bonuses (other than the official bonus itself). The company is investing in the quality of its most important asset. Mercadona considers a proud, happy employee with a balanced and satisfying life to be of higher quality than a stressed-out employee struggling to keep it all together. You've got to spend more money to have such employees, just like you have to spend more money to acquire the best real estate or the best equipment or the best legal team. If you make proper use and take proper care of what you have invested in, you'll do better in your business. That's the idea, and the results bear it out.

What Model Retailers Have in Common

Like Mercadona, the other three model retailers — Costco, QuikTrip, and Trader Joe's — view employees as precious assets and invest in them. They all deliver low prices and good service to their customers. And they all perform better than their competitors financially. Hence these four retailers have found a sustainable way to deliver superior value to employees, customers, and investors all at the same time.

Value to Employees

BETTER PAY AND BENEFITS

The four model retailers pay their employees substantially more and offer more benefits than their competitors do.[6] For example, Costco's average pay for hourly workers is $20.89 an hour[7] — over 40 percent higher than the pay at its largest competitor, Sam's Club (owned by Walmart) — and it offers benefits to all employees who work more than twenty hours a week.*

Trader Joe's employees typically start as part-time "crew members" at around $10 to $12 per hour, but they are given raises every six months if they pass their reviews. Full-time employees can make $40,000 a year, depending on the location at which they work; assistant managers, called "mates," make substantially more. Store managers, who are called "captains," make around $100,000. All Trader Joe's employees receive a 10 percent discount, and, given what the store sells, that employee discount gets used a lot. In addition, all employees — including part-timers who work more than seventeen hours a week[8] — get benefits. Employees also receive a Christmas bonus.[9]

At QuikTrip, an entry-level assistant manager makes close to

---

* As of the writing of this book, implementation of the Affordable Care Act (ACA) of 2010, which has consequences for part-time employees, is underway. Several companies that offer health benefits for part-timers have decided to change their policies. Costco has not yet announced any changes. Trader Joe's has just announced that it will stop providing health insurance to part-time employees so that they can obtain a better deal through the ACA. The company will provide a $500 subsidy toward the employees' purchase of health insurance through the ACA and may consider additional subsidies for employees on a case-by-case basis.

$40,000 per year, first and second assistant managers make around $50,000, and store managers make between $60,000 and $80,000. While part-time clerks start considerably lower — around $8 an hour — they are offered a customer service bonus after their first six months, which is typically 10 percent of their annual wage. The average salary for part-time employees is around $13,000. QuikTrip tries very hard to make sure that its part-timers are students or those who do not need the money to support a family (the average age of its part-timers is 21.75 years old). During the interview process, the interviewer asks the candidate: "Here is how many hours we can give you [typically around 20] and here is how much we can pay. Is that going to be sufficient for you? Or are you looking for a job that supports you and your family?"

All QuikTrip employees receive a range of benefits, including a Christmas bonus, tuition reimbursement, free fountain drinks and coffee when they are on duty, and an employee assistance program to help with personal problems. All employees can benefit from the QuikTrip Cares Employee Disaster Fund, dedicated to helping employees who are affected by natural disasters or life-altering emergencies such as a house fire, an accident, or a sudden illness in the family.

OPPORTUNITY FOR SUCCESS AND GROWTH

Employees who work for retailers that operate in a vicious cycle don't just have low wages, poor benefits, and erratic schedules. The lack of meaning and dignity in their jobs is a big contributor to their dissatisfaction. The design of their jobs makes it hard for them to do a good job, and they complain of a lack of respect from their managers.

For example, many employees complain that they simply do not have the right equipment to do their jobs. One employee in charge of shelving merchandise in the water area at a large retailer said he did not have access to pallet jacks to move water. There were additional jacks that were broken, but the store manager was worried about his budget and wouldn't have them repaired. Think about how heavy water is and how hard — and slow — it would be to shelve it. Another employee from the same retail chain said she always goes to work early so that she can secure one of the few "rocket carts" — specialized carts for stocking and moving merchandise around. The store didn't have enough of them and she had trouble moving heavy products, such as boxes of paper, without one.

Because model retailers invest more in their employees, they cannot afford to have them work unproductively. As a result, they make sure that employees have the resources needed to perform their jobs. Quik-Trip, for example, has its own facility support for all equipment in its stores. Say the coffee machine is not brewing properly. Store employees submit an electronic request and a deadline for when they need it fixed. A technician assigned to that store (each technician serves five stores) would then come and fix the problem.

Equipment is important, but model retailers go well beyond that basic requirement to set their employees up for success. As we will see in later chapters, they design store processes in a way that enables success and they give employees the necessary training and time so that they can carry out their tasks well. They also empower them to make decisions. Employees don't make all the decisions, but they make small decisions all the time. All this improves employee satisfaction and is an investment in the virtuous cycle.

When employees in these companies do well, they know they can move up. Almost all store managers at Costco and 100 percent of store managers at Mercadona, QuikTrip, and Trader Joe's are promoted from within, and many executives of these companies started out in the stores.

Less tangible and measurable than any of these policies, but just as important to the success of the virtuous cycle, is the feeling — expressed to me by employees at all four model retailers — that they are part of something bigger than themselves and that their job matters. Patty from QuikTrip described to me how happy she could feel at the end of the day, looking back on the work she and her team had done and the many customers they had pleased. "You look around and you're like, 'Guys, look at how good the store looks. We did this all today, ourselves. We just made it happen. We waited on over one thousand customers.'"

Some employees see their job as bigger and more important than the immediate work at hand in the same way as they may see their families as bigger and more important than today's homework assignment or sink full of dirty dishes. "[I'm] always looking for the repeat customers that always come back," said Patty. "[That] makes you build the relationships . . . they bring their kids, and eventually their kids bring their kids. And it's just an endless cycle. And that's very rewarding."

SATISFIED EMPLOYEES

A lot of employees at these retailers started out as part-timers when they were in school but then decided to make a career with their company because the pay, the benefits, and the opportunities were so good. And indeed, employees at these companies do tend to stay for a long time. QuikTrip's 13 percent turnover rate among full-time employees is substantially lower than the 59 percent rate in the top quartile of the convenience store industry. At Trader Joe's, turnover among full-time employees is less than 10 percent. Turnover for employees who stay at Costco for more than a year is 5.5 percent. And we saw before that turnover at Mercadona is less than 4 percent.

Jobs at these companies are perceived to be so good that it can be statistically harder to get one than it is to get into an Ivy League college. QuikTrip's recruiting manager, Mark Milburn, told me that in the Atlanta market, 90 percent of the applicants do not even qualify for an interview. Even so, the company ends up interviewing five people for every job opening. That makes QuikTrip's acceptance rate in Atlanta 2 percent! When Costco opened a new store in Green Oak Township, Michigan, 5,000 people applied for 160 spots; this was in 2005, when unemployment was only around 5 percent.[10]

Anecdotal evidence from Glassdoor, a popular online community in which people anonymously provide information about their jobs, also suggests that employees at these companies like to work there. Glassdoor asks people a very revealing question: Would you "recommend this employer to a friend?" (A similar question is the basis for a commonly used measure of customer loyalty.) In August 2012, Costco scored 82 percent on this question, QuikTrip 83 percent, and Trader Joe's 84 percent. In comparison, Walmart scored 47 percent, Target 62 percent, Home Depot 58 percent, and Staples 46 percent.[11]

The Payoff for Customers

LOW PRICES

Clearly, the employees are happy at these model retailers. What about the customers? To begin with, all four retailers offer their customers low prices.

Costco, of course, is a wholesale club. The low prices are why you join. According to cheapism.com, a site dedicated to informing customers about cheap products, Costco's prices are about 40 percent lower than those in a typical supermarket. Even Sam's Club doesn't have lower prices overall.[12]

The two supermarkets in our group of model retailers, Trader Joe's and Mercadona, are also known for their low prices. According to price monitoring prepared by Spain's Ministry of Industry, Tourism, and Trade, Mercadona is the cheapest food retailer in Spain. Its prices are about 2 percent lower than those of its competitor, Carrefour, which is a much larger, global company.[13] *Consumer Reports* gave Trader Joe's its highest score for low prices. In addition, Trader Joe's customers swear by the good deals they get. Some customers are so passionate that they publish their price comparisons online just to show the world how much can be saved by shopping at Trader Joe's.[14] If there is one product Trader Joe's is known for, it has to be "two-buck Chuck," the nickname given to Charles Shaw wine, which, until recently, sold for $1.99 a bottle.

QuikTrip is a price leader in the convenience store industry for the items it sells: fresh prepared foods, tobacco products, beer, snacks, grocery items, and beverages. For certain high-volume items such as soda, gasoline, and beer, QuikTrip's prices are as low as Walmart's. In most markets, QuikTrip's low gasoline prices help it maintain a higher market share than those of its competitors, despite the fact that its closest competitor in most markets has four times the number of locations.

CUSTOMER SERVICE

I often make presentations about these model retailers to executives and MBA students. When I want to make the point that these retailers provide good customer service, I just ask the audience to volunteer their experiences at Costco, Mercadona, QuikTrip, or Trader Joe's. The service that people describe is wonderful, from the speed with which the lines disappear at Costco to the Trader Joe's employee who gently reminded a customer that her pancake mix would need eggs.

In the beginning of this chapter, I described how good Mercadona's operations are. Mercadona customers have no trouble finding the products they want in clean and orderly stores. But they get a lot more than this. Mercadona's principle number seven, "the company has to prescribe," calls on employees to be knowledgeable about the selling floor and to recommend to the customers the highest-quality, most affordable, or safest products. Each section is staffed by a specialist whose job is to talk to the customers and tell them about the products. In many retail settings, there is often no employee to help customers on the selling floor, and even when there is one, he or she doesn't know all that much about the products. Mercadona constantly informs its employees about new products or about existing products turning up in new packages.

The culture of customer service pervades the organization. For example, when Mercadona managers took me on store visits, they never parked in the stores' often small parking lots even when there were empty spaces. Those parking lots were for the customers, they told me, not for them.

QuikTrip's customer service is also better than that of its competitors, according to both its own mystery shoppers and external evaluations. Mystery shoppers at QuikTrip are hired by QuikTrip's corporate office, and their identities are kept secret from the stores. These employees visit stores posing as customers and evaluate customer service. They are generally terminated if store employees discover their identities. QuikTrip mystery shoppers do the same evaluation for various competitors' stores, including fast-food chains such as Chick-fil-A and McDonald's; grocery stores such as Hy-Vee and Kroger; pharmacies such as Walgreens and CVS; convenience and gas stores such as Shell, Chevron, Exxon, RaceTrac, and 7-Eleven; and Walmart. In 2010, the composite average score for the competitive set was 76.1 percent; QuikTrip's was 94 percent.

QuikTrip also ranks among the top in customer service according to mystery shopper visits conducted by *CSP* magazine, which covers the convenience store industry. When it comes to speed of checkout, cleanliness, and merchandising, QuikTrip consistently scores over 90 percent and often near 100 percent.[15]

QuikTrip's fast checkout is a sight to behold. One thing that makes it so fast is that any employee can use any cash register at any time without making the customer wait. If you regularly shop at a supermarket, you know it's no fun waiting for the cashiers to do a changeover. The other thing that makes QuikTrip so fast is that employees have been trained to ring up three customers per minute. How do they do this? For many high-turnover items, such as soda, the cashier doesn't have to bother scanning the item. One more thing: QuikTrip employees can calculate your change in their heads. So if your coffee costs 89 cents, the employee at the register can see you and have the 11 cents ready before you can even pull that dollar bill out of your pocket. (That's a perfect example of great customer service that has nothing to do with personal interaction. It's a piece of operational excellence that makes your visit there go the way you want it to — quickly.)

Costco's customer satisfaction is as high in the American Customer Satisfaction Index as that of Nordstrom, a department store chain famous for its customer service. How could it be that customers at a wholesale club are as satisfied as customers at Nordstrom? Anyone who shops at Costco knows that he or she will find quality merchandise at low prices, that it will be in the right place, and that he or she will get in and out quickly. Even long checkout lines aren't a problem because the cashiers are so efficient.

Consumer Reports ranks both Trader Joe's and Costco high in terms of customer service. The Consumer Reports National Research Center analyzed 24,203 responses that described 42,695 shopping experiences at food store chains of various formats (supermarkets, supercenters, and wholesale clubs). The readers were asked about their overall satisfaction with their experience in these stores. One hundred percent meant completely satisfied, 80 percent very satisfied, and 60 percent fairly satisfied. Of the fifty-two retail chains, Trader Joe's and Costco were both in the top five, with scores of 86 and 83 percent, respectively.[16] Number one was Wegmans, another chain known for great employee practices; it is consistently in the top five of *Fortune*'s list of the top one hundred companies to work for.[17]

The Payoff to Investors

To qualify as a model retailer — one that pursues the good jobs strategy in low-cost retail — great operations and excellent customer service must result in great financial performance. For Costco, QuikTrip, Mercadona, and Trader Joe's, they do.

Of these retailers, only Costco is a public company, and as you may recall from chapter 1, its stock performance has been much better than Walmart's during the last decade.[18] If you had invested $100 in Costco stock in June 2003, your investment would have more than tripled in ten years. If you had invested that money in Walmart stock, your investment would have gone up by only 40 percent.

All four of these model retailers are growing profitably and managing their key assets productively. There are three key assets in retail: real estate, inventory, and people. Model retailers optimize all three. They all sell more per square foot and per employee and turn over their inventory faster than their competitors do. In other words, their space is more productive, their employees are more productive, and their inventory is more productive.

For example, Costco's sales per square foot are almost 70 percent higher than Sam's Club's is,[19] and its typical employee generates almost twice as much sales as a typical Sam's Club employee does.[20] Costco turns its inventory twice as quickly as a typical discount variety retailer does and 50 percent faster than Walmart does.[21]

Trader Joe's sales per square foot are almost triple the supermarket industry average, and its labor productivity is almost 40 percent higher than the industry average. Mercadona's sales per square foot are more than double the supermarket industry average and more than 50 percent higher than that of its largest competitor, Carrefour. Again, Mercadona's employees are more productive than those of its competitors. Its sales per employee are 18 percent higher than that of other

Spanish supermarkets and 46 percent higher than that of an average U.S. supermarket. Mercadona and Trader Joe's both turn their inventory more than twice as quickly as a typical food retailer does.[22]

QuikTrip's sales per square foot are more than 50 percent higher than the average for convenience stores. Its gas sales are twice the industry average. QuikTrip's sales per employee-hour are 66 percent higher than the industry average and 50 percent higher than the top quartile in its industry.[23]

Why are these retailers more productive in every way? Because they do not suffer all the operational problems that retailers operating in a vicious cycle suffer. Their customers find the products they want in the right place with the right price. People are so happy with the service they get that they keep coming back. As we have seen all along, area productivity and inventory productivity rest on a foundation of employee productivity. It all comes down to these companies' investments in their most important asset — their people.

A well-paid, well-trained, well-motivated, and not-understaffed workforce also helps each of these companies to control its costs better than its competitors can do. For example, while the average for shrink in convenience stores and natural and specialty food stores in the United States was 1.52 percent in 2010,[24] QuikTrip's was 0.6 percent. The difference is close to 1 percent of sales, and that goes right to the bottom line, a huge amount in an industry with razor-thin margins. At around 0.2 percent of sales, Costco's shrink is one of the lowest in all of retailing.[25]

What Is Their Secret?

Investment in employees allows model retailers to deliver better value to both customers and investors. There are obvious advantages to having a loyal and committed workforce. They work harder and they work better. You get lower employee turnover, so you have people with more experience making fewer mistakes. In addition, there are financial benefits to operating with low turnover. You limit disruptions and training costs. But as we saw at Home Depot, investment in people isn't enough. Home Depot had a loyal and committed workforce, but it still ran into trouble because it lacked operational discipline.

The virtuous cycle does not operate on its own. At Costco, Mercadona, QuikTrip, and Trader Joe's, investing in people is complemented with four operational choices (described in the next four chapters) that reduce costs, increase labor productivity, and put employees at the center of the company's success. These four operational choices are good for employees, customers, and investors all at the same time.

Though these four choices are common to each of the model retailers, they are fairly uncommon at most other retailers.

But it isn't only the four operational choices that make the model retailers as good as they are. These operational choices work as well as they do when they are executed together *and* when they are combined with investment in people. They are the hidden gears that multiply the power of a well-paid, well-trained, well-motivated workforce, turning a large investment in employees into great service for customers and high returns for investors.

CHAPTER 5

Operational Choice #1

Offer Less

C OSTCO WON'T DO a lot of things for its customers. It won't provide shopping bags. It won't put signs on the aisles that tell customers where products are located. It won't even try to offer a pleasant shopping environment — its stores have bare cement floors, industrial lighting, and bulky products stocked on top of each other. When it comes to the products themselves, Costco won't offer many choices. Want to buy diapers? You have only two options, Huggies and Kirkland (Costco's private label).

Costco won't advertise to get customers into its stores. And it won't offer extended shopping hours. The stores typically close at 8:30 p.m. on weekdays and even earlier on the weekends. They won't even stay open for holidays such as Memorial Day, Independence Day, and Easter. Oh, and you want to pay with your Visa or MasterCard? Sorry, Costco accepts only American Express or cash.

In a television program about the company in 2012, a CNBC reporter asked, "Who in the world would shop there?" The show answered its own question: "About three million fanatically loyal customers every day." In fact, it is fair to say that all those things that Costco *won't* offer its customers contribute greatly to customer satisfaction and to Costco's success.

Model retailers offer their customers less than their competitors do. As the Costco example shows, there are many ways to offer less. But in this chapter, I'll focus on two of them — offering fewer products and limiting sales promotions. These choices allow model retailers to pursue the good jobs strategy by substantially lowering their costs, increasing employees' productivity, and making employees the center of the company's success.

Offering less does not work only for model retailers; it is an important driver of success and an enabler of the good jobs strategy for companies in a wide range of settings. But it always requires companies to be very careful about what they do and do not offer. We will see later in this chapter what can happen when that criterion is not met.

Driven by "More Is Better"

Readers familiar with microeconomics may remember the "more is better" assumption in consumer preference theory. (The fancy academic name for it is "nonsatiation.") This is the assumption that consumers derive some happiness from being offered more. Perhaps it is this assumption that has pushed companies to constantly offer more to their customers and hope that their customers, in turn, will buy more.

You can see this assumption at work just about anywhere. When I was a kid, there was one flavor of Coca-Cola. Now there are more than fifteen flavors, and they each come in lots of different sizes. At McDonald's, the original menu offered three choices: hamburger, cheeseburger, and fries. Now McDonald's offers different types of burgers; sandwiches made with fish, chicken, and pork; chicken nuggets; salads; pies; cookies; yogurt parfaits; and more.

We are offered thousands of new products every year. In the United States, 18,722 new food and beverage products were introduced in 2005, including more than 5,000 types of candy, gum, and snack; 4,700 new beverages; and close to 2,000 new condiments. And if you think that's because innovative manufacturers are constantly thinking up great new products, consider the following: Close to 95 percent of new food and beverage introductions are classified as "not innovative," and in many categories, more than 90 percent of new product introductions fail.[1]

The variety is so great that shopping at a supermarket can be daunting. My local supermarket offers me around 600 choices in tea, 150 in pasta, 110 in jam, and 70 in olive oil. In some categories, such as olive oil, the choices include not only different types of product but also different sizes. When shopping there, I often think of a line that has been attributed to several famous people, including Mark Twain: "I didn't have time to write a short letter, so I wrote a long one instead." It is as if the store hasn't taken the time to really figure out what its customers want or which products will best satisfy their needs, so instead it just offers everything.

Of course, this is an exaggeration, because no retail store offers *everything*. Even supermarkets that carry tens of thousands of different products choose those products from over a million available items. But from the customer's point of view, the variety in a typical store is overwhelming.

Offering more is not limited to physical products; we are also offered more when it comes to options for retirement plans, medical treatment, phone service, life insurance, and — thanks to online dating sites — many more options for finding a partner.

We are also offered more deals. "20 percent off!" "Limited time only!" "Buy two, get one free!" "Previously $15.99, now $12.99!" "Sale ends tomorrow!" We notice that the products keep moving around the store, depending on what's on sale. If you are a careful shopper and can predict when your store will mark certain items on sale, you are probably convinced that you can save a lot of money by taking advantage of these promotions.

We're not only looking at more products and more promotions. Retail stores are now open longer hours. Need milk at 11:00 p.m.? No need to find a convenience store — many supermarkets are now open until midnight or even twenty-four hours a day. Some stores stay open during holidays. In 2012, for the first time, Walmart, Target, Kmart, Sears, and some other stores chose to open on Thanksgiving Day at 8:00 p.m. and offered customers great discounts.

The Costs of Offering More

Offering more products is supposed to help companies by improving customer service and increasing sales. Promotions, too, are intended to increase sales. When manufacturers have a new product to offer — and, as we saw previously, they constantly do — promotions are a way for them to get shelf space and to stimulate demand.

But what retailers do not realize is how much each additional product, each additional promotion, and each additional holiday they choose to stay open increases the complexity of their business. Higher product variety and more promotions, in particular, increase costs all throughout the supply chain, boosting manufacturing costs, transportation costs, inventory costs, store labor costs, and stockout costs. That's if everything goes right. More product variety and promotions also increase the likelihood of errors and operational problems in the stores.

And one way or another, as we shall see, the consequences of offering more fall all too often upon employees.

More Stockouts and More Waste — What a Great Combination!

Despite all the advances in supply chain management and all the investments in inventory-planning systems and information technology to track products, the retail industry still has trouble matching product supply with customer demand. Stores carry too few of the products that customers want and too many of the products they don't want.

The rate of stockouts has not changed during the last few decades, even for products such as pasta and diapers that should have pretty predictable demand. Studies show that in settings such as supermarkets, customers have experienced stockouts around 8 percent of the time during the last few decades. For products that are on promotion, the rate is much higher.[2]

Stockouts are expensive for both retailers and manufacturers. When customers can't find what they want in a particular store, some will buy a substitute, but more than 50 percent will either delay their purchase, buy the product at another store, or decide not to buy it at all.[3]

In other words, more than half the time, the retailer with an item out of stock won't make the sale that day.

Meanwhile, the retailer can have the opposite problem — stocking too much of something people aren't buying. In this case, the retailer suffers from needlessly high inventory costs and our environment suffers because of all the waste. The U.S. Department of Agriculture estimates that supermarkets lose $15 billion annually in unsold fruits and vegetables alone.[4] In 2008, the food waste in retail was approximately 43 billion pounds. Think about that. Forty-three billion pounds of food was grown, distributed, and shelved in stores, only to be thrown away. All the water, fuel, and other resources that were spent in the process were for nothing. Most of this waste goes to landfills; according to the U.S. Environmental Protection Agency, less than 3 percent of all that food waste was recovered and recycled in 2008.[5]

It ought to be pretty straightforward to manage inventory for products that have fairly predictable demand. So why do retailers have so many stockouts and so much waste?

Part of the blame falls on customers and their high expectations. When we go to a supermarket, we expect to find everything we are looking for, even if the store is just about to close. We also expect everything to be in perfect shape. We won't buy an apple with a brown spot, even if it's perfectly nutritious and tastes great.

Poor store execution and poor inventory planning also contribute to waste and stockouts. But two other big drivers are the sheer number of SKUs* and promotions. Inventory management is a lot more complicated when there are more products and more promotions. Higher product variety and more promotions almost always mean carrying more inventory, not just the same total inventory spread over a greater number of products. Moreover, greater inventory doesn't even necessarily mean fewer stockouts.

---

* "SKU" stands for "stock keeping unit," a term used in inventory management for a specific item for sale that can be distinguished from other items by attributes such as what it is, what company made it, what size or color it is, how it is packaged, and so on. Any two items with the same SKU are exactly the same thing; any two items with different SKUs are different choices.

Let's Talk about Inventory

Inventory management might not seem like the most exciting topic, but it is something we all do all the time. For example, we all manage the cash (or lack of it) in our wallet. We decide how frequently we should withdraw cash and how much to take out each time. Suppose there is no ATM near your home or near where you work, so you use the ATM only once a week. How much cash should you take out when you do?

First, you need to forecast how much cash you'll need for the week. Let's say you forecast your demand for cash in the coming week to be $100. But you also know it could turn out to be more. You might take a taxi or you might bump into a friend and decide to treat him for lunch at the local diner that doesn't take credit cards. Of course, you might also end up needing less than $100.

Given this uncertainty in demand, how should you decide how much cash to withdraw? Well, if you want to make sure that you don't ever run out of cash, you should definitely withdraw more than $100. On the other hand, if the cost of carrying cash around is very high — say you are worried that you might lose it or that your bank account will be down to almost nothing or that you might get mugged in a bad neighborhood — then you might decide to withdraw just the $100 you forecasted. You might even take out less, hope for the best, and deal with the inconvenience if you happen to run out.

Retailers use a similar logic when they choose how many units of a particular product to stock. In fact, for products that are staples or necessities, most retailers want to make sure they never run out.

Take toothpaste, for example. Most retailers want to make sure that when customers come to the store for toothpaste, the product is there. Managing toothpaste inventory would be pretty straightforward if there were just one type of toothpaste and it was always at the same price. It shouldn't be hard to forecast how much toothpaste a store will sell on average. Retailers generally know how many customers typically shop at the store and how frequently an average customer buys toothpaste. Like the individual deciding how much cash to carry, the store would stock the forecasted quantity plus some extra to deal with variability. In the field of inventory management, this extra stock is called "safety stock."

Offering More Means Higher Inventory Costs

But what happens if there are hundreds of types of toothpaste? There were 364 types of toothpaste in January 2011 — and that was down from 412 types in March 2008.[6] And what happens when different kinds are on promotion at different times? Now we have to forecast not only how much toothpaste we will sell in aggregate, but also how much of each type we will sell. That is not easy!

The more types of toothpaste we add to the mix, the less accurate our demand forecasts for each one will be. In fact, this is one of the universal truths of forecasting: Aggregate forecasts are always more accurate than individual forecasts. This doesn't only apply to products. Sales forecasts for a retail chain are more accurate than sales forecasts for each individual store, sales forecasts for a week are more accurate than sales forecasts for each day, and so on.

Promotions make forecasting even more difficult. When a product is on sale, demand can become distorted. Some customers will buy more than they need just because it's on sale. Then, when the sale is over, they don't buy any for a while. Finally, sales return to normal. In technical terms, we would say that "real consumption is decoupled from customers' purchasing." There will be spikes and dips even in the sale of products with flat consumption, that is, products you can't really use more or less of in a given time, such as, well, toothpaste or toilet paper. Promotions can also cause customers to switch brands, which is exactly what the manufacturer loves to see. But for the retailer, customers' switching brands makes it even harder to forecast what the demand for each brand will be.

Thus, when there are a lot of products and promotions, customer demand is more uncertain and forecasts are less accurate. What does that mean for inventory management? If we want to ensure the same level of service while increasing the variety of products — that is, if we want to offer one hundred kinds of toothpaste and practically guarantee that we are in stock when a customer wants any one of them — then we'll need to carry safety stock for each of those one hundred kinds. The total safety stock for one hundred varieties of toothpaste will be a lot more than the safety stock we would need if we only carried one or a few kinds.

So more products in a category demands more investment in inventory in order to achieve the same level of service. That means that more working capital is tied up in inventory. In addition, while certain products, such as toothpaste, may be held for a long time, some products, such as bananas and flowers, can quickly become unsellable. For such products, more inventory inevitably means more waste.

More Inventory Doesn't Always Prevent Stockouts

The benefit of more inventory is assumed to be fewer stockouts. This assumption seems to make perfect sense. In our cash example, the more money you withdraw, the less likely you are to run out of cash during the week. But when it comes to stores, reality is different than theory.

In one study, we found that increasing inventory levels increases phantom stockouts and indirectly decreases sales.[7] Why? Shelf space in stores is limited, so the greater the inventory, the more products are stored in back rooms. Employees spend more time going back and forth between the back room and the selling floor. Sometimes employees may forget to restock the shelves with the product from the back room; or even if they remember they are supposed to do it, they may not have time to do so. The store then ends up with more products that are in the back room and not on the selling floor. Many customers don't bother to ask for help when they can't find what they are looking for. Others do ask, but the employee may not be able to find what's in the back room, may not realize it's there, or just may not have time to get it. The result of all this is a sales decrease from phantom stockouts.

Offering More Increases Costs Throughout the Supply Chain

For the retailer, a high variety of products doesn't just lead to higher supply-demand mismatch costs (either too much or too little inventory). If you carry just a few types of toothpaste, you will be selling a lot of each type and can get discounts for buying in bulk. But if you carry hundreds of different types, you will buy and sell fewer units of each and each unit will cost more. In addition, retail buyers need to spend more time coordinating different products, and therefore the retailer charges higher prices for each product. More product variety also means increased costs throughout the supply chain. Both distributors and manufacturers incur higher supply-demand mismatch costs. Furthermore, higher product variety decreases labor productivity and increases overhead labor costs, rework costs, and inventory costs.[8]

Promotions, too, increase costs throughout the supply chain. Promotions cause customers to exhibit a lot of variability in their purchasing, even of products that normally have pretty steady consumption. It turns out that this variability is amplified as we move backward along the supply chain. That is, retailers' orders to wholesalers show more variability than customers' purchases from retailers. Orders from wholesalers to manufacturers exhibit more variability than retailers' orders. Orders from manufacturers to their suppliers exhibit even more variability. This amplification of variability in the upstream supply chain, called the "bullwhip effect," is expensive for every player.

More promotions saddle retailers with higher supply-demand mismatch costs. Retailers also incur higher store labor costs because employees have to keep setting up and breaking down the promotional displays, which includes shelving and unshelving products, changing prices, and then changing them back.

Distributors in retail supply chains also pay a price for promotions. High variability in their customer demand causes the same problems for them that it causes for the retailers—higher inventory costs and higher stockout costs.

For manufacturers and their suppliers, high variability in orders either means high variability in production or holding a lot of inventory, both of which are expensive. Frequent production changeovers may also invite errors. Promotions stick manufacturers with higher administrative and selling costs. And there are increased transportation costs throughout the supply chain because of the highly variable demand for transportation equipment.

....

HIGH-QUALITY BURGERS AT LOW PRICES

On a recent visit to California, my family and I treated ourselves to an extraordinary version of the most ordinary of American meals. We went to a burger chain and had hamburgers made from beef that had never been frozen and contained no additives, fillers, or preservatives. The lettuce was crisp and hand-leafed. The onions were hand-cut. The bun was freshly baked and lightly toasted. The fries were made from whole potatoes, sliced fresh right there and fried in trans-fat-free vegetable oil. My five-year-old, who is already a foodie—his favorite food is oysters!—ate his burger with gusto.

Now I understood why In-N-Out, a chain of 281 stores, has such a cultlike following. I also understood why it consistently earns one of the highest customer satisfaction scores of any fast-food chain.[9] I know—even my five-year-old knows—that hamburgers and fries are not good for us. But were these ever good!

The hamburgers were just $1.90, quite a bit cheaper than Big Macs at McDonald's or Whoppers at Burger King, which aren't made with such fresh ingredients or so much hand labor. Great quality, low prices, and yes, In-N-Out offers better jobs than other fast-food chains.[10] As of the end of 2012, the company was privately owned, so there is not much data on its financial performance, but outsiders consider the company to be extremely successful. The company has had steady sales and profitability growth, and analysts estimate its profit margins to be around a healthy 20 percent.[11] Even Warren Buffet thinks so highly of its performance that he is reported to have told UCLA students that he would love to own In-N-Out. During the same discussion, Buffet mentioned that the other company he would love to own is Trader Joe's—no surprises there.[12]

How can In-N-Out deliver great burgers at such low prices?

One factor is a menu with only six items—hamburgers, cheeseburgers, double doubles (a double cheeseburger), fries, shakes, and soft drinks. That's it. No salads, no chicken, no desserts. Given how quickly food becomes unsellable, a restaurant that operates with less waste than its competitors has a big cost advantage. Such a small menu means In-N-Out can easily forecast demand for its ingredients, reduce waste, and reduce costs all through its supply chain. The small menu also helps the chain improve labor productivity, decrease errors, and maintain consistently high quality.

....

More May Not Be More, Even for the Customers

You may be asking, What about customers? Yes, things may be more expensive for companies when they offer more products and more promotions. But isn't it the case that the more products a store carries in a particular category, the more likely it is that the customer will find what he or she is looking for? Isn't it true that the more promotions a store offers, the more customers it will attract? Doesn't this all mean higher sales?

Not always. A higher variety of products and more promotions increase the complexity of a store's operations, causing employees to make more mistakes or to cut corners. The result is operational problems, which then lead to higher prices and poor customer service, which will eventually bring down sales and profits. Higher product variety can also overwhelm a customer and lead him or her to leave a store without buying any of the choices.

Let's first take a look at the operational reasons that more choice is not always the blessing it is assumed to be. Then we will see what consumer behaviorists say about this.

Operational Complexity Degrading Customer Service

Higher product variety makes operational execution more difficult. The study mentioned earlier in this chapter found that increasing a store's product variety increases phantom stockouts, which of course *decreases* sales.[13] In some settings, the increase in sales due to offering customers more variety may outweigh the decrease due to phantom stockouts, but there are still other operational problems to consider, such as inaccurate data and pricing errors.

It's easy to see why more problems would occur with a higher variety of products. Many products in a category look similar, so employees often confuse them or don't even bother to separate them, especially under time pressure. One employee who worked in the back room at a Target store described what a pain it was to manage toothbrushes:

> You get a whole ton. I remember some of the guys would put them in the bins and sometimes it would be so many . . . sometimes they would mix up different types of toothbrushes. So a lot of times we had to . . . pull out the toothbrushes one by one, scan them to see if it was the proper one we were looking for. . . . They had a tendency of confusing certain toothbrushes because the box will look almost the same.

When things look so similar, it's easy to put them in the wrong place on the display shelves, which not only makes products hard to find but can also confuse customers about prices and force the retailer to eat the difference.

Cashiers have difficulty differentiating products, too. They may scan one product multiple times without recognizing or caring that the customer is actually buying several different (though similar) products. In this way, cashiers end up injecting errors into the inventory records and therefore into the retailer's purchasing decisions. Remember the tomato example in chapter 3, in which a supermarket chain's data showed that it had sold 25 percent more medium-size tomatoes than it ever had in stock? One contributor to that problem is offering so many types of tomatoes in a grocery store. When a cashier, especially an inexperienced one, sees a bag of tomatoes, she might enter the code for medium red tomatoes even though they're actually big beef, heirloom, roma, or plum tomatoes. Any type of tomato looks like a medium red tomato for an employee who is in a hurry or who has never been told the difference, or who, for one reason or another, couldn't care less.

More promotions also make operational execution more difficult and lead to more errors. If you walk into a store looking to buy an item that is advertised to be on sale, you may not be able to find that item.

Studies have shown that stockouts for products on sale can be more than twice as high as stockouts for regular products.[14] And that's not necessarily because of high demand. Often, there are more stockouts because of poor operational execution.

All these problems end up degrading customer service and reducing sales.

Customer Confusion

Store employees are not the only people who get confused by so many promotions and so many products; it's also the customers. Let's stick with the toothpaste example and see how bad the situation can be for customers.

When customers walk into a grocery store, they might find any of 364 different types and sizes of toothpaste. How can there be so many kinds, you may ask? Well, do you want Colgate, Crest, Aquafresh, Arm & Hammer, Close-Up, Sensodyne, Signal, Tom's of Maine, or one of the many others? Do you want it as a paste or a gel? Do you want it in a tube or a pump? We're just getting started here. Which size do you want — three ounces, six ounces, travel size, economy size? Which flavor do you want? You could have brisk mint, frosty mint, cool mint, crisp mint, cinnamint, vanilla, watermelon, bubblegum — and that's just a few of them. What are you using the toothpaste for? Toothpaste has a lot of uses, including whitening, plaque prevention, gingivitis prevention, cavity protection, tartar control, long-lasting fresh breath, and sensitivity relief.

Colgate alone offers Total Whitening, Total Advanced Whitening, Whitening with Oxygen Bubbles, Sparkling White, Simply White, and Max White with Mini Bright Strips. (Honestly, can you read this list with a straight face?)

Say you want to try a new toothpaste. What combination of use and flavor would you prefer? Are you such a toothpaste connoisseur that you can tell the difference between cool mint and crisp mint? Do you even know whether your teeth need tartar control or gingivitis relief or sensitivity relief? To most people, the differences among these different types are not even noticeable. And for many of us, the variety in the toothpaste aisle (along with many other aisles in the supermarket) is less enticing than it is aggravating.

Several studies have shown that when offered too many choices, especially when the differences among the choices are small, people end up being so confused that some decide not to buy anything at all.

Perhaps the most widely cited study of this response is the one conducted by Sheena Iyengar of Columbia Business School and Mark Lepper of Stanford University. They set up a tasting booth at a supermarket in California that is known for its wide selection. Sometimes the tasting booth offered six varieties of jam, sometimes it offered twenty-four varieties. Shoppers who took part in the sampling were rewarded with a discount voucher to buy any jam of the same brand in the store.

The researchers found that the larger selection of jams attracted more shoppers. When the tasting booth displayed twenty-four different types of jam, 60 percent of the people passing by tried a sample, but when it displayed only six types of jam, only 40 percent of the passers-by tried a sample. But trying a sample is not the same as buying. Of the people who got to taste among six choices, 30 percent took advantage of the discount and bought a jar of jam. But of those who got to taste among twenty-four choices, only 3 percent bothered to buy a jam. The rest passed.

When people were offered *more* choices, most were so overwhelmed and confused that they chose not to buy anything at all — even at a discount! Imagine the situation in ordinary — not experimental — circumstances. Besides being confused, you may be less likely to buy if a large assortment still doesn't include your favorite. Say your favorite jam is black cherry. When the supermarket carries only six types and black cherry isn't one of them, you might not mind and buy something else. But if there are twenty-four varieties, including all sorts of weird types you never heard of but *not* the one you wanted, you may just become peeved and say, "To hell with it."

Alternate versions of this study were conducted using different products and settings, ranging from selecting flavors of Godiva chocolate or selecting a romantic partner through speed dating to choosing a college essay topic or a 401(k) plan. Researchers found that having more choices not only leads to confusion but also often leads to being less satisfied with the choice. Say you sorted through twenty-four types of jam and picked apple-raspberry. Now you are home and the apple-raspberry is okay, but there *were* so many other choices, so you're wondering if apple-cranberry would have been better. Perhaps you don't think so much about a small item like jam, but you might think a lot about which refrigerator or TV or car you ultimately spent quite a lot of money on. There *were* many, many other choices. Would one of them have been better?

What does all this mean for companies? It means that they can get away with offering fewer choices to their customers without reducing sales. Lower variety may even *increase* sales, and customers could be more satisfied with what they buy if their options are limited.

Model Retailers Offer Less

We have spent all this time discussing the costs of offering more to customers so we can understand why doing just the opposite helps a company pursue the good jobs strategy and maintain the virtuous cycle.

Model retailers offer fewer products than their competitors do. While an average supermarket carries close to forty thousand products, Mercadona carries eight thousand and Trader Joe's carries around four thousand. Costco carries around four thousand products while its biggest competitor, Sam's Club, carries more than five thousand, and another competitor, BJ's, carries around seven thousand. In all the categories it offers, QuikTrip stocks only high-volume products. Model retailers also do not continually change prices to stimulate demand. They offer everyday low prices.

It is easy to see how offering less can reduce costs and allow companies to sell products at low prices. But here's the thing: If you want to offer less in order to benefit from the savings, you had better make sure that what you offer is exactly what your customers want. Offering less forces companies to be a lot more rigorous about what they offer. Let's examine how Trader Joe's determines which products it offers and how offering less affects its customers, employees, and financial performance.

Trader Joe's — A Store of Stories

Trader Joe's may have a small assortment of products compared with other supermarkets, but the products that *do* make it to the shelves are often loved by its customers. Doug Rauch, the former president of Trader Joe's, told my students that it is not uncommon for the company to receive notes from loyal customers raving about Trader Joe's products. In my class, Doug shared a photo of a couple along with the following note:

> You might think that after living in a remote village with no water or electricity for one year that we would miss things like hot showers, TV, microwave ovens, washing machines and telephones. But what we really miss is Trader Joe's Chocolate Covered Caramel Popcorn and Trader Joe's Ginger Granola.

Trader Joe's depends on its "category leaders" — what we would often call "buyers" at other retailers — to find these products. But category leaders don't just look at existing products on the market. They travel the world and visit all sorts of food businesses, ranging from restaurants to farmers markets to street sellers, to find delicious food. They then spend time with potential suppliers to convert what they've found into a Trader Joe's–worthy product, which means, among other things, no artificial flavors, no MSG, no synthetic colors, no partially hydrogenated oils, and always at a low price.

Even then, the product has to go through a rigorous taste test by an expert tasting panel before making it to the shelves. If the product doesn't pass the taste test, then the stores don't carry it.

Trader Joe's does a great job of informing its customers about the products. Apart from its store employees, Trader Joe's uses its Fearless Flyer to do that. We have all received flyers or inserts from retailers, and they typically list some products and their prices. The Fearless Flyer couldn't be more different. It describes some products, their ingredients, and how to enjoy them, and it also tells the products' stories. After all, as Doug Rauch says, Trader Joe's is a store of stories. Every product in the store has a story and a reason for being there. Look at how the December 2012 Fearless Flyer described a product called Trader Joe's Sipping Chocolate:

Grown-Up Hot Cocoa

This rich, deep, dark chocolate was inspired by memories of relaxing in an outdoor café, sipping velvety-smooth warm chocolate from a demitasse. Trader Joe's Sipping Chocolate was created with sipping in mind. Its chocolate flavors are so deep and rich that it really does invite you to savor every drop.

Each nine ounce tin of Trader Joe's Sipping Chocolate contains just four simple ingredients: sugar, cocoa, natural flavor (from soy), and a bit of salt. This is grown-up hot chocolate. Indulge in a cup any time you need an excuse to relax, because we promise that relaxation will increase with every sip. We're selling each nine ounce tin of Sipping Chocolate for the very relaxing price of $3.99.

As the description of Trader Joe's Sipping Chocolate demonstrates, the Fearless Flyer communicates what makes a product special. It is not a coupon book. In fact, there are no coupons at Trader Joe's. No promotions, no discounts. All products are sold at everyday low prices. Trader Joe's tells its customers that sale "is a four-letter word" to them and "if it makes you feel any better, think of it as all our items are on sale, day in and day out."[15]

How Trader Joe's Customers Benefit from Fewer Choices

Sales per square foot at Trader Joe's are almost triple those of a typical U.S. supermarket. Clearly, Trader Joe's customers do not mind that the retailer offers them fewer products and no promotions. They love Trader Joe's and spend a lot of money there.

Let me illustrate how lower variety helps customers. In my service operations course, I ask my students to pick two companies in a single industry and compare how they use operations to satisfy employees, customers, and investors. At the end of the semester, they do a presentation on their findings. Every year, I have several student teams that compare Trader Joe's with a traditional supermarket. One of those student teams decided to present its findings in a skit comparing the experience of buying pickles at Trader Joe's with buying them at another supermarket:[16]

TJ EMPLOYEE: Hi, can I help you find anything?

CUSTOMER: Do you know where the pickles are?

TJ EMPLOYEE: Sure, follow me. [*They walk over to the pickles.*] Here's our selection.

CUSTOMER: Oh, do you only have these three types? I usually like the unsalted dill.

TJ EMPLOYEE: Yeah, but all three types are great! These two are organic, but the bread-and-butter ones are my absolute favorite.

CUSTOMER: Hmm, are you sure?

TJ EMPLOYEE: Yeah, I buy them all the time. In fact, if you'd like to try one, they're over at the tasting station today. I can walk you over there.

CUSTOMER: No, it's okay. I trust your judgment. You guys always have great suggestions for new items.

Then the same customer goes into another supermarket:

CUSTOMER: Excuse me, can you tell me where the pickles are?

EMPLOYEE 1: Sure, aisle fifty-eight. There should be someone over there if you need more help.

CUSTOMER, *Turns in circles, lost*: This place is huge — where is aisle fifty-eight? [*Finally finds it.*] Oh, wow. That's a lot of pickles. [*Turns to a nearby store employee.*] Excuse me, can you help me? I'm trying to decide between these pickles. Any advice?

EMPLOYEE 2: Wow, we really do have a lot of pickles. Hmm, I wish I knew more about pickles. I hear the organic ones are healthier. My friend likes them.

CUSTOMER: Oh, that makes sense. Wow, seven dollars . . . I guess these look good. One more question, where are hamburger buns?

EMPLOYEE 2: Oh, back toward the front, aisle three.

As the students went through the skit, they showed photos of the pickle sections. Pickles at Trader Joe's were only $2.29, $2.99, and $3.49. The same size pickles at the other supermarket were a lot more expensive, most of them more than $5.

The skit shows how customers benefit from fewer choices. The obvious benefit is low prices, which is one of the reasons why people shop at Trader Joe's. The bread-and-butter pickles, which were the most expensive kind at Trader Joe's, were only $3.49. Because Trader Joe's sells just three kinds, it can leverage economies of scale in purchasing and can reduce all the complexity costs I mentioned earlier.

In addition, limited variety leads to high inventory productivity, which means lower costs for Trader Joe's and ultimately lower prices for customers. Trader Joe's inventory turnover is extremely high compared with that of its competitors. While the average inventory turnover in the food retail industry is around eleven times, at Trader Joe's it is around thirty-eight times. That means that an average product stays on the shelf for a little more than a month at a typical supermarket and only about ten days at a Trader Joe's store. In New York City stores, Trader Joe's turns its inventory fifty-two times a year, so an average product stays on the shelf for only a week.[17]

The difference, however, is more than just low prices. Even though Trader Joe's offers fewer pickles than its competitors do, customers feel that they are getting more when they shop there. The employees are so knowledgeable that they can tell you how the product tastes, how good the ingredients are, and how you can mix it with other products to create a delicious meal. Employees know so much that you trust that they know what they are talking about and you follow their recommendations.

With less variety, customers can get in and out of the store much more quickly. They don't have to evaluate — and often be confused by — lots and lots of options. There are just three kinds of pickles. Pick one and you're done.

Another benefit is hinted at in the skit. Many retailers offer us a huge selection but not nearly enough help sorting through all those choices — sometimes no help at all. Model retailers, by narrowing down that choice, can be seen as customer advocates. They do the research, they try to get the best products and the best deals for us. That's how Mercadona feels about its "prescription" approach, and that's how its customers feel, too, as do customers of Trader Joe's.

There is yet another benefit that doesn't come out in this skit. Because Trader Joe's customers know that they will always get low prices, they don't have to stuff their pantries with sale items they won't actually use for weeks. Trader Joe's customers save themselves from clutter, and their more rational and predictable shopping patterns save the company's supply chain by reducing the bullwhip effect.

Less Is Not Always More

Trader Joe's and other model retailers thrive by offering less. Their costs are low, and their customers are happy and buy a lot. But while offering less would reduce pretty much every company's costs, it won't always make customers happy. Walmart's recent effort to reduce product variety provides a good example.

In 2008, Walmart announced Project Impact, a strategic initiative that included, among other things, reducing product variety and making the stores less cluttered in order to improve the shopping experience and to improve operational efficiency. Stores were expected to reduce product variety by about 15 percent overall and by even more in certain categories. In the microwave popcorn category, for example, the plan was to reduce variety by 25 percent, and in tape measures, by 83 percent (from twenty-four types to four).[18] Many experts applauded this strategy, predicting that Walmart, already known for excellence in supply chain management, would benefit from even greater efficiency.

But Project Impact had an unintended impact at Walmart stores. In some categories, such as salty snacks and granola bars, sales at competitors grew while sales at Walmart shrank. For the first time on record, Walmart's sales increase in the cereals category underperformed that of its competitors.[19] Soon these effects started showing up in financial statements. Same-store sales growth started falling. In March 2010, the company announced that it was dialing back and reintroducing three hundred of the products it had eliminated, but sales kept on declining. In July 2010, after the fourth successive quarterly decline, the company announced the departure of the chief merchandising officer, John Fleming, who had been behind the effort. Walmart's sales decline continued for five more quarters.

Offering less clearly did not work for Walmart. It came at the expense of customer service — that is, customers' finding what they had hoped to find — and sales. Yet offering less works for model retailers. Why? One reason is that these retailers pursue the good jobs strategy.

Investment in employees helps model retailers better identify what their customers want. Model retailers are sophisticated users of information technology and analytics. Mercadona, for example, was the first retailer in Spain to use bar code scanners. It invests hundreds of millions of euros every year to equip its stores and supply chain with the latest technology. But when it comes to choosing what products to carry, model retailers do not rely solely on the sales data they collect from the stores. They also rely on their people.

Collecting and analyzing data are powerful. Data can help us make better decisions. But there is one thing companies miss when they rely solely on data. Data can show what customers have bought, but not what customers *would have bought* if the store had carried different items. Frontline employees who talk with their customers all the time *can* do that. And at model retailers, they do.

Investment in employees also helps model retailers explain their offerings better to customers. Employees are able to tell customers all about the products and their prices. They can explain why a certain product is not there, which product is a good substitute, and how much the customer saves when the store carries fewer products or does not run promotions. Customers may even see the model retailers as their advocates. They trust these companies to offer the best mix of products and the best deals. When the bread-and-butter pickles at Trader Joe's are priced at $3.49, customers do not question how fair that price is. All told, a customer is far less likely to go away annoyed. In fact, a customer is likely to be impressed and to come back — and the retailer is on its way along the virtuous cycle.

Given how understaffed Walmart stores tend to be, I doubt that many of its employees can do the same for their customers. First, it's hard to find an employee there who is not busy, and even if you find one, chances are he will not know much about the products. How would he, given the company's high employee turnover and the tens of thousands of products it carries?

Offering Less Is Not Just for Retailers

Other types of companies, not just model retailers, can benefit from offering less. And offering less doesn't mean only offering fewer products and fewer promotions. Successful companies in a wide range of industries thrive by offering less than their competitors do in one way or another. In the field of healthcare, Shouldice Hospital in Thornhill, Ontario, focuses entirely on hernia surgery. Earlier in this chapter, I explained how In-N-Out offers an extremely limited menu. Apple offers a limited number of SKUs in all its product categories.

Southwest Airlines is another great example. For decades, Southwest built a reputation for offering low fares to its customers, good jobs to its employees, and great returns to its investors. In 2002, *Money* magazine identified Southwest as the American company that has given the greatest return to shareholders over a thirty-year period, and that success has continued. In 2012, the company had its fortieth consecutive year of profitability — extremely impressive in a cyclical industry. Southwest definitely offers less than its competitors: no seat assignments, no meals, no baggage transfer to other airlines, no first class, no upgrades. As Colleen Barrett, the former president of Southwest, said, "Southwest doesn't purport to be all things to all people, and we're very upfront about it. We tell our customers why we don't do this, that, and the other — why we don't have assigned seating, for example. And then we just kill them with kindness and caring and attention."[20]

Offering less has not meant low customer satisfaction for Southwest. In fact, Southwest is the only airline to have won the "triple crown" of airline service — the highest level of customer satisfaction, the best on-time arrival record, and the lowest level of lost baggage — and it did so multiple years in a row. In 2011, as it had in previous years, Southwest earned the leading customer satisfaction score, according to the U.S.

Department of Transportation, with 0.32 complaints per 100,000 passengers. The airline had the highest score among all airlines in the American Customer Satisfaction Index for seventeen years in a row, only losing the top place to JetBlue in 2012, after Southwest's acquisition of AirTran in May 2011.

How Offering Less Enables the Good Jobs Strategy

Now that we have taken a detailed look at one of the four operational choices that underpin the good jobs strategy, let's build upon that to get a better picture of what the good jobs strategy really is and how it works. I had originally planned to move systematically through the three groups — employees, customers, and investors — showing how the strategy was good for each one in turn. But I gave up on that because the effects for each are so connected to the effects for one or both of the others — which is the whole point. So if what follows seems like a great swirl of effects, bear with me. That, in itself, will give you an important view of what the good jobs strategy really is.

We have seen that offering less — be it products, promotions, services, or amenities — while also investing more in employees, such as through more training, more stability, or more pay, helps companies reduce their own costs and therefore helps them reduce costs for customers. Offering less makes operations more efficient and accurate, which in turn improves customer service and hence sales. Since improving operations helps employees do a better job — sometimes in ways the customers can see with their own eyes — employees feel greater pride and joy in their work. (Most people *like* being helpful to other people.) This, in turn, contributes to greater dedication and lower turnover, both of which are good for service, sales, profits, growth, continuous improvement, and return on investment.

See what I mean? The good jobs strategy is a bit like a healthy human body. There are so many things being done right all at the same time — metabolism, body temperature, calcium levels, semicircular canals, white blood cell counts, and on and on. But it's the combination of everything, not any particular thing by itself, that makes you healthy. The concept of synergy has already inspired more than its share of blather and hot air. I certainly did not set out to promote an abstract concept, such as synergy. I was motivated to discover *empirically* how certain companies manage to be so good for so many stakeholders without someone — particularly the employees — getting the short end of the stick. The phenomenon was real — model companies were doing all this long before I came along and wondered how. What I found when I did my research is similar to what my colleagues who have previously studied high-performance human resource practices have found.[21] Just like the human resource practices that work best when they are combined, a certain set of operational practices work well together, producing intertwined benefits for employees, customers, and investors.

Let's see some more of these interconnected effects in action. By improving operational efficiency, offering less helps to improve labor productivity. Fewer products and promotions decrease the physical work in the stores. Employees don't have to go back and forth so often between the selling floor and the storage room. They don't need to keep moving things around and changing prices as promotion displays come and go. Here, again, there is a complex interaction between operations and the company's investment in its people. We saw that offering less and doing it *successfully* (as model retailers do and as Walmart did not) depend on whether a company has invested in a well-trained and well-motivated workforce that can provide the necessary information "from the trenches" about what customers want and what they can do without. At the same time, offering less rewards investment in labor by making that labor more productive. Labor productivity is a very important metric for low-cost retail. The fact that one operational choice both requires and rewards an investment in labor is emblematic of why the virtuous cycle is indeed a cycle and thus emblematic of how the good jobs strategy works.

With fewer products and promotions, employees can also process customers more quickly at the checkout. Haven't we all waited and fidgeted — with a combination of pity and aggravation — while some poor cashier tries to remember the product code for Barcarole romaine lettuce or to figure out what to make of two contradictory coupons? The low variety at model retailers makes the cashier's job a lot easier. Avoiding tie-ups in the checkout line obviously makes customers happy, and you can be sure the cashiers don't like having a line full of people glaring at them. Labor productivity is higher, which, as we will see later, allows stores to make better use of cross-training, which in turn has many benefits for employees, customers, and investors.

Offering less enables retailers to leverage their investment in employees in still other ways. When Trader Joe's doesn't carry a particular product that a customer wants, or it is simply stocked out of it, its knowledgeable employees can recommend something else — and the customer feels that the employee really knows what he's talking about. (This makes the employee happy and motivated, too.) Hence, an investment in employees' knowledge can be a substitute for an investment in inventory — a great deal for retailers. And investment in employees' knowledge has cumulative effects that an accumulation of inventory will never have. In short, investment in employees yields more "return" than investment in inventory.

Companies that successfully offer less also leverage their investment in employees to better understand what their customers want. We will see later what employees who know what their customers want can do for their company's profits, growth, continuous improvement, and ability to capture strategic opportunities.

Offering less even gives employees greater job security because it increases efficiencies and reduces waste. When there's waste — which means higher costs for the company — labor is often the expense to be cut. That's largely what drives the vicious cycle — seeing labor as a kind of fat that's easy to trim. But when retailers reduce waste by offering less, employees benefit because now there is more to spend on them. Model retailers know — they don't just believe, they know — that by spending more on their employees, they are investing in their own success. That's what powers the virtuous cycle.

CHAPTER 6

Operational Choice #2

Standardize and Empower

Q UIKTRIP HAS STANDARDIZED and timed every operational task, from receiving merchandise to opening boxes to ringing up customers. Say a new shipment comes in a red box. You are supposed to shelve the contents of a red box in a particular way and it's supposed to take you thirty-four minutes. If a customer comes through the checkout line with a cup of coffee, it should take you five seconds to ring that up if the customer pays with cash. Management's attitude is that "if you are not going to have a way to inspect what you want people to do, then don't bother asking them to do it." There is a tight monitoring of *how* tasks are performed. Doing it the wrong way in the right amount of time won't do.

Though this approach to operations is efficient and provides consistency, you might think that the employees must hate it. Don't they feel humiliated that they have to follow instructions so precisely and aren't trusted to use their judgment? Don't they feel that what they do doesn't matter because anyone else would have to do exactly the same thing? Whatever happened to empowerment?

Ah, but QuikTrip is big on empowerment. Store employees make a lot of decisions ranging from how much inventory their store should carry each day to how to handle customer complaints or problems. They even have a say in how products and processes should change over time. You might wonder, though, if this is really a good idea. Can QuikTrip maintain consistency this way? Is this much autonomy scalable? Can the company really rely on tens of thousands of people to make the right decisions? Won't they game the system?

In fact, this blend of standardization and empowerment works very well. Despite all the standardization and monitoring, QuikTrip employees feel they are treated with respect and dignity. The company has been on *Fortune*'s "100 best companies to work for" list for eleven years in a row. Turnover among employees who spend over a year there is almost nonexistent. In spite of its employees' empowerment, Quik-Trip maintains tight control over its operations and provides highly consistent service to its customers. It operates more than six hundred stores, so its model is clearly scalable, and its employees consistently make decisions that end up being good for customers and investors.

QuikTrip is hardly alone in successfully combining standardization with empowerment. While most of the debate in work design seems to be about whether employees should follow standardized processes *or* be empowered, operationally excellent companies in a wide range of industries tend to choose the best of both.

Let's look at each part of this combination.

Standardization

Standardization tends to get a bad rap. Consistency and efficiency sound like good things, but if you think of them as repetition and obedience, you may find yourself thinking of factories full of employees doing the same mindless task over and over, with supervisors watching to make sure no one slacks off for even a moment. Dignity is crushed.

Standardization implemented in this way deserves its malevolent reputation. But there are different ways to implement standardization. Some companies have been able to use it as the basis for empowerment, improvement, and — ultimately — dignity.

Scientific Management

Standardization has its roots in so-called scientific management. Frederick Winslow Taylor, widely known as the father of scientific management, was an interesting character. He was born in 1856 to an upper-class family. His father was a Princeton graduate and his mother was an abolitionist and feminist. Taylor was accepted to Harvard College, but instead of taking his spot there, he chose to work on the factory floor at Midvale Steel Company. Between 1878 and 1884, he advanced from laborer to chief engineer and, during the same period, also completed his mechanical engineering degree from Stevens Institute of Technology.

It wouldn't be an exaggeration to say that Taylor was obsessed with improving efficiency not just in factories but also in life. He reportedly wore slip-on shoes to save time, invented his own golf putter and tennis racket to play the sports more efficiently, and insisted that even shoveling could be turned into a science.[1] Taylor thought inefficiency in factories led to a lot of suffering because it hurt employees' wages, companies' profits, and even nations' prosperity. According to Taylor, this inefficiency came in part from not knowing the best way to perform a task, but also from laziness. He wrote:

> Underworking, that is, deliberately working slowly as to avoid doing a full day's work, "soldiering," as it is called in this country, "hanging it out," as it is called in England, and "ca canae," as it is called in Scotland, is almost universal in industrial establishments, and prevails also to a large extent in the building trades; and the writer asserts without contradiction that this constitutes the greatest evil with which the working people of both England and America are now afflicted.[2]

Taylor thought the remedy for inefficiency was scientific management, which included scientifically developing the best way to do the job, the best way to select people who were most capable of doing the job that way, and the best way to train them to do the job right. Scientific management also included close monitoring of workers by supervisors and the creation of financial incentives for workers to do their work as quickly as possible and to exceed the performance standards developed by industrial engineers, based on detailed analysis of time-motion studies.

In Taylor's scientific management, there was a clear distinction between planning and doing and between those who did each. Management did the planning and thinking and workers simply did the work. No thinking was really necessary on the worker's part.

There were many critiques of Taylor's scientific management. Many found his methods inhumane and his assumptions about human behavior — that people are inherently lazy and do not want to do a good job — unrealistic. Starting in the 1930s, a human relations movement arose that argued against the de-skilling of work and the view of employees as interchangeable parts. Studies, including the famous Hawthorne studies, showed that workers' motivation, satisfaction, and social relations all contributed to employees' productivity.

In addition, scientific management was often associated with bureaucracy, top-down control, resistance to change, and static rules and procedures. Some even challenged how "scientific" scientific management really is.[3]

Despite all these criticisms, Taylor had a huge effect on both academia and industry. The field of industrial engineering has its roots partly in scientific management, and the principles of scientific management became widely used, from factories to restaurants. Those who practiced scientific management divided labor into narrow tasks and had each person perform the task over and over. Repetition of well-designed and narrow tasks was understood to increase efficiency. Close monitoring and, in some contexts, a piece-rate incentive system motivated employees to work as quickly as they could. The results were consistency, efficiency, and a high level of control by management.

Standardization in Services

Taylor's way of standardization also has proponents in service industries. The renowned marketing professor Theodore Levitt, who argued that businesses would do better if they focused on meeting customers' needs rather than on selling products or services, was a believer in the application of standardization in services. He maintained that factories could produce consistently high-quality products because manufacturers thought in technocratic terms, ensuring that their success depended on the design of the tasks rather than the performers of those tasks.

Levitt wrote in a *Harvard Business Review* article in 1972, "While it may pain and offend us to say so, thinking in humanistic rather than technocratic terms ensures that the service sector of the modern economy will be forever inefficient and that our satisfactions will be forever marginal."[4] Offering McDonald's as an example of a service company that applied factory methods of standardization, Levitt continued: "Discretion is the enemy of order, standardization, and quality."

In many ways, Levitt is right. When the success of a service is largely dependent on the person providing it and not on the process or design of the job, we as customers get inconsistent quality. We also pay more, although we don't see that.

Let me offer an example. Our family loves Chipotle, a fast-food chain serving Mexican food such as burritos and quesadillas. We like the ingredients — tomatoes, onions, cilantro, and avocado — and we like the fact that they are all fresh, often organic, and locally grown whenever possible. So we go every two weeks or so, but each time, we have to decide which location to go to. There are two near us. One has great parking, while finding a place to park at the other is a huge pain. But the food is never as good at the one with good parking. The chicken is almost always dry and sometimes even burnt. The burritos are sometimes made in such a sloppy way that they fall apart. Someone must mix up the spoons used for spicy and mild salsa because sometimes our children's burritos, which are supposed to have mild salsa, turn out to have jalapenos in them. At the other one, though — the one with terrible parking — the food is always great.

How could a Mexican restaurant consistently botch the most basic of Mexican foods? And given that all Chipotle stores are company-owned, you would think that as long as one of them could make great burritos, they all could. Maybe if every Chipotle store had mercilessly

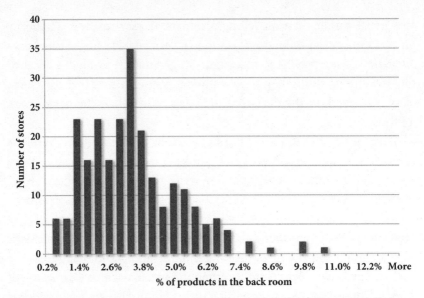

Figure 6.1. Percentage of Products That Were in the Back Room but Not on the Selling Floor at the Time of the Physical Audit for 242 Borders Stores in 1999

implemented Taylor's scientific management, we could get the really good burritos without the parking hassles.

This kind of variation within the same chain is quite common. There is a lot of evidence from various studies. The histogram in Figure 6.1, for example, shows data from 242 Borders stores in 1999. The performance being measured in this study was the percentage of products that were in the back rooms but should have been on the selling floors. The height of each bar in the graph represents how many stores had that particular percentage. From the customer's point of view: What were the odds that the store you were in had the book you wanted but not where you could find it? As you see, there was a lot of variation in performance across the stores — some had less than 1 percent of their books in the wrong place and some had 8, 9, or 10 percent.

When there is variation in how a product tastes or whether a customer is able to find a product in the store, there is variation in customers' satisfaction. When it comes to customer engagement — a measure that, according to Gallup researchers, includes customers' satisfaction and their emotional attachment to the company — variability among the stores within a chain is often much larger than variability between different chains. In one retail chain with 1,100 stores, the researchers found that the best store's customer engagement was 3.5 times better than that of the poorest performer.[5] So maybe a good dose of standardization is in order.

Arguments Against Standardization in Services

There are also many opponents of standardization in services. They often cite standardization as a driver of low employee and customer satisfaction. When employees are asked to follow tasks mindlessly, they are not engaged in their work, and that shows up in how well they do their jobs and satisfy customers. If you have ever found yourself dealing with an employee who can only keep repeating the same information even though it isn't addressing your particular problem, you know exactly what I mean.

Nowhere is this more prevalent than at call centers. A lot of call centers make their employees follow standardized scripts. Just like Taylor's supervisors did on the factory floor, these call centers monitor employees' adherence to the script. Do the words "This call may be recorded for quality assurance" sound familiar? Managers also ensure that calls are handled efficiently by measuring call time, idle time, and talk time, providing goals for all these. Sometimes operators read their scripts so quickly that you can't even follow them.

But research shows that all those scripts and all that monitoring and measurement contribute to an environment with low job satisfaction, high burnout, and a widespread desire among employees to find a better job.[6]

So what if employees are not engaged? After all, when knowledge resides in routines, processes, and rules, employees can be considered interchangeable parts. The success of call centers should depend on the quality of the scripts and the technology that allows the scripts to be used effectively, right? Well, not really. Despite all the investment in the scripts and technologies, the most important driver of customer satisfaction in a call center still seems to be the individual who takes the call and makes you feel like someone wants to help you, not just deal with you.[7]

Where do all these arguments for and against standardization leave us? Is standardization in service industries something we can't live with or something we can't live without? The key seems to be to implement standardization in a way that allows people to retain a sense of dignity, to respond to customer needs, and to contribute to continuous improvement. You may think such a miracle would call for a magic wand, but not only is it possible, there are companies at which it happens every day.

Empowerment

How many times have you requested something you thought was completely reasonable from a frontline employee, only to be told, "I'm sorry, this is against our policy" or "Let me ask my manager." My husband and I were celebrating Valentine's Day at a fancy restaurant. I had been drinking a glass of wine chosen to go well with my lamb, but toward the end of the meal, my glass was almost empty. All I needed was one more sip of wine to enjoy the end of my meal, so I asked our waiter if he could give me just a little splash.

No — they sell wine only by the full glass. He would have to ask his manager if he could give me a bit more. By the time he came back with his manager's okay, it was too late — the meal was over. Next time we want a special night out, we'll go somewhere else.

Restaurants generally make a hefty 75 percent margin on wine. One little splash more would have cost the restaurant close to nothing, especially in comparison with what we were already spending on our meal. Furthermore, restaurants are particularly reliant on word of mouth, and where we live, customers have hundreds to choose from. So why was the waiter so reluctant to make such a small decision in which the restaurant had everything to gain and only pennies to lose? Because even at this high-end restaurant he had to follow standardized rules and processes instead of making his own decisions about how to satisfy his (that is, his employer's) customers. Clearly, he was not empowered. And in this case, rather than standardization contributing to a consistent customer-pleasing performance — the kind my family keeps hoping for at our local Chipotle — it prevented customer satisfaction.

As a contrast, let's take a look at Zappos, an online apparel store that started by selling shoes and has one of the largest assortments of shoes in the world. Zappos is famous for its outstanding customer service. Nowhere is the emphasis on customer service more apparent than when a customer calls the customer service number.

Zappos employees are not given a script and they don't need one. They know quite well what they are expected to do: deliver a "wow" experience to each customer. According to its CEO, Tony Hsieh:

> At Zappos, we don't measure call times (our longest phone call was almost six hours long!), and we don't upsell. We just care about whether the rep goes above and beyond for every customer. We don't have scripts because we trust our employees to use their best judgment when dealing with each and every customer. We want our reps to let their true personalities shine during each phone call so that they can develop a personal emotional connection with the customer.[8]

Empowerment, then, is almost the opposite of standardization. Empowered employees do not need to follow one best way. Instead of obeying scripts, documents, or rules that describe how each step of a process should be performed, empowered employees are encouraged to make their own decisions to arrive at the desired outcome. The desired outcome could be wowing a customer or it could be making sure that the store is clean or that the products are where they are supposed to be or that the mild burritos are mild.

Why Empowerment Works in Services

Empowerment especially works in service industries because customers bring a lot of variability in this context. It is almost impossible to anticipate precisely what every customer will want, how each will behave, and what will make each one happy, and to create a script or rule book to achieve that. That means that a combination of judgment and caring may often be more effective than rules and protocols. Companies that have tried to create scripted responses in advance to as many situations as possible — such as the call centers mentioned previously — have not become noted for their customers' satisfaction.

Empowered employees can often respond more quickly and appropriately. If our waiter on Valentine's Day had been empowered, he would have evaluated my request in the context of what I was ordering and perhaps how much wine was left in the bottle and responded to me right away. I don't doubt that he could see that for himself and that he would have liked to accommodate me. In the end, he was allowed to do the right thing, but too late.

Empowered employees can also provide better service because they themselves are more satisfied. As my colleagues who study motivation have shown so clearly, autonomy is great for motivation. Which is just what you would expect. Lack of autonomy and its association with mindless work and lack of dignity were indeed one of the main criticisms of Taylor's scientific management.

....

A CASE OF EMPOWERMENT

One of the most fascinating examples of empowerment can be found at Affinity Plus, a federal credit union based in St. Paul, Minnesota, that offers traditional financial services (such as savings and checking accounts, ATM cards, and Visa service), investment portfolio accounts (such as money market savings and certificates of deposit), and loans (such as automobile loans, home mortgages, and student loans).[9] Before 2002, Affinity Plus was managed like a typical financial institution, with policies and procedures to guide how things were done. In 2002, the firm underwent a dramatic transformation. Policies and procedures for everything from waiving fees to underwriting loans were replaced by employee judgment.

Employees were to use a simple framework: "Member, Organization, Employee," or simply "MOE." Here's how the CEO explained it to the employees: "Not sure what's right in a particular situation? Run it through MOE—in priority order—remembering that the member always comes first and trumps the other two. In other words, if a solution is right for the employee or the organization but does not position the member for future success, we will not proceed." He also said, "No employee will ever get in trouble for doing what is right for the member. . . . There is only one operating policy or guideline you ever need. Trust your feelings . . . Do not consider the system capability, policy, or procedure . . ."

Think about the magnitude of this change. Tellers and call center employees were now being empowered to make decisions on product pricing, general services, and even loan structuring. The management of the firm's operations changed significantly as a result. At its call centers, for example, employees used to be driven by efficiency. They were encouraged to finish calls as quickly as possible to meet the target average wait time of 1.41 minutes. But with the MOE framework, efficiency could no longer be the sole or even the primary objective—not if what was efficient for the bank was less than satisfactory for the member. Members had to come first. So the call center employees started spending more time with their callers, really listening to their problems and suggesting solutions.

Over time, call center employees started creating personal relationships with some members, and more members started calling with bigger needs. It sounds wonderful, but weren't members having to wait longer and longer on hold while the staff had ever-longer conversations with each caller? Interestingly, the waiting time was reduced to thirty seconds without significantly increasing the number of call center employees. How did they do this? By making another of the four operational choices—the one we will discuss in the next chapter. They cross-trained all employees in the organization to handle transactions. If all call center employees were busy, a call could be routed to any other employee in the network. Affinity Plus also started to invest more in its labor force by recruiting people who were not experienced in financial services but who did have empathy for customers. The firm also invested in mechanisms to help employees make better decisions, such as white papers that showed examples of the effective use of empowerment and systems that captured the rationale by which employees made exceptions for customers.

For Affinity Plus, putting employees at the center of its success made for plenty of success. Even while many of Affinity's competitors were pulling back from lending, especially from real estate lending, Affinity's membership grew and so did its lending portfolio, with more business being done per member. The credit union survived the 2008 financial crisis, and at the end of 2008, its performance was in the top fifth percentile of all U.S. credit unions, with over one billion dollars in assets.

....

Arguments Against Empowerment in Services

Despite the arguments for empowerment and the success stories of companies such as Affinity Plus and Zappos, there are several arguments against empowerment.

The main criticism, of course, is Theodore Levitt's argument that when the performance of a task depends too much on the performer — the employee — the outcome could be harmfully inconsistent. A related criticism is that empowerment means lack of managerial control, which many executives and managers find scary. It requires trusting thousands of people to make the right decisions all the time, with no one making sure they do. What if an Affinity Plus employee writes a bad loan? What if a Zappos employee gives merchandise credit unnecessarily? Customers who know which companies have empowered employees could make a habit of abusing the system.

Ever heard the Nordstrom tire story? A customer walks into a Nordstrom store in Alaska to return snow tires. If you're familiar with Nordstrom, a high-end department store chain, you're probably puzzled: Does Nordstrom even sell tires? No, it doesn't. The customer brought the snow tires there because he had bought them from the store that had been in that location before Nordstrom took the spot. In any case, according to legend, the Nordstrom store manager decided the customer had made an honest mistake and took the tires back anyway. It's a lovely story, but can you afford to have your employees taking back products you don't even sell?

How about that waiter who wasn't allowed to just give me an extra bit of wine? Had he been empowered to do that for me, his employer would have had to trust in his goodwill toward the restaurant and its management. What if he decided to give free drinks to his friends and relatives, just to make a few more customers truly satisfied?

Yet another criticism of empowerment is that it requires competent employees. (Heaven forbid!) Hiring truly competent employees may mean paying more, although that isn't always the case. A lot of low-cost businesses simply assume — and wrongly so — that this would be too expensive.

Investment in Employees and Job Design

Environments that implement standardization and empowerment call for different levels of investment in employees. Standardization can be seen as an antidote to high turnover. This is consistent with a study I conducted with my colleague Robert Huckman from Harvard Business School.[10] Using four years of data from Borders stores from 1999 to 2002, we examined the effect of employee turnover on two types of store performance — profit margin and customer service. We found that, on average, employee turnover had a negative effect on both. But within that average, we found an exception: Employee turnover did *not* hurt performance at stores when employees consistently followed standard operating procedures and did not use their own discretion. If you have created a system in which employees really are interchangeable parts, then it won't do the business any harm to interchange them.

Indeed, our study shows that in settings in which high turnover is unavoidable, standardizing processes and ensuring conformity with standardization can mitigate the negative effects that high turnover normally causes. This is why McDonald's is known to deliver its burgers, fries, and shakes with great consistency even though it operates with high employee turnover.

If everything is documented in procedures and rules and no discretion from employees is necessary, investment in employees would likely be a needlessly expensive approach. But if work is designed in a way that requires judgment from employees, then investment in employees is important. The combination of high turnover and high need for judgment will produce operational problems, bad decisions, low customer service, and poor financial performance. This is why investment in employees and a reliance on their discretion typically go hand in hand. (The results of the various combinations of high and low employee judgment and high and low turnover are shown in Figure 6.2.)

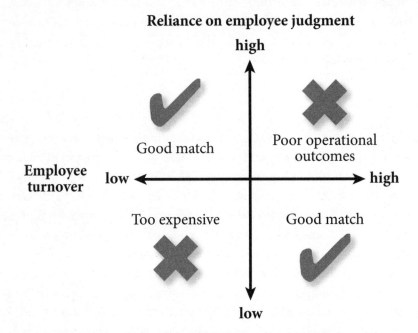

Figure 6.2. Employee Turnover and Reliance on Employee Judgment

Why Not Standardize *and* Empower?

So far we have seen that (a) both standardization and empowerment have their merits and their costs and that (b) standardized and empowered environments call for different levels of investment in employees. So how does a particular business decide whether to use standardization or empowerment? Keep in mind, the premise of this book is that a business needs to decide what is best for its employees, customers, and investors — all three and all at the same time. That's part of the good jobs strategy.

• • •

One of the dominant views is that we should examine the work environment and see whether it is suited best for standardization or for empowerment.[11] Standardization is often seen as appropriate for manufacturing environments in which routine tasks are performed repeatedly or for those service environments in which the interaction between customers and employees is limited (for example, a fast-food chain). These environments do not require much employee investment. They can be managed with a workforce that is unskilled and inexperienced. Empowerment, on the other hand, is seen as appropriate for service environments that depend heavily on customer-employee interaction. These environments require a lot more investment in employees.

Although there is truth in this categorization, I find it limiting. Manufacturing companies such as Toyota show us that there is a lot of merit in empowering employees, even on the assembly line. Toyota's empowered employees can stop the production line when they see a problem. They also actively engage in problem solving. On the other hand, service companies such as Four Seasons, a high-end hotel chain that provides outstanding customer service, show us that even in environments with a lot of customer-employee interaction, standardization can work wonders. Four Seasons uses 270 operating standards — worldwide — that detail tasks from how to place a coffee pot to how to greet guests to how to book reservations.[12]

The question should not be whether to standardize or to empower in a particular environment, but which tasks to standardize and which tasks to trust to empowered employees. Standardization works great for routine operational tasks that do not depend on local business conditions or on individual customers' needs. Preparing the food at a restaurant chain, unloading trucks at a retail store, and making beds in a hotel are all great candidates for standardization. These tasks should be performed consistently, efficiently, and in the safest way. Having employees exercise judgment in the performance of such tasks is a recipe for inconsistency and low customer satisfaction.

Tasks that are nonroutine or that depend heavily on local conditions or on the idiosyncratic needs of individual customers are great candidates for empowerment. Employees in a call center, for example, find themselves handling certain problems over and over. It's probably a good idea for those problems to be handled in a consistent way, honed by companywide experience, so that the company doesn't get a reputation for bungling something it ought to be able to handle in its sleep. On the other hand, those same employees can find themselves working with customers who have complicated or simple problems, who are familiar with or bewildered by the company's product or service, who are quick to understand or too dim to understand, who are angry or good-natured, who are honest or dishonest. Employees will also face problems that they themselves cannot solve. Here, then, is where empowerment can really delight the caller (and be gratifying for the employee) while standardization can be totally frustrating for both.

Combining standardization with empowerment — like the other operational choices that underlie the good jobs strategy — is easier said than done. Standardization needs to be implemented without compromising employees' dignity and satisfaction while empowerment needs to be implemented without losing control. We saw how Home Depot lost control when its employees were highly empowered during its first two decades. Customer service started declining, there were inefficiencies, and stores were simply not safe for employees and customers. But when the company tried to instill more discipline — in some cases, with more standardization — it forgot that it still needed to keep its employees at the center of its success. It started seeing employees as interchangeable parts, replacing experienced full-time employees with part-timers. While supply chain management at Home Depot benefited from increased standardization, the super-helpful employee-customer interactions that made Home Depot what it was were not at all of the kind that could be carried out by "interchangeable parts." Lack of investment in employees therefore caused further decline in customer service and hurt sales.

Combining Standardization with Empowerment at UPS

Mike Eskew, the former CEO of UPS, told my students that UPS is a measurement company. "We measure everything that moves. And if it doesn't move," he added with a smile, "we make it move."

Indeed, at UPS, everything is timed and measured. They know how long it takes for a driver to take a package to his truck, depending on whether he has to take it off a shelf or pick it up from the floor and whether or not he has to open the rear door of the truck to get the package in. They know where each driver goes, how fast he drives, and whether or not he buckles his seatbelt. Every movement in and out of the truck is standardized, down to which finger to use to carry the keys. A driver should place the key in his right ring finger so that it is in position for the index finger and thumb to turn it in the ignition and pull it out in one motion.

When it comes to delivering a package, UPS drivers know that they have to follow the UPS way every single time. That's how UPS achieves efficiencies and prevents accidents and injuries. Yet drivers also know that they are empowered to delight the customer. If they need to go around the block to give the customer time to get ready to receive them, they are free to do that. They don't need to ask headquarters for permission.

UPS does a great job of giving its drivers the best way to be safe and successful while, at the same time, letting their human spirit come alive through customer service. More important, UPS lets the drivers understand how important they are for the company. In his book *Punching In,* Alex Frankel, a journalist who worked under-cover as a frontline employee at a number of companies, describes his experience as a UPS driver, right after delivering packages for Christmas:

> In my mind right then, we were part of a higher calling — connect-ing people with love, desire, loss, friendship, and family. If your job was to deliver all year, then Christmas presents pretty much epito-mized the idea that by creating real meaning for customers, people find true meaning in their jobs.[13]

Model Retailers Standardize and Empower

Like UPS, Toyota, and Four Seasons, our model retailers use a lot of standardization for routine tasks. At Costco, for example, there is no employee judgment in how to conduct a "safety walk" or how frequently that has to be done. There is no employee judgment in which store equipment needs to go through maintenance and how that is to be done. There is also no judgment in how to process customers at the checkout. Two employees work in a team: One starts the process by taking the customer's membership card. Then she or he starts scanning while the other employee helps the customer unload the cart, making sure that heavy items stay on the cart, which is faster and also saves employees from hurting themselves by lifting out something too heavy. That's their protocol — every time.

At the same time, Costco and other model retailers rely on empowerment. They let employees decide how to solve customer problems, how to improve processes, and even how to display merchandise in accordance with the needs and tastes of local clientele. Some even let their employees order merchandise.

Let's take a look at how QuikTrip combines standardization with empowerment. In QuikTrip's early years, store managers, like those at Home Depot, had considerable autonomy. There was no officially sanctioned best way to perform store tasks, and each store manager had his or her own view of how to achieve results. When the company was small, this approach worked fine, but as the company grew larger, the CEO, Chester Cadieux, realized that the lack of standardization was causing not only inconsistencies in performance but also inconsistencies in how employees were treated.

The problem was that QuikTrip expected great results from its stores, but when it was left to each store manager to decide how to get those results, some began to ignore how important it is to treat employees with respect and dignity. Cadieux therefore sent the following memo to all managers:

TO: All Management Personnel[14]
DATE: February 27, 1984
RE: Practicing the Golden Rule

QuikTrip customers expect and deserve well-groomed employees who give them fast, friendly service. They also expect and deserve attractive, clean and well-merchandised stores. Just as there are minimum standards for customer service, appearance and store operation, there are minimum acceptable standards in the management of our employees. QuikTrip employees expect and deserve intelligent, positive, factual supervision. They do not deserve to work for an asshole. I am more tolerant of poor operation than I am of poor treatment of employees.

I am writing this memo not as a threat or because I perceive we have a problem, but as the result of a discussion held in one of our Management Committee meetings. Everybody seemed to understand what the minimum standards of customer service, employee appearance, and operation were, but there was no clear definition of minimum acceptable human relations skills. Some failed to realize that the way we get good results is just as important as the results.

Because of different personalities and experiences, we handle employees differently and I would not try to teach one set method. I would just say we cannot tolerate obnoxious, oppressive, abusive, tyrannical despots (assholes).*

Please be sure that you always treat your employees the way you want to be treated. That is the minimum expected standard of management at QuikTrip.

  * Obnoxious — highly offensive

    Oppressive — unreasonably severe; depressing to the spirit

    Abusive — characterized by verbal abuse

    Tyrant — a ruler who exercises absolute power oppressively or brutally

    Despot — a person exercising power abusively, oppressively, or tyrannically

    Asshole — an easily understood American vulgarity for all the above

This memo helped improve the culture — employees knew for certain that they should be treated with respect and dignity — but store managers were still free to run their stores differently from each other. "Who you worked for was the employee book," said Ron Jeffers, QuikTrip's vice president of operating systems.

How QuikTrip Implemented Standardization Without Sacrificing Employees' Dignity

To improve operational consistency, QuikTrip initiated a big reengineering effort in 1995. The objective was to map store operations, time them, and standardize them. These standards would be shared with all stores, and all employees would be asked to follow them. This sounds like Frederick Taylor's brand of standardization, but there was one key difference. Instead of hiring industrial engineers to map out processes and standardize them, QuikTrip chose thirteen of its store managers to work side by side with the director of operations for a year and a half on the standardization effort.

The store managers, in turn, collected input from employees and customers. They talked to thousands of customers in different markets to understand what they valued and what they would like to see changed in their QuikTrip shopping experience. These interviews all took place inside the stores, not over the phone, and became the basis for QuikTrip's mystery shopper evaluations.

The store managers also worked with employees to define the standards, an approach that generated a huge buy-in from employees at all levels. As Jeffers explained, "The managers were the ones mapping the processes, timing them, and talking to customers. And once we were finished, it was the managers who explained what we did and why to everyone."

QuikTrip also made sure to address a problem that had been growing: Employees didn't always understand why they had to do things in a particular way and were no longer always willing to take the boss's word for it, as had earlier been the case. Jeffers explained:

> Until the draft ended in 1973, most employees had served in the military and were used to an autocratic system. In the years after, new employees without military experience clashed with our "Yes sir, no sir" type of mentality. We had two cultures clashing . . . the generational differences were starting to show between the baby boomer generation and the culture that it had, to the generation Y coming in

now, and you can see people were questioning it. Questioning why we did what we did. Why is it the right way to go?

Once standards had been decided, employees were not simply told what to do, as they would have been before. They were told *why* they were doing things in a particular way and how that helped them and their customers. Employees could see for themselves, during the in-store customer surveys, that the standardization was being driven by their customers' needs, not by remote, out-of-touch corporate types. Even employees who were not personally involved in the standardization effort heard what customers said and saw their managers taking notes. In addition, because store managers had worked closely with employees in developing the standards, the employees found the standards to be fair. It wasn't company executives imposing unattainable goals such as shelving products at impossible speeds. The employees themselves and their managers had arrived at these numbers.

To this day, QuikTrip employees know that these standards are not set in stone. The employees are in charge of improving them, and there is a definite process for doing that. For every position in the store, from part-time clerk to store manager, there is a resource group in each geographical division. The resource group members accumulate employees' input on product and process improvement opportunities and share it with other members in their division. The division managers then take the recommendations from their resource group meetings and share those with other division managers. Good ideas from these meetings are eventually implemented.

Through the resource groups, employees can see that their input is taken seriously. In addition, Chet Cadieux, the current CEO of Quik-Trip (and son of previous CEO Chester Cadieux), reads the notes from every resource group meeting to make sure that employees know how important their thoughts are to him and to the company. Employees know that their ideas are heard and that their ideas are important enough that the CEO is going to make reading them a priority.

In sum, by involving employees in initially defining the standards and then in continuously improving them, QuikTrip was able to gain the benefits of standardization without hurting employees' dignity and satisfaction — without pushing employees away from the center of its success, as Home Depot had done. In fact, everyone in the company started seeing standardization as something that helped them do a better job and feel prouder than ever of the work they did.

MEASURING CUSTOMER SERVICE AT QUIKTRIP

I have never seen any retailer put such emphasis on tracking customer service as QuikTrip does. They use mystery shoppers, as many other companies do, but QuikTrip's mystery shopper program is by far the most rigorous I have seen.

Far too often, mystery shoppers' evaluations are based on questionnaires prepared at the headquarters with limited involvement from frontline employees or from customers. "I think this is still one of the things our competitors miss out on," said Jeffers. "They want to tell people how to do it from up here. But nobody goes and talks to the real consumer. They want to set a standard based on their beliefs from their day and time, and, in many cases, I think they miss the boat because they're not listening to the people who really bring the money in."

Not with QuikTrip. The mystery shopper questionnaire is based on customer feedback. Since the first questionnaire in 1995, the company has changed the questionnaire every two to five years or whenever QuikTrip stores went through a major change, such as changing layouts. Updating the questionnaire is an intensive process. Two store managers from each division interview one thousand customers (five hundred from urban and five hundred from suburban settings) in their division. These interviews last fifteen to twenty minutes and the customers receive a five-dollar gas card for their participation. QuikTrip combines this feedback with Internet surveys that gather about fifty thousand customer responses.

Armed with this carefully prepared questionnaire, QuikTrip mystery shoppers visit every store once a week. They are hired by the corporate office and paid twice the industry average. They evaluate employees' behavior — how friendly and courteous they are, how accurately they calculate change, and how good the stores and employees look on a variety of standards. Their identities are kept secret from all store employees, and if they are discovered, they are generally terminated. To top it off, they get mystery-shopped themselves. Periodically, a second mystery shopper visits a store to make sure that the first mystery shopper evaluated it correctly.

Why does QuikTrip go to all this trouble to measure customer service accurately? Because employees' bonuses, which make up about 10 percent of their pay, are based on mystery shoppers' evaluations. In addition, if a store scores 100 percent — and 20 percent of the stores typically do — the employee who was on the checkout at that time gets a fifty-dollar bonus.

How QuikTrip Empowers Employees Without Losing Control

QuikTrip doesn't stop at empowering employees to identify product and process improvements. Employees can use their judgment when they order store inventory. They can choose how to interact with customers and how to solve their problems. They are even empowered to use their heads at the cash register. At almost every retail chain, employees have to scan products, but because speed matters more than accuracy at QuikTrip, certain fast-moving products such as soda and coffee do not need to be scanned. There is a speed key for these products. When employees spot these products, they hit the appropriate speed key, take the money from the customer, and calculate the change in their heads.

But how does QuikTrip do this without losing control? How do they make sure that thousands of employees in hundreds of stores make the right decision every time?

Hire the Right People

Dennis Campbell of HBS uses data from Affinity Plus to show that one way to ensure that empowered employees make the right decisions is to hire the right people in the first place.[15] When Affinity Plus empowered its workforce, it changed its hiring methods so that it hired people who were comfortable making their own decisions and who would be able to put the member first in making those decisions. The new system worked. Campbell compared employees who had been hired into the old system with those who had been hired into the new system and found that the newer ones not only exercised more decision-making authority in granting and structuring consumer loans, but really did make better — that is, less risky — decisions, not only for members but for the credit union.

QuikTrip, too, wants to retain control — that is, to make sure its empowered employees consistently make the right decisions — and therefore it, too, relies heavily on hiring the right people. Here are a few of the things QuikTrip does:

1. *Get referrals.* QuikTrip is a company obsessed with data analysis. Having studied the predictors of high performance among its employees (characteristics such as level of education, retail experience, and military service), the company found that 40 percent of the best employees were referrals from other employees. Now the company gives bonuses to any employee whose referral brings in a new employee who then reaches various milestones. Yes, it's a plural — "bonuses" — because you get a $100 bonus when the person you referred finishes training and again when he or she makes it through three months, six months, and one year of employment.

   At Affinity Plus, more than half of the employees hired into the new system were referrals from employees already working there. This is consistent with the benefit that other companies have found in using referrals and employees' social networks for hiring.[16]

2. *Have professionals do the hiring.* A lot of retailers rely on store managers to do the hiring. Not QuikTrip. Hiring at QuikTrip is done centrally in each city by QuikTrip employees who specialize in it. Mercadona follows the same approach. Hiring centrally not only saves store managers time and lets them focus on managing their stores, but also ensures that employees are selected in a rigorous way.

3. *Start out with competence.* How many times have you heard "Hire for attitude, train for skills"? Well, QuikTrip does hire for attitude, but it also looks for specific skills. Because employees have to handle numbers in their heads, QuikTrip starts the interview process with a simple math test that includes questions on calculating change and ordering products based on last week's sales. If you can't pass this test, you're not going any further.

During the interview, the personnel manager asks questions to see if the candidate is comfortable exercising judgment. For example: "If you were working the night shift alone and a customer came in and said he had spilled gas while pumping, what would you do?"

Monitor Employees

We have already seen QuikTrip's intensive mystery shopper program. Another way QuikTrip ensures control is through constant monitoring. Store managers and supervisors constantly monitor employees and help them improve. "Trust but verify" is the mentality here. And to do that, QuikTrip relies both on technology — especially IT systems — and on personal observations. Security cameras inside the store, which are on par with those at most banks, are directed at the cash register. If, for example, the store's sales and the money collected do not match at the end of the day, QuikTrip can use the video footage along with cash register transactions, which can be pulled in fifteen-minute increments, to figure out what went wrong and who needs some extra training. If an employee is stealing, this can help catch him or her.

Given QuikTrip's mix of standardization and empowerment (common to all four model retailers), monitoring employees helps to evaluate not just whether they are using their judgment well, but whether they are adhering to the standards. QuikTrip knows all too well that just because it standardizes a process doesn't mean that employees will adhere to it. Remember my visits to the two auto plants that had the same standards on paper but very different behavior on the factory floor? Standards need to be enforced. Apart from investment in employees, QuikTrip uses monitoring by mystery shoppers, store managers, and supervisors to ensure that they are.

This may sound too much like Big Brother Is Watching You, but when there is trust between the company and its employees, monitoring can be a powerful way to improve performance. One company that successfully uses monitoring is Toyota. Worksheets detailing an employee's standardized work are posted to face outward, away from the operator. The operator is well trained in the standardized procedures he has to follow, so he doesn't need to keep looking at the written instructions — a good example of high investment in employees, by the way. The only reason the worksheet is posted at all is so the team leaders and group leaders can check to see if it is being followed by the operator.

Measure Performance and Provide Incentives

Performance measurement and incentives can also work to motivate employees to make the right decisions. At QuikTrip, employees are highly motivated to serve the customers because half of their bonus is based on mystery shoppers' evaluations. They are also motivated to make sure that orders are made properly and that cash transactions are handled accurately because the other half of their bonus is a percentage of their store's and their division's operating profits. And because employee bonuses depend on how well the store and the division are performing, the bonus system encourages teamwork and increases peer pressure in a constructive way.

How Standardization with Empowerment Enables the Good Jobs Strategy

Now let's step back and review how this second operational choice — a blend of standardization and empowerment — combined with investment in employees is good for employees, customers, and investors.

Standardization certainly helps model retailers lower their costs. Many of the tasks inside retail stores are operational tasks that do not require customer-employee interaction. When there is conformity to standards, there are fewer problems such as phantom stockouts, price mix-ups, back room jungles, and the like. When there are fewer operational problems, costs are lower, and when people can find what they're looking for, sales are higher.

As we have seen, retail operations are not always as rote and mindless as people imagine; employees are constantly having to use their judgment to decide whether to shelve a few extra tubes of toothpaste that don't really fit or take them back to the back room. Store employees using their own judgment have a lot more to do with a store's success than management typically realizes. Some of these individual decisions *ought* to be standardized — not because employee judgment can't be trusted but because the very need for individual employee judgment indicates inefficiency or a poorly designed process.

Remember the bookstore employees hiding stashes of books behind other books? They were exercising judgment, but only because they were forced to make the best of an inefficient situation. This is a case where it would have been better for the retailer (or at least the store manager) to address the problem head-on and then either work out rules (based, as they were at QuikTrip, on the employees' direct experience and on customers' experiences) or at least work out guidelines for individual judgment. For example, is it a higher priority for the customer not to have to wait for an employee to go find a book in the back or for the store to always know where every book is? If employees understand the priorities — and *why* they are priorities — they can be trusted to make pretty good judgment calls.

At QuikTrip, speed at checkout is more important than accuracy of sales data because speed is what customers value the most and because QuikTrip does not use point-of-sale data for centralized ordering — store employees do the ordering. But in many retail settings, accuracy of sales data is important because the retailer relies on those data to make centralized inventory-planning decisions. A supermarket cashier at such a setting may think he is doing the store a favor by scanning different items with the same price as if the customer were buying several of the same item. Hey, it's faster and it's the same amount of money, right? But if this employee is given a clear understanding of how that affects inventory and replenishment and how those, in turn, come back to make it hard for customers to find what they need and hard for employees to help them, he will be able to take time to ring things up correctly without feeling that he's making customers wait just on account of some silly corporate rule.

This brings to light yet another way that standardization benefits employees, customers, and investors. Standardizing forces managers and employees to give detailed thought to exactly how a task is being done and how else it *could* be done — perhaps even how it could be eliminated. You are forced to examine what may simply have been an organizational habit. Thinking about any one task or process in that way is likely to bring other tasks and processes under scrutiny.

Model retailers invest in their employees with much more extensive training than their competitors provide. Standardization can play a big role in this because it is, of course, easier to train someone to carry out a standardized task than it is to teach him or her to exercise good judgment, which is often based on experience. So the more a company can standardize those tasks that *should* be standardized, the more it can impart competence at those standardized tasks during an employee's initial training. That's good for everyone. In some stores, new employees are sent onto the selling floor and expected to figure it out, partly because no one has standardized the tasks they will have to figure out. If you want to lower your firm's labor productivity, that's a perfect way to do it.

One of the beauties of combining the seemingly unlikely pair of standardization and empowerment is that it makes it much easier for a company to adjust and improve its processes. Empowered employees at model retailers can discover a better way to do something and they have effective mechanisms by which to share what they have found. In some cases, it might be better to make a new rule; in others, to relax, refine, or make exceptions to an existing rule. The point is that the company always has a choice of what to be rigid about and what to be loose about, rather than trying to make a rule for everything or leaving too much to individual discretion.

All of this is good for employees in a number of ways. Most obviously, it sets them up for success by making it that much easier to deliver good service. Most employees would rather spend a workday sat-

isfying customers than spend it frustrating them. We saw how happy
Patty felt to give her customers a little bit of satisfaction during the day.
One of the wonderful things about the human race is that Patty is not
at all unusual.

When operations are more efficient due to standardization and employees are empowered to use judgment, then employees have both
the time and the freedom to help a customer with a problem that can't
be solved quickly. Remember the employee in chapter 2 who described
the adversarial relationship between her and the customers? Employees of retailers that follow the good jobs strategy are less likely to feel
that way. They are less likely to think, "If I show this woman exactly
where the electric toothbrushes are and explain the differences among
them and what makes the really expensive one actually worth the price,
I'll be in trouble for a pallet of unshelved laundry detergent." Service
that thorough has to be thought of not only in terms of the immediate
sale (perhaps of a very expensive electric toothbrush) but also in terms
of future sales from a person who is going to choose to come back to
this store rather than to any of the others that sell the same thing.

Service that thorough also creates more opportunities for improvement because employees find out more about what their customers
need or want and what might keep them from buying something. Even
if there were no such thing as stockouts, customers can still be prevented from getting what they want or need because they don't fully
know what they want or need. This is the insight underlying Mercadona's philosophy of "prescribing" to its customers. A customer might
also rule out a product because she doesn't realize it is worth what it
costs. By the same token, a retailer may be missing out on sales of a
product simply because it doesn't realize it is something people want.
A retailer may also be missing out on a chance to improve the customer's experience by solving a problem that isn't quite serious or annoying enough to generate formal complaints.

Let me conclude with a final observation about employee dignity.
I have had many, many conversations with retail workers. One thing
I have heard over and over is how motivating it is for them to be able
to help one person after another. Though what they help customers
with may not be of earth-shattering importance, each time they can

make a bit of someone's day go better, they feel proud of themselves. What's more, if they feel their employer is helping them do this, they feel proud of their company and not only glad but even grateful to work there. Employee motivation like that is priceless. Of course, if employees consistently feel that they have to fight their own company in order to do right by the customers, that's another story.

CHAPTER 7

Operational Choice #3

Cross-Train

W HEN I ASK Trader Joe's customers why they love the company so much, they almost always mention friendly employees who give you whatever help you need. If you have a question about a product, you don't have to find the "right" person to ask; chances are, any employee you see can help you. If there is a long line at the checkout, chances are someone shelving cans of soup or arranging the flowers will come over and open another cash register.

Trader Joe's employees can do these things because they are cross-trained. Investing in employee training ensures that all employees know how to operate a cash register, how to shelve merchandise, and how to do any number of other useful things. Trader Joe's also makes a number of operational decisions that allow employees to perform a wide range of tasks. Offering fewer products makes it possible for employees to be familiar with most products. Putting produce in packages so that employees do not have to remember the product codes makes the checkout process simpler and easier to learn. So does eliminating sales promotions.

Trader Joe's is not alone in this. Other model retailers, as well as companies in other industries, use cross-training to achieve flexibility, which, for the purpose of this book, I will define as the ability to respond to variations in customer demand. Whatever business you are in, it's seldom if ever that you know exactly what customers you'll have when and what they will want. A restaurant owner knows that Friday night will generally be busier than Thursday night — except when a whole office decides to go out for dinner together on Thursday and everyone stays home Friday to watch a series finale on TV.

In service industries, customer variability has many effects on operations — some obvious and some not. A firm's ability to handle customer variability has many effects on service and profitability — some obvious and some not. In this chapter I'll focus largely on a particular example of variability, called "arrival variability," and explain how cross-training helps accommodate that variability. Of course, cross-training has benefits that go well beyond accommodating variability.

Variability from Customers

Figure 7.1 shows how hourly traffic into a department store can vary within a week — not only day by day but also throughout each day. Each bar on the chart represents the number of customers that arrived at the store in that hour. On Saturday morning, between 10:00 a.m. and 11:00 a.m., 498 customers walked into this store. But the traffic picked up later on, and from 4:00 p.m. to 5:00 p.m., 1,651 people, more than three times as many, came in.

Much of this variation is predictable. Any department store manager knows that Saturdays will be busier than Tuesdays and that fewer customers will show up during opening hours than later in the day. For this particular store, close to 80 percent of the variation in traffic can be explained using day of the week, time of the day, and whether the day is a holiday or not.

But then there is that other 20 percent, which cannot be predicted as easily. A change in the weather forecast, promotions run by the store or by a competitor, a construction site nearby — even a concert by Madonna, as we saw in chapter 4 — can all make a difference in how many customers will walk into the store. And to some extent, it's just a matter of whim and happenstance.

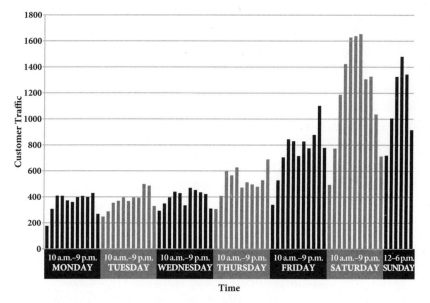

Figure 7.1. Hourly Traffic into a Department Store

What Variability Means for Operations

Predictable or not, these large fluctuations in customer traffic present a challenge for operations. When there are more customers, there are more people to be served at the checkout, more carts need to be returned from the parking lot, and more products need to be brought from the back room or from distribution centers. There are also more problems. For example, some customers routinely take things off the shelves, decide not to buy them, and just leave them somewhere else in the store, which contributes to phantom stockouts. When a customer can't get help because the employees are too busy with too many other customers, the store might lose a sale even though it has exactly what the customer wants.

Figure 7.1 shows only the variation in the *number* of customers who walk into that department store. But there is more variability than that. Not only may one individual need more help than another (or perhaps enjoy chatting more than another), but ten people looking for a bottle of marinated artichoke hearts will require more work than ten people looking for a bottle of stuffed olives if the store has twenty bottles of stuffed olives on the shelf but only five bottles of artichoke hearts.

If companies do not manage traffic variability well, they can get into a lot of trouble. If they have more employees than they need, they will end up paying for employees who sit idle. If they have too few to handle all the workload, then their stores will have plenty of operational problems and their customers may leave the stores aggravated, empty-handed, or both. Indeed, that's what I observed at the department store represented by Figure 7.1. *Conversion rate,* which measures what percentage of the customers who walk into a store actually buy something, varied greatly over time and depended, among other things, on how many sales associates were present per customer.

Understanding Variability

The first step toward managing traffic variability is to understand it. That requires two things: the right data and local knowledge.

A lot of companies rely on store managers' intuition alone to manage traffic variability, but that is not sufficient. The manager of the particular department store in Figure 7.1, for example, told me that on weekdays, traffic into his store built up until late afternoon and then dropped until the store closed. He had been managing that store for more than ten years, so he ought to know, right? But my analysis of the traffic data showed that the busiest times during weekdays were often in the evenings, after 6:00 p.m. These were also the times when the store had the lowest staffing and hence the lowest conversion rate.

Why did the store manager get this so wrong? Because, like many other store managers, he was basing his assertion on sales data rather than on traffic data. Traffic counters had only just been implemented at this store, so he hadn't seen the traffic data yet. To estimate traffic, he was simply looking at how much the store sold and how many customer transactions took place during different hours. But both the number of transactions and how much is spent on each transaction depend in part on staffing levels. If there aren't enough salespeople, there will be lower sales than there could have been with the same traffic. Hence, sales or transactions are not good proxies for traffic, especially in contexts such as department stores where conversion rate can vary a lot from one part of the day to another. Since the store manager was already convinced that there were fewer customers in the evenings, he staffed the store with fewer sales associates at that time. Obviously, when he looks at his sales, it *looks* as though there isn't much action at night, which confirms his false impression.

Data alone are also not enough for understanding traffic variability, because not all traffic is the same. There may be times when people are visiting the store not to buy anything but just to look around or hang out. There may be times when parents shop with their children, making traffic appear greater than it really is. This is where local knowledge becomes necessary. People on the selling floor observe not just how many people show up, but what types of customers show up when and what they need. A couple years ago, I visited Family Mart, the third-largest convenience store chain in Japan after 7-Eleven and Lawson. At the time, Family Mart operated 14,000 stores worldwide, yet the company executives I met raved about one store that had outstanding performance thanks to its store manager, who had been operating it for many years.

When I visited the store I was surprised to be greeted by a store manager who was in her seventies. This woman worked from 11:00 a.m. to 10:00 p.m. every day. She told me that part of her secret was understanding her customers and matching her employees to particular customers' needs. Early in the mornings and in the evenings, her customers are people on their way to work or coming back from work, so they want fast service. That's when she schedules her younger employees. During the daytime, however, a lot of housewives visit her store, not only to shop but also to hang out. They bring their small children and are eager to have conversations with the staff. That's when she schedules her older employees. They aren't as quick on the cash register but they are more comfortable chatting with mothers and enjoying the children. Some of the older staff may be lonely and treasure this addition to their social lives.

Strategies for Managing Variability

Once companies understand the specific variability in their own traffic, they can start managing it. In his classic *Harvard Business Review* article "Match Supply and Demand in Service Industries,"[1] Earl Sasser describes two main approaches for managing customer variability. One is to alter customer demand for the service in order to make the demand smoother and more predictable; for example, by lowering prices to stimulate demand during nonpeak periods, as some restaurants do with their "early bird specials." Another technique is to require customers to make reservations, which is what most healthcare providers do.

The second approach is to control the supply of the service, and Sasser describes two ways companies can do this. One is to get customers to deliver at least some of the service to themselves. A lot of companies are already doing this. Airlines have their customers do the check-in themselves. Car-sharing services such as Zipcar have their customers make reservations, pick up the cars, and return them to the right place without ever interacting with employees. A restaurant that offers a buffet is getting its customers to customize and serve their own meals. But outsourcing work to customers who are not recruited, not trained, and often not offered any motivation to perform well can have drawbacks.[2] A customer at an airport who cannot figure out how to check in can make the wait a lot longer for everyone else in line. A Zipcar customer who does not return the car on time can make life miserable for the next customer who needs the car for something important.

The second and much more common way to control supply is to manage the company's capacity to handle variable workload. Employees perform most of the work in service environments, so managing capacity ultimately means managing labor capacity.

Managing Arrival Variability in Retail

Which of these two approaches can be used more effectively in retail? Altering demand to make customer traffic smoother is a hard sell for most retailers. Busy people want to shop when it's most convenient for them. With the exception of some high-end retailers that offer personalized help, retailers generally don't ask their customers to make reservations to shop. Nor have retailers generally taken the approach of charging different prices depending on the time of day in order to encourage customers to shop during nonpeak periods. If anything, retailers make traffic variability even worse by keeping stores open longer hours and offering more promotions.

Asking customers to get involved in production also seems like a less effective way to manage retail traffic variability. Some stores have begun encouraging customers to do their own checkout. But customers can't always figure out how to use the self-checkout equipment, which can be fussy and confusing, so employees end up spending time walking the customers through the transaction. Sometimes customers think they have checked an item through and paid for it when they actually haven't. Either the store loses the money or the customer is embarrassed when he or she is stopped by an employee on the way out. Promotions, price discrepancies, and coupons can all make self-checkout even more complicated. In environments such as supermarkets and warehouse clubs, where people tend to buy dozens of products, customers can be very inefficient at checkout compared with employees and can frustrate other customers who are waiting. All this may explain why self-checkout, which was first used during the late 1980s by supermarket chains such as Publix and Kroger, is still not as widespread as had been predicted. Some retailers, such as Albertsons — another supermarket chain — experimented with self-checkout and then abandoned it.[3]

Even if self-checkout prevails, most of the work at retail stores will still be done by employees. Customers will not be invited to receive merchandise on the loading dock, shelve merchandise, move merchandise between storage locations and the selling floor, or change prices.

Hence, the main approach retailers use to manage traffic variability is to alter labor capacity. Model retailers do this, too, but they differ significantly from other retailers in *how* they do it.

General Strategies for Managing Capacity

We will get to how model retailers use cross-training to handle traffic variability, but first we need to understand a little more about the way most other retailers handle it and why they handle it that way. To do that, we'll need to take a detour into the world of manufacturing.

Highly variable demand is not unique to service businesses. Many products have seasonal demand, so the factories that produce them have to think about how to manage their capacity accordingly. Pencils, for example, are in high demand when students go back to school and in much lower demand at any other time. The two main strategies for managing demand variability — the level strategy and the chase strategy — are illustrated in Figure 7.2.

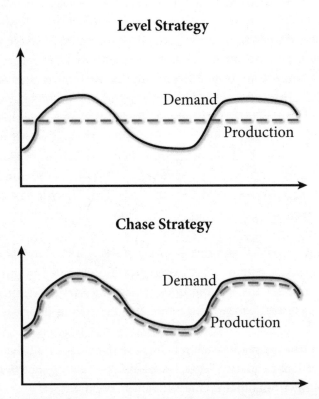

Figure 7.2. Level and Chase Strategies for Managing Demand Variability

In the level strategy, companies run production at a fairly constant level. For simplicity, let's say we have a factory that makes only one type of pencil and that the demand for pencils is normally 1,000 per week but jumps to 3,000 per week for four weeks during September, at the beginning of a new school year. So the total demand for a year is 60,000 pencils (or about 1,150 pencils per week on average). A factory following a level production strategy will produce 1,150 pencils every week. During the 48 weeks when the demand is only 1,000 per week, the factory will accumulate 150 pencils in inventory each week. Then when the demand jumps up to 3,000 per week, the factory will draw on that inventory.

In the chase production strategy, on the other hand, production varies with demand. When demand is 3,000 pencils per week, the factory makes 3,000 pencils per week, and when demand is 1,000 per week, the factory makes only 1,000 per week.

Both level and chase strategies have their costs. In the level strategy, the factory needs to hold a lot of inventory. If inventory-carrying costs are high (as they are for products that go obsolete quickly, such as electronics), then a level strategy will be expensive. A level strategy is also expensive when it is hard to forecast demand. What if, one year, the demand for pencils turns out to be only 30,000? Then the factory would be left with a lot of unsold pencils. Or what if, one year, the demand were 100,000? Then the manufacturer (and perhaps the retailers that it supplies) would end up incurring stock-out costs.

In the chase strategy, the difficulty is that the factory needs to be able to keep changing its capacity. That can be expensive, especially if changing the capacity for some bottleneck process that determines the capacity of the whole operation — perhaps a certain piece of equipment — is very expensive. In a level production system, that machine can work at its capacity throughout the year. In the chase strategy, on the other hand, there will need to be extra machines to take capacity up to 3,000 pencils per week, and those extra machines will remain idle forty-eight weeks of the year.

This is an overly simplified example. Production systems are rarely entirely chase or entirely level. Usually, we see hybrid systems where the earlier part of production is run on a level strategy and the later part is run on a chase strategy, with manufacturers using inventory to separate these two parts.

How Retailers Alter Labor Capacity

Service companies cannot store labor capacity in inventory the way a pencil maker can store extra pencils. At any given moment, labor capacity has to be used or it is wasted. As a result, most service companies, including most retailers, need to follow a chase strategy or else they will incur high costs. Imagine what would happen if a supermarket calculated its average daily demand for labor and used that same number of employees every day. A lot of employees would be idle on slow Mondays and a lot of customers would complain about long lines and messy stores on busy Saturdays.

Yet model retailers and retailers that operate in a vicious cycle differ greatly in the degree to which they follow the chase strategy. Retailers that operate in a vicious cycle follow the chase strategy in increments as short as fifteen minutes. They forecast customer traffic for 10:15 a.m. to 10:30 a.m., for 10:30 a.m. to 10:45 a.m., and so on, and try to match the number of employees to the traffic.

Retailers that operate in a virtuous cycle do not have to match store labor to traffic in such short increments because they cross-train their employees. Once they determine how many employees they need in a given day or shift (we will see exactly how they do this in chapter 8), they can have their staff perform different tasks throughout the day, depending on customer traffic.

Vicious-Cycle Retailers

Following a chase strategy in general requires two things: Obviously, you have to be able to forecast customer traffic reasonably accurately. But you also need to be able to match your labor capacity to your forecast. That is, you need to be able to staff your operation with more people at one time and fewer at another.

For vicious-cycle retailers, these requirements lead to problems. In chapter 5, I mentioned that one of the universal truths of forecasting is that aggregate forecasts are always more accurate than individual forecasts. That same concept applies here. Even with investment in traffic counters, a lot of historical data on customer traffic, and the best analytical techniques, forecasts for customer traffic every fifteen minutes or every half hour will always be less accurate than forecasts for a whole day or a whole week.

Retailers that want to follow a chase strategy in short increments will therefore have to live with less accurate customer traffic forecasts; that is, their forecasts are going to be wrong a lot of the time. Here is another universal truth of forecasting: Forecasts for short time-horizons are more accurate than forecasts for long time-horizons. We will always have a better sense of what customer traffic will be tomorrow versus two weeks from tomorrow. For example, weather tends to be an important predictor of customer traffic. If we know what the weather will be like tomorrow — that it will be rainy in the morning but sunny in the afternoon — our customer traffic forecasts will be more accurate. But we cannot know this very far in advance.

This point about forecasting has important implications for managing employees. If retailers want to make the most accurate forecasts possible and then use them to manage their labor capacity, they will want to keep their forecasts as short term as possible and then schedule their employees as late as possible. Even better if they can make last-minute changes. Say we find out in the evening that the weather forecast has changed and there will be rain the next morning. Rain means fewer customers. So why not call a few employees and tell them not to come in after all?

Even if a retailer can come up with perfect forecasts and is free to alter people's work schedules right up to the last minute, that's not enough. Retailers also need flexible labor, that is, employees who can work in short chunks of time. Suppose the forecast for a particular day is to have one hundred customers from 9:00 a.m. to 10:00 a.m. but two hundred customers from 10:00 a.m. to noon and then one hundred customers again from noon to 2:00 p.m. A perfect chase strategy would start at 9:00 a.m. with, say, ten employees, bring on ten more at 10:00 a.m., then send that extra ten home again at noon. It's helpful for the retailer if employees work short shifts. If you could get away with having employees work one-hour shifts, it would be much easier to follow a chase strategy.

These are the reasons for what we saw — largely through the employees' eyes — in chapter 1. Retailers use a lot of part-time employees, ask them to work short shifts, and let them know their schedules only one or two weeks in advance. They also constantly make changes to those schedules during the week, depending on last-minute forecasts. Moreover, vicious-cycle retailers do not apply the chase strategy just to part-time employees. Even full-time managers can have schedules that vary all the time.

Now you can see that retailers don't do this because they are evil. They do it because they think it's good business. Employees will be there when the store and its customers need them, but will not wait around idle when they are not needed.

Walmart spokesperson Sarah Clark made the business case pretty clearly: "We will benefit by improving the shopping experience by having the right number of associates to meet our customers' needs when they shop our stores."[4] Perfectly matching labor supply with customer traffic is intended to improve efficiency and service at the same time. Yes, this may be hard on employees, but the conventional wisdom is that this is just the way it has to be in the low-cost retail industry.

....

JUST-IN-TIME APPLIED TO THE WRONG CONTEXT

In the retail industry, scheduling employees at the last minute is called "just-in-time" scheduling. If you are not an operations junkie like me, when you hear the phrase "just in time," you probably think about this strategy as it has been used successfully by manufacturing companies such as Toyota. You may have heard that JIT (as operations people call it) reduces waste, improves quality, and brings many other benefits. So you might ask, "Isn't that a good thing?"

But if you have had experience with operations, you might be scratching your head and thinking, "Really? They call this way of scheduling employees 'JIT'? Don't retailers understand that JIT would not work in this setting?"

In a nutshell, JIT is a strategy where you make only what is needed, when it is needed, and in the quantity that is needed. Companies such as Toyota have championed this philosophy and have shown all its benefits. But JIT does not operate in a vacuum. In fact, implementing it requires a relatively smooth production. Think about our pencil example. If your customers need 1,000 pencils one week and 3,000 the next week (when school starts), how practical would it be to produce 1,000 pencils one week and 3,000 the next? What would be the implication for your suppliers, who will have to supply you with the lead and wood for 1,000 pencils one week and 3,000 units the next?

JIT works well for companies such as Toyota because it is complemented with what the Japanese call *heijunka*—what we saw earlier as level production. For various reasons, Toyota managers believe level manufacturing allows them to achieve higher quality, lower cost, and continuous improvement. That being the case, JIT makes very good sense, as the Toyota suppliers who have to deliver "just in time" are not likely to be taken by surprise.

Retail, as we have seen, is a very different story. A supermarket's demand for labor cannot be kept level like a Toyota plant's demand for tire rims. The labor hours cannot be held in inventory. The "suppliers" of labor—the employees—are therefore constantly taken by surprise, much to their disadvantage. This is, in fact, an excellent example of applying a good principle to the wrong context. It is also an excellent example of a systems perspective and how operational choices such as JIT and *heijunka* work better when they are practiced together.

....

Unintended Consequences of Following a Chase Strategy in Short Increments

The effect of "extreme chasing" on employees is clear. We all know that employees don't like their schedules to change all the time because it makes it hard for them to live normal lives or even to earn decent livings. What is not widely understood is that retailers are not benefiting from this way of managing labor as much as they think they are. By focusing too much on one dimension of performance, they are missing the big picture.

Yes, perfect chasing of store traffic may sound more efficient. If you have employees exactly when customers are there, customers will get better service. If you don't have employees when customers are not there, you won't waste money on idle labor. However, when companies shift the cost of their uncertainty about customer traffic onto employees, they not only affect the lives of employees but also the customer's store experience and the company's profits.

Employees who find it hard to manage their lives, or even just to get by, because of unexpected changes in their hours and hence their incomes do not come to work motivated or happy. Who would enjoy getting a new schedule every week or having his or her schedule changed the night before or working in really short shifts? Unhappy employees are less likely to be committed to their jobs and less likely to stay.

With a chase strategy practiced this way, we often see high turnover, absenteeism, and tardiness. This, in turn, makes matching labor supply to customer traffic even more difficult because now we have not only a lot of variability in traffic but also a lot of variability in our labor supply. We don't know who will quit, who will be late tomorrow, and who just won't bother to show up.

In addition to greater variability in the quantity of labor, we also see greater variability in the quality of labor. Some employees may work hard and some may not; some employees may know what they are doing and some may not; some employees may still care and some may not. All of this further complicates matching labor capacity to customer demand.

Furthermore, we know that when employees' morale is low and turnover is high, employees will make more mistakes or take shortcuts; sometimes the shortcuts are just a way to deal with the understaffing. There will be more phantom stockouts, more data inaccuracy, more shrink, and more customer service problems. Here we are, back in the vicious cycle of retailing.

Virtuous-Cycle Retailers

Retailers that operate in a virtuous cycle also experience significant variability in customer traffic throughout the day, albeit less than that of the vicious-cycle retailers since they offer less to their customers. However, they manage traffic variability in a very different way. Rather than constantly change the number of employees, they change what their employees do.

You are probably familiar with the off-peak hours between 3:00 p.m. and 5:00 p.m. in Spain, when most people take a short nap after a long lunch. Resting is such a tradition there that a lot of small shops and banks still close for a few hours in the afternoon. Until 2006, government employees had two- or three-hour breaks in the middle of the day. If you are a foreigner visiting Spain, you might even be annoyed by these off-peak hours.

When you visit a Mercadona store between 3:00 p.m. and 5:00 p.m., it's practically empty. Traffic doesn't really pick up again until early evening. Nevertheless, the number of employees at a Mercadona store stays pretty much the same all day. Approximately 85 percent of Mercadona employees are salaried full-timers who work 6.6 hours a day, six days a week. Yet Mercadona's labor cost as a percentage of sales is lower than that of its competitors. How can this be? How can Mercadona be so efficient without trimming the head count to match the customer traffic? How can all those seemingly unnecessary employees actually be profitable?

The answer is cross-training. Every new Mercadona employee goes through four weeks of training, during which he or she not only learns about the company's values but also learns how to perform a broad range of tasks. The fruit and vegetables specialists, for example, are trained to help customers, manage product flow, order products, perform inventory checks for four to five hundred products to make sure that the physical inventory matches the system inventory, and regularly check their sections for product or process problems. During busy periods, these specialists stay in front of their sections and spend their time exclusively helping customers — answering questions and prescribing products. During off-peak hours, on the other hand, they perform all their other tasks that do not directly involve customers. They conduct inventory checks, bring products from back rooms, arrange their shelves, look for problems and improvement opportunities, and order more stock.

The same is true for cashiers, who are cross-trained not just to operate cash registers but also to shelve and to clean. During low-traffic periods, cashiers who aren't busy help the specialists shelve products or help cleaners clean the store.

Most retailers cannot shift their labor around like this because they do not invest enough in training. Having given a cashier just enough training to run a cash register and having given a cleaner little or no training at all, they have no choice but to have employees perform narrow tasks and to keep alternating between idle work capacity and undone work. The only way such stores can respond to variations in customer traffic is by changing the number of employees, and that can rarely be done on the spot.

Cross-training may become even more valuable in the Internet age. More and more, retailers are trying to figure out the best way to integrate their physical stores with their online stores. One answer might be to use idle labor inside the stores to help with customer service online. Many companies with online sales now offer their customers live chat with customer service people. Retailers could use their store employees to help provide that service when they are not busy with in-store tasks — but only if those employees have been given the training to do it well.

Companies do not have to train every employee to do every job. In fact, it is widely known in the field of operations management that small levels of cross-training can go a long way in accommodating variability. This is good news because in many contexts, full-skill cross-training would be very expensive. Think about a Costco store. First, the place is huge. An average store is about 150,000 square feet. There are lots of different departments and different skills are needed in each. Employees in the food court, for example, need to know how to cook the food, operate the cash registers, and keep the area clean. Bakery employees need to bake, wrap the baked items, shelve them, and keep the area clean. In the meat section, employees need to know how to cut the meat, wrap it, shelve it, and keep the area clean. Cross-training every employee to do all the tasks in the bakery, the meat section, and the food court *and* to run a cash register *and* to do general shelving would be extremely expensive. But cross-training employees within the food court or within the meat section or within the bakery or cross-training employees who do merchandising or shelving to also operate cash registers can provide enough flexibility to deal with changes in customer traffic during the day. And that's exactly what Costco does.

How Virtuous-Cycle Retailers Manage Last-Minute Changes

Cross-training helps manage variability in traffic throughout the day, but what about variability at a higher level? What if Saturday is much busier than forecasted and Sunday is a lot quieter? What to do then? As we will see in detail in chapter 8, even if customer traffic during a particular day is heavier than expected, model retailers rarely suffer from having too few employees because they use some slack when they decide how many people to have on any given day. But what if there are too few customers and not enough work to do?

When you enter a Costco store, the first person you see is the greeter, who checks your membership card and records how many customers enter the store. If traffic is turning out to be a lot lower than expected and there are good reasons to believe that it will remain lower, then the store manager goes around asking if anyone wants to take a few hours off. This is not forced time off — the manager simply asks if anyone would like to take time off, and there are often more than enough employees who would.

Believe it or not, that's something for Costco to be proud of. Costco employees, unlike most retail employees, are well paid and have great benefits. Even part-time employees are guaranteed twenty-five hours of work every week and have benefits. As a result, they don't have to worry about whether they will be able to put food on the table each night. Given a chance to take some time off during the day to get ahead on errands that were planned for the weekend or a day off, some employees tend to take that opportunity. If there is no one who wants to take the time off, then Costco eats the cost of having too many employees. But for model retailers, this cost is not as high as you might think.

HOW QUIKTRIP MANAGES BUSY SUMMERS AND QUIET WINTERS

Customer traffic at a convenience store changes significantly from season to season. Summers are the busiest because people consume a lot more cold drinks. Here's how QuikTrip manages these fluctuations.

An average QuikTrip store employs about fifteen people. Five of these are managers with fixed schedules throughout the year and the rest are full-time and part-time employees who have more flexible schedules. In 2011, a little less than 40 percent of QuikTrip's employees were part-timers. Many of the company's part-timers are high school or college students who are not yet trying to support a family or even to entirely support themselves. These students often want forty hours of work a week in the summer and are happy to work for as few as fifteen hours a week in the winter.

QuikTrip offers a stable schedule—a "level strategy"—for its managers and many full-time hourly employees, and it uses part-timers for dealing with fluctuations in traffic. Sounds intuitive, doesn't it? Yet, as we saw with Janet, retailers that operate in a vicious cycle apply the chase strategy even to their managers.

Part-timers who are not students can get more hours by working at more than one store. The reason they can do this is that QuikTrip has standardized processes and even standardized stores, so that pretty much anyone can work at any store at any time. Once again, we see the interaction of the operational choices—standardization and cross-training.

Cross-Training Beyond Retail

Scholars in fields ranging from economics to operations management have discussed the costs and benefits of cross-training. The main costs are the cost of the training itself and the loss of efficiency — and hence potential loss of output — when employees are not specialized. Specialized employees who do the same task over and over are expected to do it more quickly than employees who are not specialized. In addition, it is cheaper to train an employee for one task than for several tasks. The main benefits of cross-training, on the other hand, are the increased flexibility and the increase in workers' motivation.

In service environments in which there are some tasks that involve customers and some that do not, the benefits of cross-training will often trump its costs. We saw in chapter 6 how Affinity Plus used cross-training to handle call volume from its customers without increasing its staff. Flexibility is just as important in manufacturing environments. Most factories produce a wide range of products whose demand and specifications change all the time.

Let's consider a production line with many stations. There are at least two types of variability that cross-training can help the firm to manage. Sometimes different machines or tasks on the same line require different processing times. Sometimes different products or jobs take different amounts of time on the same machine. In either case, one station can accumulate a lot of work while others are waiting for work. If operators are cross-trained, such bottlenecks can be alleviated.[5]

Not surprisingly, a lot of manufacturing companies use cross-training to manage flexibility. Toyota is a great example. The assembly line at a Toyota factory is divided into stations. In each station an employee performs several tasks, typically in under a minute. But Toyota factory employees do not work at only one station; they typically rotate among different stations every two hours or so. That way they are familiar with tasks at different stations and can be assigned to different stations as the need arises.

Rotating employees among stations clearly helps Toyota achieve flexibility. But the benefit goes well beyond that. Job rotation also improves quality. How? Working on an assembly line does not typically qualify as enriching work. After all, people do the same task over and over, and their piece of the total effort is often so small that it's hard for them to feel any sense of their work's significance. At Toyota, performing multiple tasks allows the employees to keep their minds active by paying attention to multiple stations that require different standards. The need for active thinking is so much a part of the Toyota Production System that some people say that TPS stands for Thinking Production System. Being able to perform different jobs helps Toyota employees understand how their work fits into the big picture. Switching from task to task also keeps boredom at bay and leaves employees less vulnerable to fatigue and even injury from repetitive actions.

How Cross-Training Enables the Good Jobs Strategy

Cross-training helps companies satisfy customers, employees, and investors all at the same time. By making it possible for employees to be busy with something useful even when there are no customers, it improves labor productivity. That, in turn, allows companies to improve customer service and sales without even increasing their costs.

There is another, less obvious way in which cross-training puts employees at the center of a company's success. If you have ever read accounts of start-ups, or been involved in one yourself, you know that one of their common, distinctive, and essential features is that there are only a few people on the team and anyone might end up doing anything as the need arises. Founders tend to remember this aspect of the start-up very fondly, and once the company grows to the point where that doesn't make sense anymore, they miss it.

In a large and established company, cross-training offers some of that same kind of excitement and sense of being part of the group effort. The effects are probably not as electrifying as they are in a start-up — "all for one and one for all!" — but they are valuable indeed and confer benefits on customers, employees, and investors.

We know from years of research in job design that one way to improve motivation is to make the job more meaningful. What makes a job meaningful? According to the renowned psychologist Richard

J. Hackman and his colleague Greg R. Oldham, the three important qualities are (1) the chance to use a variety of skills, (2) the chance to see a job through from beginning to end, and (3) the chance to do something that makes a difference.[6] Cross-training offers all three. Being cross-trained doesn't mean an employee will perform every step of selling a product from unloading the truck to ringing up the sale on the cash register, but it does mean he or she will perform more than just one of those steps and will therefore have a sense of being a part of the whole process.

Cross-training also gives employees a greater sense of making a difference because it emphasizes the importance of each job and removes some of the barriers between employees and their managers. At Trader Joe's, for example, all managers spend part of their workday unloading boxes, helping customers, and being cashiers. So do the managers at QuikTrip. Ron Jeffers, QuikTrip's vice president of operating systems, told me, "The number one reason people stay with QuikTrip is not the money. It's because their managers will do the same jobs they do. They have never worked anywhere else where the management will do the worst parts of the job such as clean the bathroom, empty the trash, work in the freezers, and clean the gas islands." Experiences like this do several things. They give employees a much stronger sense of being part of the *team* that accomplishes the company's purpose. They also allow employees to identify much more strongly with the top managers, who clearly do make a difference. And they endow the employees' work with more significance; if it's important enough for higher-level people to pitch in to make sure it gets done, then it must be pretty important. All these effects feed into employees' loyalty and longevity.

Something similar goes on at Southwest Airlines, where anyone involved in getting an airplane ready for its next flight can be called upon to help with whatever needs to be done. If the plane isn't turned around on time, the whole team is marked down, so it doesn't pay to take a "that's not my job" attitude. If need be, pilots will help unload the baggage and gate attendants will help provision the next flight. If there is a problem, the team's responsibility is first to solve it, then to figure out how to keep it from happening again. And then, as Donna

Conover, executive vice president of customer service, explained, "You can talk later about who should have done what."[7]

We have seen throughout this book that making it possible for employees to enjoy their jobs and lives brings important benefits to customers and investors as well. Cross-training allows for more stability. From the employees' perspective, knowing your schedule and knowing that it won't change gives you peace of mind. You can plan your life around that schedule. When employees have this stability, they are happier.

Happier employees who have more stability in their lives keep the virtuous cycle going. They tend to show up at work on time and they rarely quit. All model retailers have low employee turnover. Less variability in labor supply makes it easier for these retailers to deploy the number of people they need at different times of the day, the week, or the year. These employers get the flexibility they want in their head count without making life miserable for their employees.

Employees who are happier and more committed of course make fewer errors and are less likely to take shortcuts. Not only are they less likely to be in a rush due to chronic understaffing, but they are also more likely to care about doing a good job because it's a job they want to hold on to. As a result, companies that use cross-training can have fewer operational problems and lower costs.

At the same time, cross-training allows customers to enjoy not only lower prices but also better service. Products are where we want them to be, stores are tidy, employees are knowledgeable and available, and we spend less time in the checkout line finding out way too much about the latest celebrity scandal from the gossip magazines.

Apart from all this, employees who are committed and who know a broad range of tasks — employees who can see the forest for the trees — can suggest improvements.

Making jobs more enjoyable also gives a company more potential employees to choose from. We saw in chapter 4 that applying for a job at QuikTrip can be as competitive as applying for an Ivy League college. When Trader Joe's talks about careers in its stores, it makes a point of how much fun it is to work there *because of* cross-training. Here is part of the company's online job description for an entry-level "crew" position:

> The Crew is the heart and soul of the Trader Joe's operation. They do it all. And all that they do is dedicated to creating a WOW experience for our customers. Most importantly, they have fun while doing it. So what exactly do they do?
>
> As a member of the Crew, you'll handle a lot. But that's the thing; so does everybody else. What's more, you won't be stuck in one role here. Take over the register, have fun helping customers, bag some groceries, build a display, or stock the shelves — there will never be a dull moment in your day! All you need is a passion for people and fervor for food. We can teach you the rest.

The four operational choices we have been going through result in various benefits when all four choices are carried out together and when they are complemented with an investment in people. They also serve as opportunities for improvement without necessarily being causes of that improvement. While making your company more attractive to potential employees does not force you to revamp your recruitment processes, it does suggest that you do so and gives you a golden opportunity to do so. With more applicants to choose from, you can think about how to make better choices.

What's more, companies that provide extensive training are motivated to invest more in their recruiting to make sure that investment in training pays off. When QuikTrip hires someone, it makes sure that the person will be a good fit — both in the sense that the person will do good work for QuikTrip and in the sense that QuikTrip will not be taking advantage of someone who needs more income than the position will provide. As we saw earlier, the hiring process even includes math tests.

Cross-training interacts productively with offering less. One reason that all Trader Joe's employees can operate the cash register is that it's much easier to operate a cash register there than at an ordinary supermarket. First, there are fewer products at Trader Joe's, so it's easier to learn them. Second, most of the produce there does not need to be weighed, because it's in packages that are already weighed and priced, so the cashiers don't have to learn product codes for hundreds of produce items.

Cross-training also interacts with a policy of setting high expectations. The satisfaction of being cross-trained is not that you can do several things, but that you can do them all well. Otherwise, a company would just be spreading people's mistakes around. Without high standards (and the training to make them achievable), it would be better to let an employee stick with one job and improve at that one only.

Cross-training works well for model retailers for all the practical reasons I have mentioned. But it also works well because it reflects the overall mind-set that employees are at the center of a company's success. It perfectly expresses the realization that employees are human beings and that most human beings are capable of many different things and aspire to do great things, even if on a small scale.

CHAPTER 8

Operational Choice #4

Operate with Slack

MOST LOW-COST RETAILERS work hard to reduce waste and are proud of their efforts. They buy directly from suppliers, control highly efficient distribution centers, work with their suppliers to improve packaging, and try their best to match their labor hours to their exact needs — hour by hour, or even more finely than that. Walmart has established a tremendous reputation for eliminating waste in its supply chain and for squeezing what it considers to be every last bit of waste from its labor expenses.

But for all that, these companies still waste a lot. As we have seen, many retailers produce inventory waste by having high product variety and having a lot of promotions, that is, by providing customers with more than they actually need. They waste employee productivity by (a) restricting employees to narrow tasks and then having some of those people idle when traffic is low and frantic when high, (b) forcing employees to waste time dealing with so many operational errors, and (c) forcing them into inefficient work patterns just to deal with the immediate demands caused by understaffing. All this waste eats into profits and customer satisfaction, not to mention that it creates a lot of headaches for beleaguered store employees and their beleaguered managers.

Model retailers are just as obsessed with eliminating waste as other low-cost retailers are, and when it comes to making their supply chains more efficient, they do many of the same things the other retailers do. Because of their much higher investment in people and the four operational choices they make, however, they can do more than other retailers do to eliminate waste. When I was visiting Mercadona, I saw that it had replaced hand-cream bottles that had convex tops with bottles that had flat tops. That made them easier to stack, lowering the cost of transportation and the time needed for shelving. But the product didn't look as pretty. Mercadona was able to get away with this because employees were always on hand to explain to skeptical customers that it was the same product, just with smarter packaging to save them some money.

Other retailers would be well aware that those rounded tops can be a hindrance to operations, but the tops seem to be necessary to attract buyers who are guided only by how svelte the bottles look on the shelf. Mercadona shoppers, however, have Mercadona staff to guide them. Therefore, the extra-attractive shape of the bottle is not absolutely necessary and can, in fact, be treated as a type of waste to be eliminated.

This example raises the point on which model retailers differ most greatly from other retailers in their efforts to cut waste — the last of the four operational choices that underlie the good jobs strategy. Model retailers cut waste everywhere they can find it *except when it comes to labor*. There, they like to err on the side of too much labor — or overstaffing — which would be seen as a fatal mistake anywhere else. It's not even a matter of "erring"; model retailers deliberately build slack into their staffing.

Let's have a look at how unintuitive overstaffing really is. If you pay someone a lot more than your competitors would do, give him or her a lot more training, and provide all sorts of benefits, you would want to make full use of that person, right? But for all that Mercadona invests in its employees, it doesn't try to achieve that type of efficiency. It deliberately staffs its stores with some slack. In other words, it makes sure to have more labor hours on hand than what it expects the workload to be.

It's clear that having more people at the stores would improve customer service. However, Mercadona doesn't operate with slack solely for better service. Well-staffed stores also reduce costs. How can having too many employees on hand reduce costs? First, by preventing the operational problems that come from understaffing. Second, by allowing employees to be involved in continuous improvement in the form of waste reduction, efficiency and safety improvement, and product and process innovation. By creating time for continuous improvement — and by empowering employees — Mercadona makes it possible for its people to identify problems and suggest improvement opportunities. We're not talking about the legendary "suggestion box" that leads nowhere. Mercadona makes sure that employees' ideas are heard and that good ideas are successfully implemented in its more than one thousand stores.

Mercadona is not alone in empowering employees and providing them with enough time and other resources so that they get involved in continuous improvement. Employee involvement is in the DNA of model retailers and other operationally excellent companies.

For companies that simply view employees as costs to be minimized, enabling employees to be involved in continuous improvement is a lot more challenging. When minimizing labor costs is the objective, having too many employees on the job rather than too few is viewed as waste that cannot be tolerated. And when a little slack in the system is seen as waste and the definition of getting the most out of your employees is to have them work as quickly as humanly possible, who has time for continuous improvement?

How Many Employees Are Enough?

In the previous chapter, we discussed the strategies companies use to manage variability in customer traffic. Being smart about who does what and when can significantly increase flexibility without adjusting the number of employees in the store. But regardless of which employee does what task, retailers as well as companies in other industries still have to figure out how many employees are enough to do everything that needs to be done during any particular period — say, a shift or a day.

How many employees a retailer needs in a day depends on how much workload there will be, which is uncertain. There is uncertainty from customers: How many will come? What will they want to buy? How much help will they need from employees? There may be some uncertainty from suppliers: What products will be delivered? When will they arrive? How much will be delivered? How many defective units will there be? On top of all this, there may be uncertainty in the way work is done. Mary may shelve a case of peanuts in ten minutes but Mark may take twelve minutes.

Say the average workload on a typical Monday is 500 labor-hours ($\mu = 500$). But of course, some Mondays the workload is higher and some Mondays it's lower. You have found that workload is normally distributed (as shown in Figure 8.1) and the standard deviation of workload (σ) is 50 labor-hours.

How many hours of labor should you have at the store to maximize profit? Should it be 500 hours? Although the average workload is 500, the actual workload varies from day to day and is only occasionally exactly 500. Each day, there is (a) nearly a 50 percent chance that the workload will be higher, in which case you will not have enough labor-hours to get everything done and your customers will likely be unhappy, and also (b) nearly a 50 percent chance that the workload will be lower, in which case you will end up with idle labor-hours that you have paid for and can't possibly use.

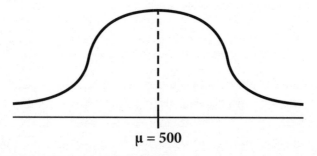

$\mu = 500$

Figure 8.1. Normal Workload Distribution

Not getting all the work done almost half the time won't do. What would be a safer bet? When we look at the normal distribution, shown in Figure 8.2, we can see that almost 99.9 percent of all outcomes fall under the average plus three standard deviations (the shaded area below the curve). That means that if you always staffed the store with 650 hours of labor (the 500 plus an extra 3×50 labor-hours), then you're almost guaranteed to have enough labor nearly 99.9 percent of the time. This also means that you will almost always have more labor than you need.

That level of safety may be so expensive that the store ends up losing money. What is exactly the right level of staffing to maximize profit? That depends on how much it costs you to have extra labor — your *over-staffing cost* — versus how much it costs to have too little labor — your *understaffing cost*. Without getting into the math, let's think intuitively about how this would work. Your estimate of how much labor you need each day (or each shift or hour) is almost always going to be at least a little bit wrong — too high or too low. What you want is to make the less-expensive mistake more often and the more-expensive mistake less often. If the costs of overstaffing and understaffing were identical, then you would have no reason to prefer one to the other and it would make sense to staff the store with exactly 500 hours of labor every day. But if, say, your overstaffing costs are higher than your understaffing costs, it would make sense to staff the store with fewer than 500 hours of labor. If your understaffing costs are higher than your overstaffing costs, on the other hand, it would make sense to staff the store with more than 500 hours of labor, though not necessarily as many as 650 hours.[1]

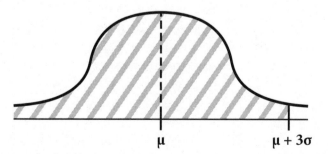

Figure 8.2. Staffing Level That Ensures That Workload Will Be Completed 99.9 Percent of the Time

Why Understaffing Is Everywhere

More and more, customers complain about understaffed stores. Chapter 3 offered empirical evidence for persistent understaffing, with retailers choosing staffing levels that do not maximize profits. Now we are in a position to understand why we see that so often.

Optimizing staffing is easier said than done. First, a lot of companies do not have a good idea of the workload distribution in their stores. Many use sales as a proxy for workload and make their staffing decisions accordingly. For example, if a store is expected to sell $50,000 worth of goods in a day, the manager may assume that using, say, 500 hours' (or $5,000) worth of labor would do the job. But an assumption like that can be quite wrong. "A bottle of whisky sells at over ten times the price of a bottle of water," Jaime López, a regional manager from Mercadona, told me, "yet they require the same amount of labor time to unload and shelve."

In addition, even if a company does have an accurate forecast for the workload in its stores, it is not simply a matter of plugging in numbers for overstaffing and understaffing costs, because it is far from obvious what those costs are.

Let's take understaffing costs. What happens if we have fewer labor-hours than the actual workload? Then we'll have employees rushing, taking shortcuts, unable or unwilling to spend time with customers. We will have stores with misplaced products, messy shelves, long checkout lines, a lot of wasted inventory, and a lot of unhappy customers. Do retailers know for sure how much this costs? Or how much the lack of staffing contributes to these problems, which can also exist for other reasons? Hardly. The cost of having too few employees is very difficult to quantify. Some of the cost can be long term and indirect. A customer may not give up on a store because of one frustrating experience there, but she may eventually give up after five such experiences, or ten. What is the effect of that customer telling her friends why she's fed up with that particular store?

Calculating overstaffing cost, on the other hand, is more straightforward. For most companies, it is simply the employee's hourly wage, and it has to be paid the very next payday. This cost is immediate, direct, and very easy to quantify.

When it comes to trading off the cost of having an extra unit of labor and the cost of not having that extra unit of labor, which one do you think wins? We humans are wired to emphasize the short term at the expense of the long term. People still smoke, even though there is plenty of evidence that it can kill them. We still eat that high-calorie dessert even though we know it's bad for us. And there are those among us who stay up to watch two more episodes of *Breaking Bad* even though we know we're going to be tired and sorry the next day.

We know from previous research that when managers are called upon to weigh costs that are obvious and easy to measure against benefits that are indirect and not immediately felt, they tend to pay too much heed to the obvious costs and make suboptimal decisions. So we would expect retail managers to pay more attention to the costs of more labor than to the benefits of having more labor, and, indeed, that's mostly what we see.

Vicious-cycle retailers put even more emphasis on the costs of labor because that's how they view employees — as costs to be minimized. As we have seen in chapter 3, store managers are constantly measured on how well they manage labor costs, sometimes even on a daily basis, and are under a lot of pressure to reduce them. Not surprisingly, store managers often choose to have too few employees rather than too many, even if doing so will not maximize profits and even if they *know* it will not maximize profits. For the individual store manager, the cost of being seen by the corporate management as overspending on labor is simply not worth the benefits that extra labor would bring.

Understaffing as a form of cost-cutting causes a lot of problems and unhappy customers. Marshall Fisher of Wharton makes the connection perfectly. A root cause for why we, as customers, tend to have a bad experience at retail stores is "business-school thinking gone wrong," he argues. "We teach our students to be rigorous and manage by the numbers. Not a bad idea, except that it leads to over-weighting the measurable and under-weighting what's hard to measure. In a store, what's measurable is the payroll checks a retailer writes every week to its stores' staffs. What's hard to measure is the impact that stores' staffs have on revenue."[2]

Retail is not the only business in which this scenario plays out. Executives from a wide range of industries, including manufacturing, have told me that they, too, suffer from understaffing. It's not only hourly workers who tend to have more work to do than they can do well. It's also salaried employees. You may have experienced this in your own job — having too little time to do everything that you have to do. In all these instances, people end up rushing through their tasks, making mistakes, or just not getting it all done.

WHAT HAPPENS WHEN EMPLOYEES DON'T SHOW UP?

Even if you plan your staffing levels so as to have enough people to perform all the necessary tasks at your store, there is no guarantee that everyone will show up. People get sick, their children get sick, or there are emergencies. When you employ thousands of people, these things happen all the time. If you don't plan for them, you may end up with an understaffed operation even if you have scheduled enough people.

In some settings where the costs of understaffing are extremely high, companies hire extra people for contingencies. Airlines, for example, hire reserve pilots — who may be called at any time during their on-call periods. It is worth almost anything for the airline to avoid incurring the cost of a canceled a flight, which causes trouble for hundreds of passengers and damages its own reputation. We also see contingency employees in education, with substitute teachers; in healthcare, with on-call technicians, nurses, and doctors; and in theatre and opera, with understudies.

You would think that the cost of understaffing would not be high enough in convenience stores to justify employing contingency workers. Nevertheless, QuikTrip consistently employs "extra" employees — 15 percent more than it theoretically needs — so that they can fill in for regular employees who have emergencies, get sick, or are taking vacations. Every day, these relief employees call QuikTrip's help desk in Tulsa and ask to which store they should go that day. A relief employee with no assignment for the day just reports to her base store and helps out there. Having 15 percent slack labor may seem like a wasteful luxury, but it's not that expensive after all when you consider what having slack labor enables companies to do and what understaffing costs them.

Why Model Retailers Prefer Too Many Employees to Too Few

Companies such as QuikTrip believe that it is important to have enough employees to get everything done and to have a little extra on hand for contingencies. How can companies, especially those that compete on the basis of low cost, afford to operate with deliberate slack? If you ask their managers, they will give you a simple response: How can we afford not to?

These companies know that their understaffing costs are higher than their overstaffing costs. In addition, because they offer less, combine standardization with empowerment, and cross-train their employees, they are in a position to forecast the workload at their stores more accurately than their competitors can do.

Forecasting Workload

Mercadona does an excellent job understanding how much work needs to be done in its stores. Instead of using sales as a proxy for workload to make its staffing decisions, Mercadona looks at the work itself — not only tasks that are purely operational but also those that require interaction with customers. And thanks to the operational choices I have just mentioned, Mercadona has a pretty good sense of how long these tasks actually take.

Because Mercadona cross-trains its employees, it doesn't have to worry about forecasting workload in short increments like fifteen minutes. It can use a much longer period — as long as a day — for forecasting workload. Remember the rule about forecasting: Aggregate forecasts are more accurate than individual forecasts. Hence, forecasts of how many customers will visit a store in a day and how much they will buy in a day will always be more accurate than forecasts of how many people will visit that store and how much they will buy every fifteen minutes during the day.

In addition, Mercadona enjoys less variability in its customer demand than its competitors do. Offering less — especially operating with low product variety and everyday low prices — reduces variability in customer demand. Low variability in customer demand combined with years of historical data on customer shopping behavior allows Mercadona to forecast its workload pretty accurately.

Mercadona also enjoys less variability in supply. All product deliveries come from the chain's own distribution network. As a result, Mercadona has a better idea of when trucks will arrive and what they will bring. Because of its operational excellence, Mercadona can also ensure that all the pallets that arrive at a store are in good shape and are easy to open and shelve.

On top of all this, Mercadona does a great job of understanding how many hours of labor are necessary to do all the work that needs to be done at each store, because it standardizes the in-store logistics tasks. Remember that Mercadona has neighborhood stores that are all different from one another. Some are freestanding, some are under apartment buildings, some are inside old markets. The same task can take different times at different stores. Mercadona is careful to figure out how many hours of labor are necessary to do a particular job at a particular store, so that employees are not held to a standard that may be the average for the chain but is impossible to attain at their own store. For example, unloading takes longer when trucks cannot park right next to the store; replenishment takes longer when the back room is far from the sales floor; and shelving takes longer in a crowded store. It also goes the other way: Using a chainwide average may overestimate the amount of time needed for particular tasks at particular stores.

Finally, Mercadona does not have to deal with as much variation in employee capability as other retailers do. Because it has invested in its people, every employee knows how to perform the assigned tasks in the given time and in an accurate way.

Once Mercadona can calculate that it has so much work to do in a given day or a week, it can calculate pretty accurately how long and how many of its employees it will need to do that work.

Determining Staffing Levels

Mercadona's managers repeatedly told me that they always plan a little more than the expected workload. They would rather have too many employees than too few, which of course means that Mercadona believes that the cost of understaffing is higher than the cost of overstaffing.

For one thing, Mercadona's understaffing costs are typically higher than they would be elsewhere. If products are not shelved in the right place at Mercadona and customers can't find them, the company incurs lost sales just as any other company would. If products are damaged because employees didn't have time to properly shelve them, Mercadona incurs the same shrinkage costs that any other company does. But Mercadona's employees, unlike those at other retailers, have an active role in recommending products and providing information to their customers. Hence, their absence can mean even more lost sales.

Mercadona's overstaffing costs are also much lower than they are for others. What would happen if there were more employees than needed at a Mercadona store? Well, because employees are cross-trained, they can find lots of useful things to do: checking inventory, ordering more stock, tidying up their sections, and so on. They can also spend more time with customers, help customers carry their shopping bags, or just have some fun with them. Asking customers "Can I help you find anything?" or "Which of these soups do you like best?" is not just chatting — it's gathering valuable information for the retailer while giving customers attention they often appreciate. This can even be seen as a form of training. Earlier I discussed an employee who knew she could help a customer decide among the confusing choice of electric toothbrushes and that she could explain to that customer why the most expensive brand was actually worth the money. That employee may know about the high-end electric toothbrush from her training, but she may very well have learned about it from talking with some other customer who knew all about it. That is, of course, if she is empowered to carry on such conversations. For a retailer that is operating in the virtuous cycle, all this chatting with the customers is money in the bank.

Remember, companies that operate in a virtuous cycle and pay their employees well have one other benefit: If they feel that they are too overstaffed, they can ask their employees if anyone wants to take time off. We already saw, in the previous chapter, how Costco does this. QuikTrip uses the same approach. Chet Cadieux, the CEO, told me that QuikTrip pays its employees so well that most of the time people can afford to and want to take unpaid time off and enjoy their day. In fact, many times there are more volunteers to take unpaid time off than are needed. When that happens, QuikTrip randomly selects who can take time off.

Time + Empowerment = Opportunity for Continuous Improvement

The cost of overstaffing is not the only important thing here. It's the opportunity cost of not having slack. Store employees operating in an environment with some slack can add tremendous value that employees pushed to the limit cannot. Employees who are not always swamped with immediate tasks and who are empowered can use their extra time to identify problems, come up with solutions, and communicate both the problems and the solutions. For example, if many customers are asking for a product Mercadona does not carry, employees can use the extra time they have to communicate that information to field employees who work with the marketing and purchasing departments.

John Matthews, the senior vice president of human resources and risk management at Costco, told me that store employees constantly help the company reduce costs. They come up with suggestions to improve packaging or shipping or how a product should be displayed. They also suggest bigger changes. A particular Costco store in Florida had some landscaping, like most other Costco stores, and it cost the company money to water it. One of the hourly employees there suggested that they were in a good location to have their own water well.

"What a great idea!" John told me. "And all those years no one had thought about it." They dug the well and saved a lot of money.

Stories like this can travel throughout a company to encourage others to come up with ideas and to promote a culture of waste reduction. If each person can come up with an idea that takes one or two cents off the price of some product, that adds up to huge savings. Employees who find it hard just to finish the tasks at hand are not likely to have time to think about improvement opportunities, and even if they do, they are not likely to have time to share their ideas with management. Further, they are likely to conclude — from the "mismanaged chaos" all around them — that management wouldn't listen anyway.

I saw a particularly impressive example of employee involvement in continuous improvement when I studied Arrow Electronics, one of the world's largest distributors of electronics parts and computer products. Arrow serves companies in a wide range of industries, from electronics manufacturing to aerospace to medical imaging. Electronics distribution is a highly competitive industry with razor-thin margins; Arrow's competitive advantage comes from operational excellence.

Arrow strives to get the right product to the right customer with the right paperwork more quickly and more cheaply than any other distributor can. Every day, Arrow's sales and marketing people receive orders from customers and promise same-day delivery for all orders received before 4:00 p.m., based on what the inventory system says is available in Arrow's network of distribution centers. Let me point out that many retailers who want to fulfill online orders from their physical stores would not (or should not) dare to make such promises because they can't trust their own inventory data. In many cases, a customer would look up a product online, the inventory software would say it was at a store, but a store employee trying to fulfill the order couldn't find it. Arrow's sales and marketing people never worry about having the rug pulled out from under them like that because more than 98 percent of the products in Arrow's distribution centers have accurate data at the part-location level. In some distribution centers, the accuracy is 99.8 percent.[3]

Achieving such accuracy is very impressive, especially given how big Arrow facilities are and how many tiny little resistors, capacitors, and semiconductors they stock. One way Arrow maintains such accurate data is by involving the lowest-level employees in finding problems and then in solving them.

Every day, Arrow employees are given time to do routine checks of inventory accuracy. For example, when a picking operator finds a part that is physically stocked out, he or she verifies that the system inventory is also zero. Or when the system inventory for a particular part is zero, operators are instructed to verify that the physical inventory is also zero. Whenever there is a discrepancy between the physical and the system inventories, it means there is a problem. Warehouse operators are not only in charge of finding these problems, but also in charge of fixing them. When needed, they change the inventory data in the computer systems to reflect the physical inventory.

When I asked BJ Hess, the former senior vice president of worldwide operations at Arrow, why they involved warehouse operators in finding and solving problems, her response was quite intuitive and also consistent with what a lot of operations management scholars and thought leaders have argued for many years. The people closest to a problem have the best chance of spotting it and spotting what causes it. They are also the most motivated to solve it because it's causing them pain every day and putting them behind schedule. "Headquarters types" and managers would never be as enthusiastic about what to them would be long-distance drudge work, so they wouldn't give it the focus and tenacity that is required to keep such a complicated inventory at more than 98 percent accuracy every day. Hess also told me that Arrow's warehouse operators take pride in keeping their own house in order rather than being treated as mere extensions of the conveyor belts. It's humiliating to have to ask someone higher up to fix something you could easily fix yourself, as if you were too stupid to be trusted. I would also suggest that a reasonably intelligent person finds it annoying to keep encountering the same mistake or inefficiency over and over and will be motivated to fix it — given a chance to do so — just to make it go away.

For all these reasons, Arrow finds it better to have the operators themselves take care of their problems and have headquarters monitor and support them.

Involving warehouse operators in making inventory adjustments sounds intuitive. Yet, Hess told me that Arrow has acquired more than sixty companies, and there hasn't been one in which warehouse operators were allowed to make inventory adjustments. Only corporate office managers were allowed to make the changes, because changing inventory data in a computer system is seen as a big deal. If you mess it up, bad data can cause many problems down the line. Management simply didn't trust the workers — neither their competence nor their honesty. Yet when you think of it, although you have to be careful when you correct inventory data, it's not rocket science. Trained employees can do it just as well as someone at headquarters can, and in fact, quite a bit better for being there on the spot. In addition, a well-paid and well-respected warehouse employee has no more motivation to deliberately screw up the system or to steal products than the guy at headquarters does.

Listening to Employees

Involving employees in continuous improvement is in the DNA of other operationally excellent companies, just as it is at Arrow and Costco. But that doesn't mean such companies find it easy to do. Allowing time for improvement (by operating with slack) and empowering employees are both important, but even these momentous steps are not enough, especially in large chains with hundreds or thousands of locations.

In some cases, employees cannot fix the problems or implement the improvement opportunities they see on their own, no matter how empowered they are. If a product is difficult to shelve because it's poorly designed, store employees can identify this problem, but they can't fix it. The problem needs to be communicated to the supplier. Even when employees can fix problems or implement improvements, the benefit may stay within one store — maybe only when a particular employee is there — unless there is a process by which employees can communicate what they have found or done and by which the company can institutionalize improvements.

Jesús Echevarría, chief communications officer of Inditex, Zara's parent company, told me that employees are full of great ideas but the hard part is being able to truly hear them. Zara knows the importance of listening to employees. Its success relies heavily on understanding what customers want, and designing, making, and delivering those products quickly. To understand what customers want, Zara relies on frequent communication among stores, headquarters, and field employees.

Every day, Zara's employees observe their customers — what they buy and what they do not buy. Just as important, Zara's employees talk to their customers and find out what they would have bought if Zara had carried it. This is something that no point-of-sale or inventory data can ever tell you. Employees communicate this information informally to the managers responsible for their sections. The section managers (for the women's, men's, and children's sections) communicate this information to headquarters-based product managers. Each of these product managers works with about forty stores within a region.

Store managers may tell the product managers that customers are asking for different colors or variations of products — maybe they want this blouse with long sleeves instead of short sleeves. The store managers may even ask for completely new designs based on their observations. If a lot of stores make similar requests, the product managers communicate these changes to the designers. Zara's supply chain designs and delivers the products to the stores within just a few weeks and in some cases within forty-eight hours. This is how Madonna's concert outfit got into the closets of Spanish customers in just a couple days.

Employees' suggestions are heard not just for what products should be made, but how products should be displayed and how operational and customer-related processes should be carried out. For example, Zara is very conscious of communicating the same brand image to customers all around the world. Part of that communication is to display merchandise in a similar way in all its stores. Teams of merchandisers at the headquarters decide on the store look, take photos of how they want items to be displayed, and send these to the stores. If a store employee comes up with a better idea for displaying merchandise, he or she can take a photo of the changed layout and send it to the regional and central merchandisers for approval. If approved, the new display idea will be shared with all the other Zara stores.

Benefiting from employee suggestions requires Zara to invest in field employees who do not work at any particular store but work closely with numerous stores. These are the regional directors, human resource directors, regional merchandisers, and window dressers who are in direct contact with the stores. They not only gather ideas from the stores but also play a key role in implementing the ideas and monitoring conformance.

At Zara, products change all the time, so decisions often have to be made quickly. There may be no time to test different ideas, compare how well they work, and then broadly implement what seems to be the best one. In settings such as supermarkets, warehouse clubs, and convenience stores, on the other hand, the selection tends to be more stable. New cabbages don't come and go quite so quickly as new fashions. These retailers can use a scientific approach when implementing new processes or when testing new products or their presentation.

At Mercadona, each store process has a process owner who works closely with store employees to design the process. Say a store comes up with a faster way to shelve merchandise. First, this change would be communicated to the owner of that process, who would test the new way at one store and quantify its effect. If the shelving method was indeed faster and did not compromise safety, accuracy, or customer service, the process owner would test the change in a larger geographic area with several stores. If similar improvements were observed, then the change would eventually be implemented throughout the chain. There is a similar mechanism for communicating product ideas from the stores to the headquarters.

At Costco, employee suggestions from each store are communicated to the corporate office, where they are reviewed and sorted. When Costco executives and country managers get together for budget meetings every four weeks, they talk about ideas that have come up from the warehouses. As we saw earlier, some of those ideas are ultimately put to very good use.

Trust Is the Foundation of Employee Involvement

Previously, we saw the importance of trust from the managers' perspective. For empowerment to work, managers need to trust that their frontline employees will make good decisions. For employee involvement to work, employees also need to trust their managers and their companies. Employees in many companies believe that if the company gets its hands on a more efficient way to do something, it will decide it needs fewer employees. Unless employees can trust that their jobs and their friends' jobs will be safe, they will not be enthusiastic about suggesting improvements.

Model retailers make it clear that they will not eliminate employees as their processes become more efficient. QuikTrip, for example, has never laid off an employee.[4] Ron Jeffers told me, "One of the reasons our employees come to us and plan to stay with us is because they or their family have lived through the layoff process elsewhere and they want to go somewhere where they feel secure."

Knowing that one's job will not be compromised is an important ingredient to employee involvement in the Toyota Production System, both at Toyota and at other companies that have adopted the system. According to Mark Hogan, a former manager at NUMMI, the previously discussed Toyota-GM joint venture:

> There is no question in my mind that the commitment to no layoffs and the ability of managers to operate on a day-to-day basis in a way that supports this underlying philosophy are absolutely crucial to our success. Team members know that when they contribute ideas for more effective operations they are not jeopardizing anyone's job. And that's fundamental since they know more than any manager or industrial engineer about how to improve our efficiency and competitiveness.[5]

Mark Graban, an expert on lean implementation, makes a similar observation:

> In many Lean implementations (including mine in hospitals), we insist on "no layoffs due to Lean" and management makes that

pledge. If employee input is critical to Lean improvements, layoffs will understandably kill most of the enthusiasm for Lean. We try to think of employees as partners in providing value and improving quality, not "heads" to be cut.[6]

How Operating with Slack Enables the Good Jobs Strategy

Operating with slack, like the other three operational choices, simultaneously benefits employees, customers, and investors. The benefits for customers are obvious. Just think back to the last time you wandered up and down the aisles of a large store, thinking, "Hello? Does anyone work here?"

For employees, the benefits are many. The ability to complete one's work and do a good job provides both pride and pleasure. Helping customers or improving how the store operates is a lot more fun and satisfying than chasing after misplaced products, dealing with unhappy customers, and doing a half-baked job because that's all you have time for.

Slack also allows employees to live more normal, balanced lives. I mentioned earlier that QuikTrip has a lot of relief employees. Of course, that spares the stores from getting caught understaffed, but it also allows regular employees to take time off when they need to for family, medical, or other reasons that most of us would agree are important. When Patty described why she likes to work at QuikTrip, she mentioned the ability to attend her kids' school activities. QuikTrip's target is to offer regular employees time off when they want it 95 percent of the time, and thanks to relief employees, it achieves that target.

Better-served customers and employees who aren't constantly frustrated — combined with operations that are not only good but always getting better because there's time to do things right and to solve problems — mean plenty of benefits for investors. Cutting waste, improving processes, and improving labor productivity also make an investment in people possible. When cost reductions are translated into lower prices, customers benefit, too.

Less obvious is the way that operating with slack helps companies hire better employees. When an employee leaves a store at which the other employees were already struggling to get everything done, there is often a lot of pressure on managers to get someone new as quickly as possible. That is hardly conducive to finding the best possible person. Operating with slack allows companies to sort through applications carefully and find the best fit for the job. More careful hiring benefits all stakeholders — employees, customers, and investors.

Allowing for some slack in the workforce doesn't sound like all that much on the face of it. But of the four operational choices we have seen, it is the ultimate expression of putting employees at the center of a company's success. It is a choice that recognizes that employees, although they do have a cost like anything else the company makes use of, do not have a fixed use or value.

We have seen that one reason offering fewer products can work for a company is that committed, empowered, well-trained employees *who aren't rushing desperately from task to task* can actually do more than having a vast variety of products to help customers get what they want or need. We have seen that committed, empowered, well-trained employees *who aren't rushing desperately from task to task* make higher performance standards possible because they *like* having high standards they can actually achieve. One can feel so much more proud of oneself when one does a really good job, especially for customers. We have seen that committed, empowered, well-trained employees *who aren't rushing desperately from task to task* are a huge source of ideas about improvement and are often the means by which those ideas can be implemented. An uncommitted, unempowered, poorly trained workforce would not be able to make these same ideas work. It is no surprise, then, that companies that pursue a good jobs strategy can pull off improvements and transformations that other companies cannot manage.

CHAPTER 9

Seizing Strategic Opportunities

W E SIMPLY EXECUTE our business plan better than our competitors exercise theirs," said John Shields, the former CEO of Trader Joe's, describing why the company has been so successful since its beginning in 1958.[1] Indeed, better execution is an outcome of the good jobs strategy and leads to higher sales and profits, which further feeds the virtuous cycle. The result, as we have seen, particularly in chapter 4, is better financial performance than that of competitors in a wide range of metrics.

Apart from stellar financial performance, companies that pursue the good jobs strategy enjoy two other strategic advantages that keep them competitive over time. First, they can better adapt to changes that regularly knock companies off balance, such as shifts in customer tastes, new technology, or new regulations. Second, they have a better shot at keeping their customer base loyal by giving them a reason to shop *there* rather than at other physical stores or online. Beyond offering low prices and good customer service, model retailers can make emotional connections with their customers by creating communities in which people form relationships and feel a sense of belonging.

As we have seen in chapter 3, companies that pursue the bad jobs strategy, on the other hand, suffer from poor execution and end up in a vicious cycle. Beyond the problems we have covered and their financial implications, poor execution limits these companies' strategic options. Such companies find it difficult to adapt to changes, as we saw with Walmart in chapter 5. They also find it difficult to differentiate themselves from their competition and to give their customers a reason to shop there beyond low prices.

The following case study provides a wonderful opportunity to examine a company that was following the bad jobs strategy and that not only failed to adapt to changes in its environment but also failed to give its customers a reason to shop there.

Let Me Guess. You Did Not Buy This Book at Borders.

Remember Borders? Once it was a highly successful retailer of books and music. Borders is no longer around. It declared bankruptcy in February 2011 and announced its plans to close all stores and liquidate in July 2011. This was sad news for a lot of Borders employees and customers. It was also sad news for me. Borders was the research site for my doctoral dissertation. From 1999 to 2002, I visited dozens of Borders stores, interviewed over one hundred Borders employees, and collected and analyzed a lot of data from Borders stores. You've seen some of that research in this book.

As I mentioned earlier, Borders is where I first learned about what happens when companies do not invest in employees and how much seemingly small operational problems such as phantom stockouts can hurt a company's bottom line. It was through my research on Borders that I started seeing evidence of the vicious cycle of retailing.

It was also at Borders that I first saw how poor execution can prevent a company from acting on strategic opportunities.

Borders was founded in 1972 to offer its customers a wide assortment of books and music at low prices. An average Borders superstore during the late 1990s carried around 180,000 titles. Borders was what is typically called a "category killer," a big box store that offers a wide assortment of items in a single category such as office products (Staples), toys (Toys"R"Us), or home improvement products (Home Depot). Like other category killers, Borders experienced strong growth in the 1990s, expanding from nineteen stores in 1992 to around three hundred superstores in 2000.

The customers who shopped at category killers loved having access to tens of thousands of products at low prices. There was such enthusiasm for this type of store during the 1990s that many companies were able to grow successfully despite less-than-stellar operations and despite a lack of investment in store employees.

Borders was in some ways an exception because it traditionally carried out one aspect of operations really well — getting the right product to the right store at the right time. Borders's "expert system" for merchandising was one of the best in retailing; it got the sales data from the stores, forecasted demand for products, and decided on the assortment and the quantities. The system customized an assortment for each location based on sales data. A store in Alaska, for example, would have more books related to small planes than a store in Boston, which would have more books related to the Celtics.

Borders's sophisticated use of analytics and information technology came in part from its cofounder, Louis Borders, who was an applied mathematician from the Massachusetts Institute of Technology. He always thought about using technology to improve the customers' experience. Even in the late 1980s, he thought about giving customers floppy disks containing a store's inventory so they could check a product's availability from their homes.

Apart from the expert system, Borders equipped its stores with computer stations that allowed employees to search for products and, if needed, special order them for customers. During the late 1990s, Borders added computer stations that customers could use by themselves. The station displayed a map of the store and showed you where the book you wanted was located. If that book was not in stock, you could order it yourself and have it delivered to the store or to your home.

During Borders's glory years, under the CEO Bob DiRomualdo from 1989 to 1999, Borders was highly profitable. In addition, it was the most popular book superstore, generating better returns than its main competitor, Barnes & Noble. Borders had the highest sales per store in bookselling, roughly $7 million per average store versus $4.9 million for Barnes & Noble superstores. In 1997, its sales per square foot were $260 versus $224 for Barnes & Noble.

Failure to Adapt to Changes

Starting in the late 1990s, forces in Borders's environment began to make life difficult for the company. Internet retailing, mostly by Amazon, started taking away book sales. Digital music started taking away music sales. Opportunities for growth seemed to be narrowing, and Wall Street responded by reducing Borders's stock price by more than half within an eight-month period from July 1998 to March 1999.

At the same time, the opportunity for Borders to fully integrate its brick-and-mortar retail stores with its own online store arose. Interestingly, Borders had already been thinking about this strategic opportunity in the late 1990s. Plenty of other retailers are still puzzling over it today. With integration, Borders could offer its customers the best of both worlds — the convenience of online retail and the instant gratification and personal experience of stores. A Borders customer shopping online would not have to wait to get the book in the mail. If the book were available at a nearby store, she could go over and pick it up that very day.

In many ways, Borders was in a great position to achieve this integration, because it already had a highly sophisticated IT system. But there was one problem. Frequently, the IT system would say that a book was in stock, but no one in the store could find it. In fact, approximately 18 percent of customers who asked a Borders salesperson for help experienced this problem — a phantom stockout.

There was no way Borders could seamlessly integrate its physical stores with its online store with such a high frequency of phantom stockouts. Imagine what would happen if, 18 percent of the time, online customers who zipped over to a store because the book they wanted was supposed to be there found that it wasn't — or at least, found that no one could find it. You're always going to disappoint a customer from time to time, but 18 percent of the time, especially when a product wasn't available after a customer had been told otherwise? That would be intolerable.

Why did these phantom stockouts occur? Employee turnover, understaffed stores, lack of training, operational complexity, and poorly defined processes all contributed. Borders lacked what other companies that follow the bad jobs strategy lack — the ability to execute operationally.

Poor operational execution and the resulting phantom stockouts contributed to Borders's inability to act on a great strategic opportunity even though it was so well qualified in other ways to do so. Because Borders could not integrate its physical stores with its online store and because there was a belief that competing with a company like Amazon head-to-head online would not work (after all, Amazon had access to a lot of cash and could afford to lose over $2 billion in its first seven years), Borders gave up online retailing altogether. It sold Borders.com to Amazon in April 2001. Amazon would maintain the website and handle fulfillment; Borders would get a share of revenues and pay an up-front fee.

Failure to Differentiate from Competitors

Borders did not just fail to adapt to the changes in its environment because it could not execute well enough. It also failed to give its customers a reason to continue shopping in its stores. At a time when the demand for bookstores was declining, the only way for Borders to stay competitive was to capture more of the existing demand by differentiating itself from other bookstores. But instead of doing that, Borders chose to focus on pleasing investors in the short term. In a declining market, it kept opening new stores to show — or rather to fake — growth to investors, and it spent all its cash to buy back its stock in order to "return value" to shareholders.

Meanwhile, Barnes & Noble started getting ahead. The retailer gave its customers loyalty cards offering substantial discounts. Borders chose not to follow that strategy immediately, and its customers left the company for better deals at Barnes & Noble. On top of this, when things got tough, Borders reduced its investment in people and compromised its customer service.

To increase flexibility, the company increased the percentage of part-timers from 37 percent in 1999 to 51 percent in 2001. Each employee started getting fewer hours, and they did not like this. One store manager explained that the single most important reason for turnover was reduced hours. Turnover of full-timers increased from 54 percent in 1999 to 69 percent in 2001, and turnover of part-timers increased from 96 percent in 1999 to 112 percent in 2001. As you can imagine, Borders was deep in the vicious cycle of retailing during the early 2000s.

When things got worse and labor budgets shrank further, Borders eliminated "community relations coordinators" from many of its stores. Community relations coordinators localized the stores and made them part of the community. They created special in-store events such as book readings and visits from authors, sometimes as many as twenty per month. Customers looked forward to these events, and leveraging them may have been a great way for Borders to compete against other retailers and its online rivals. It would certainly have been worth a try, and they already knew how to do it; it seems a shame they let it go so easily.

Who knows where Borders would be today if it had had the ability to act on its strategic opportunities or the ability to differentiate itself from its competitors? But it certainly would not have been the first large book retailer to declare bankruptcy.

Seizing Rather Than Missing Opportunities

Just as poor operational execution can prevent companies such as Borders from acting on strategic opportunities, good operational execution can help companies seize opportunities, respond to changes in the business environment, and satisfy new needs of their customers. And just as lack of differentiation can cause companies that follow the bad jobs strategy to lose their customers, ability to differentiate can help companies hold on to their customers. Let's visit each of these strategic advantages.

Strategic Advantage #1: The Ability to Adapt

How UPS Adapted to Changes in Its Business Environment

UPS loves logistics. If you have not seen UPS's "we love logistics" commercial, it really is worth watching. You'll hear phrases such as "on time" and "in synch," and you'll see clues to sustainability and an increased bottom line. You'll also see UPS employees at the center of all this, smiling, appearing competent, walking with urgency to deliver packages on time, and their customers just loving them. The UPS commercial emphasizes two things: First, amazingly efficient operations that get the right package to the right place at the right time. Second, happy employees.

Yes, this is a commercial and yes, commercials often make things look much happier and nicer than they are. But UPS really is a company that has pursued the good jobs strategy for more than one hundred years. It has always combined its investment in people with operational excellence. Even during the early 1900s, UPS paid its drivers higher wages, gave them more training and better and cleaner equipment than competitors, and created processes that enabled them to deliver great service at low rates.

As early as 1927, UPS allowed its drivers to own equity in the company:

> The founders were not extending equity because they needed financial capital. Instead, it was *human capital* they were after. UPS needed commitment and faith and a level of performance from their people that would go well beyond a typical corporate employee-employer relationship. They needed heart. The goal behind the new policy, Jim Casey [the founder of UPS] explained in a letter to the credit agency Bradstreet, was to invest in the company's people "in the building of its business."[2]

UPS's ability to execute helped it to transform package delivery by innovating and by adapting to new technologies, new business environments, and new needs of its customers. UPS is now the world's largest package delivery company. In 2011, it generated more than $53 billion in revenue and made $1.3 billion in profit. It now delivers more than 15 million packages every day in 220 countries.[3]

One example of the kind of transformation UPS went through during its history occurred in the 1920s, when UPS was a delivery consolidator for retailers in metropolitan areas. Clean UPS trucks with well-paid, courteous drivers would take the products from department stores and quickly deliver them to the right customers' homes.

Two changes in the business environment had a profound effect on UPS's business. World War II and the imposition of wartime rationing reduced department store sales. Their sales decline meant declining business for UPS. But even after the war ended and consumers' spending increased, UPS's business kept declining because the spread of automobiles and the emergence of shopping malls meant that there was less need for local delivery.

While Borders could not react to changes in its environment, UPS could. Just like Trader Joe's and the other model retailers, UPS executes better than its competitors. Even when business plans change, the ability to execute remains. During the early 1950s, UPS decided to exit the declining delivery consolidation business and make use of its operational excellence to become a common carrier competing with the postal service. By 1975, UPS offered delivery service to every address in the forty-eight contiguous states. Think about the magnitude of this change. During the next several decades, UPS would start its own airline, start its own third-party logistics business, go global, start its online business, and even more.

How Frito-Lay Adapted to Changes in Regulation

Frito-Lay, the largest salty-snack company in the United States, provides another example of how the ability to execute operationally can help companies act on strategic opportunities. In the early 1980s, the trucking industry was deregulated and private carriers were allowed to transport products from other companies.[4]

Deregulation presented an opportunity for Frito-Lay. The company's trucks carried its own products from warehouses and plants to distribution centers and other storage locations, but they returned empty. Of the 69 million miles those trucks drove per year, 35 million were driven empty. If Frito-Lay could use the empty miles to haul other companies' products, called "backhauling," then it would get a lot more use of its trucks and generate a lot of revenue.

Pulling off backhaul, however, was extremely challenging. Pretty much everyone in the organization, from quality control to sales, was opposed to it. Quality people worried that the trucks would be contaminated. Salespeople thought that Frito drivers would not be able to deliver their own products with the same on-time delivery performance because their focus would shift to carrying others' products. The legal department had concerns about product liability. The logistics department thought the extra work could be difficult to handle.

When I teach the Frito-Lay case in my MBA courses, most of my students, presented with the choice that Frito-Lay's top management faced, advise against implementing backhaul. They think it is too difficult and they are somewhat right. It is very difficult, but not *too* difficult for a company like Frito-Lay, which executes extraordinarily well.

Like our model retailers and UPS, Frito-Lay has a tradition of investing in its employees. In 1983, when Frito-Lay was considering the backhaul decision, its drivers were making around $35,000 a year, far above the average in their industry. Their 3 percent employee turnover was extremely low, and the drivers were highly committed to their jobs. Inside Frito-Lay, the truck drivers were seen as essential to the company's success. If they did not deliver the goods on time and in good condition, customer service would suffer. Just like employees of model retailers, Frito-Lay truck drivers felt that they were part of something bigger. To emphasize their role in the company and to give them the pride and respect they deserved, Frito-Lay prepared a driver motivation video that likened its truck drivers to the Blue Angels pilots, the Navy's top-notch flight demonstration squadron. In the video, Frito-Lay drivers demonstrate precision and excellence in driving, just as Blue Angels pilots demonstrate their precision and excellence in flying and in preparing to fly.

Frito-Lay's investment in its drivers and in its operating system, as well as its culture of excellence, allowed its drivers to deliver products on time 99.1 percent of the time, within very short windows (just two hours). Many drivers have gone hundreds of thousands of miles without an accident.

Frito-Lay went ahead with backhaul, and it was this execution capability that made the move a great success. Backhaul is now a big part of Frito-Lay's logistics operation and generates significant revenue.

How Model Retailers Adapt to Change

The ability to execute well enables model retailers to act on strategic opportunities. When the environment changes or customers' needs change, model retailers can capture even more market share because they can act on those changes quickly. They have not only the ability to see what's coming and formulate plans to accommodate it but also the ability to carry out those plans and do it better than their competitors do.

Mercadona, for example, emerged from the global recession as a stronger company than before because it could do things its competitors could not. Knowing that customers would become more price-conscious during the recession, Mercadona announced in 2008 that it would reduce its prices by 10 percent. For those readers who are not familiar with the supermarket industry, let me remind you that these companies operate with very low margins. Mercadona's profit margin in 2008 was a very slim 2.24 percent. (Note, though, that even this was higher than the 1.77 percent profit margin of its largest competitor, Carrefour.) A 10 percent decrease in prices, therefore, is a huge deal.

Yet within just a few months of the announcement, Mercadona had made substantial changes to its operations to reduce prices. One big change was to reduce the variety of products at its stores from nine thousand to eight thousand. At nine thousand, Mercadona's product variety was already lower than that of its competitors, but the retailer saw more opportunities for simplification.

Over time, the number of choices within each category had grown. In 2008, Mercadona carried 72 types of milk, 112 types of juice, 100 types of coffee, carrots of every shape and size, and several types of tomato sauce. Some of the products varied only slightly. So Mercadona cut 1,000 products from its assortment.

Remember how Walmart tried to follow the same strategy in 2008 in reaction to the economic environment? Cost reductions there came at the expense of sales because customers were not happy that the retailer did not carry the products they wanted. For Mercadona, cost reductions came along with *higher* sales because Mercadona's employees helped the retailer understand what its customers wanted. Employees were there to explain to customers why certain products were no longer being sold, which products would be good substitutes, and how much the customer was saving as a result of the reduction in variety.

Store employees were also there to correct the company's mistakes. When Mercadona reduced product variety, there were several branded products that customers really did miss, but it didn't take Mercadona too long to find out. Its store employees are in close contact with customers all the time, so they hear about what customers are missing. In addition, store employees have the time and organizational structure to communicate their needs — or, more important, their *customers'* needs — to headquarters.

Another major change was the way Mercadona sold fruits and vegetables. Here again, employees played an important role. Before 2008, Mercadona sold fruit and vegetables in packages. This policy incurred a monetary cost: Waxing the fruit and vegetables and putting them on trays covered with film cost 25 euro-cents per package. It also incurred a cost in customer service: Customers who wanted to buy smaller quantities just couldn't. Apples came in packs of six, and if you wanted only two, you either had to buy six anyway or go somewhere else.

The company realized that selling fruit and vegetables individually would reduce costs and improve sales substantially by improving customers' satisfaction. But that meant changing operations throughout the supply chain, from the way fruit and vegetables were prepared at the suppliers to the way they were distributed in Mercadona's logistics network to the way they were shelved in the stores. Mercadona was able to implement this change in just a few months. The result was annual savings of €175 million, and these savings were passed on to the customers in the form of the reduced prices the company had announced.

Mercadona's employees played an important role in changing the way fruit and vegetables were sold there. Not only were they the first ones to identify this opportunity to reduce costs, but they were crucial in implementing the change, from helping to design new processes for shelving to suggesting ways to display the loose merchandise. At most other stores, fruit and vegetables are stacked on the displays one by one, but Mercadona employees suggested that they be shelved in plastic crates, speeding up the shelving process and reducing shrink by eliminating extra handling.

In addition to this big change, Mercadona implemented many other small changes to reduce costs, including:

- Herbs and spices: Change from glass to plastic containers. Annual savings = €150,000.
- Ice cream, yogurt, and desserts: Reduction in weight and size of cardboard boxes. Annual savings = €1.2 million.
- Bottles of water and boxes of milk cartons: Reduction in weight of plastic and cardboard. Annual savings = €2 million.
- Cans of anchovies and tuna: Changes in packaging. Annual savings = €700,000.
- Wine and oil: Reduction and elimination of duplicate labels and unnecessary ink. Annual savings = €900,000.
- Cereals and nuts: Reduction of air in packets. Annual savings = €900,000.

The result of these modifications was the promised 10 percent reduction in prices, which saved an average household €720 in annual grocery spending. All these efforts paid off for the company as well. From 2008 to 2012, Mercadona's market share in Spain went from around 15 percent to over 20 percent.[5]

QuikTrip provides another example of how a retailer using the good jobs strategy can act nimbly to exploit a strategic opportunity. QuikTrip's customers often used to buy prepared foods and heat them at home. During the mid-2000s, customers kept telling QuikTrip they wanted to buy fresh food there that they could eat while traveling, often in their cars. In 2007, QuikTrip made the decision to start selling fresh food such as sandwiches, wraps, and pastries, which, in that company's culture, meant that it had to become *the best* gasoline, convenience, and food retailer in the eyes of its customers, employees, and competitors. With the addition of fresh food, QuikTrip's competitors would include not only the other convenience store chains but also fast-food retailers.

Selling fresh products at these stores is no easy task. It adds a lot of complexity to store operations, and employees who do not have training, experience, or time would be lost in this complexity. But QuikTrip's employees do have training, experience, time, and a well-honed ability to execute, which enabled the company to seize this opportunity quite successfully.

Strategic Advantage #2: Differentiation

In addition to adapting to changes that affect the entire retail landscape, from the arrival of Amazon to the burgeoning preference for organic products to an economic crisis, retailers with a good jobs strategy are able to keep their customers loyal by giving them a reason to continue shopping at their business. Creating and sustaining customers' loyalty in a world of endless options is not easy. It is accomplished by differentiation, which is much more attainable by a company that has operational excellence and that puts its employees at the center of its success.

As we have seen, model retailers provide their customers more than just in-stock merchandise, clean stores, and fast checkout. Their operational choices combined with their investment in people allow them to offer their customers advice on products, assistance with their shopping, and a fun and friendly environment. Many employees at model retailers see their roles as making a difference in their customers' lives, and they are empowered to go beyond their official job descriptions to do so.

Doug Rauch, a former president of Trader Joe's, said that a checkout person there had once paid for her customer's groceries when the customer realized she had left her wallet at home. The employee said, "Just pay me back next time you are here." I recently saw a comment on the *Atlantic* magazine's website by a reader who wanted to share her Trader Joe's experience: "A few months ago a man at the register even pulled a dollar out of his pocket when I was short and was reaching to put something back, and just said 'Pay it forward and have a great night.' It seriously stuck with me for a week (and I did). I worked retail for a lot of years and can't say I ever had the urge to do that. Which makes me sad in retrospect."[6] Model retailers do not just offer customers a fast, convenient shopping experience. They also have the ability to touch their customers' hearts.

Let's not forget that the model retailers also offer low prices. So, apart from breaking the trade-off between low prices and good jobs, they also break the trade-off between low prices and good service. (Trade-offs between cost and service are represented in Figure 9.1.) We are used to believing that if a company has the lowest prices, then it must have bad service. But model retailers manage to offer low prices *and* good customer service, operating on a different trade-off curve than their competitors do. What they achieve is similar to what world-class manufacturers such as Toyota achieve by offering higher-quality products at low cost.

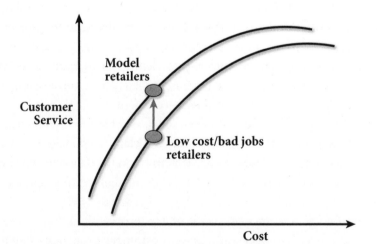

Figure 9.1. Trade-Offs Between Cost and Customer Service

The ability to offer low prices and good service allows model retailers to achieve better financial performance than their competitors do. It will become even more strategically important as online retail becomes more dominant and more of a threat to brick-and-mortar businesses. According to Forrester Research, U.S. online retail sales were about 7 percent of total retail sales in 2012. This percentage is expected to increase to 9 percent by 2016.

When it comes to shopping for many products, from soap to paper clips to lightbulbs, many people couldn't care less where they go. If there's someplace more convenient than where they went last time, they'll just switch. If the Internet is more convenient, many will switch to the Internet. In order to compete against online retail, brick-and-mortar stores have to give their customers a reason to shop *there*. The reason has to be more than instant gratification, because many customers are willing to wait a day or two to get a better price. What's more, if trends continue, online shoppers may even get same-day delivery for some products.

The choice about where to shop cannot be based solely on low prices, either. Competing with Amazon solely on the basis of low prices is bad business. Amazon is getting bigger every day — its sales were $61 billion in 2012 — and it has several advantages over brick-and-mortar retailers even beyond its enormous economies of scale. It doesn't have to operate thousands of stores, it can fulfill customer demand from its centralized facilities with a lot less inventory, and its cash-conversion cycle is faster. For many product categories, such as office supplies, electronics, and books, it's hard for anyone else to compete with Amazon given these economics.

What brick-and-mortar retailers can do that online retailers will find very hard to do is to create face-to-face personal connections with their customers. As Abraham Maslow, the psychologist renowned for creating the "hierarchy of needs," emphasized, people have an inherent desire to belong and to be part of something greater than themselves. People want relationships — not just transactions.

You may have read or heard the story of Johnny the Bagger.[7] Barbara Glance, a customer service consultant, advised the staff of a supermarket chain to try to "create memories" for their customers. Johnny, a bagger with Down syndrome, took this to heart and began putting a "thought for the day" in each customer's bag, having prepared them on slips of paper each night before work. These became so popular that one day, when the store manager saw a long checkout line and tried to move customers to other lines, the customers wouldn't go. They wanted Johnny's thought for the day. Other employees were inspired by Johnny to touch customers in their own departments. According to the store manager, "Now when the floral department has a broken flower or unused corsage, they find an elderly woman or a little girl and pin it on them." All this brought customers back more frequently and brought in new customers as well, drawn by what they had heard from their friends.

Forging Relationships with Customers Requires Inspired Employees

Model retailers are, by their very nature, able to create emotional relationships with their customers and make their customers want more and more. But you may ask: Does my company need to be operationally excellent in order to create such relationships? Can't we just hire nice people who treat customers well?

First, being nice is not enough. If a grocery story is frequently out of milk, if an airline constantly loses luggage, if a restaurant keeps serving meals late, if the bathrooms are usually a mess, it doesn't really matter how nice the employees are. Customers will find somewhere better to go. I don't know if the store where Johnny worked was operationally excellent or not, but I am confident that even Johnny couldn't have saved a supermarket where customers were constantly frustrated.

Second, even the nicest employees will have a hard time creating relationships with customers if they are constantly rushing from task to task; are not empowered; don't have enough time, training, or other resources to do a good job; or if their employers convey to them that they don't matter. I will never forget the interview I had with a young cashier. She told me how excited she was to get that job because she knew that she was the last person the customer would deal with, and if she left a good impression, the customer would keep coming back. She thought her job was really important, but after a few months, she felt her job did not matter at all.

"I wasn't rude to any customers," she said, but then she paused and added, "I probably was, but I wasn't rude to customers all the time." When I asked her what had changed, she said, "My job was important to me, but when you're dealing with a whole bunch of stuff from the managers — the lack of hours and the lack of respect and stuff like that — it's kind of difficult to see your significance at that job."

Employees of model retailers find meaning in their jobs. So do the employees of UPS and Frito-Lay. As we saw earlier, Alex Frankel, the journalist who worked as a UPS employee so that he could report on the experience, thought that UPS drivers were "part of a higher calling — connecting people with love, desire, loss, friendship, and family." After only three weeks there, he said he "felt what it was like to represent UPS, to *be* UPS."

QuikTrip's purpose, "to provide an opportunity for employees to grow and succeed," also inspires QuikTrip employees to connect with their customers. Patty said to me: "You're working with twelve or fourteen people, they go out and they touch twelve or fourteen people. So I get to make a really big impact in so many people's lives, just by trying to get them to see what QT's ending goal is and that's for everybody to be successful, you know, and everybody to be happy."

Alex's job at UPS was to deliver hundreds of packages every day. Patty's job involves cleaning toilets and gas pumps. In both cases, the design of their jobs made it possible for them to see their jobs as something much bigger than that: making a difference for their customers.

Return on Relationships

Creating relationships with customers doesn't cost much for companies that pursue the good jobs strategy. It is a natural outcome of following this strategy. But the return on this minimal investment can be huge, including more sales to loyal customers (like Johnny's) who keep coming back.

I am one of those customers. I love the fact that when we go to

Costco, the person checking my receipt on the way out draws a smiley face on it and gives it to my kids. I love the fact that when we go to our favorite local restaurant, the waitresses are so good-natured with my children, who, I must confess, do not always behave so well. So I keep going to those places, even when it might be easier to go somewhere else.

I also try my best not to take my children to stores or restaurants where I know, either from my research or from having been there before, that employees are not treated with respect and dignity. I want my children to see people at their best, not at their most disengaged. I want them to be around people who are kind and respectful to each other so they know that kindness and respect are part of the society we live in.

Beyond inspiring return visits, social interactions can also give stores valuable information about what their customers need and want. As we saw earlier in this chapter, when Mercadona reduced its product variety, it made a few mistakes, discontinuing some products that customers really wanted. But it took no time at all for Mercadona to realize its mistakes. It wasn't necessary to spend months collecting and analyzing data to see how many customers were substituting different products or how much the company was losing in sales in those categories. They were able to get this information immediately from the specialists who talk to customers every single day.

Creating relationships is also free advertising. Model retailers do not spend much on advertising; their customers do a lot of it for them. They tell their friends. They tweet. There are Trader Joe's and Costco customers with blog sites dedicated to these companies.

Relationships also build trust. What is the return on that? Hard to quantify, I admit, but I think we can all agree that it's well worth it.

CHAPTER 10

Values and Constraints

Throughout this book we have seen that the good jobs strategy requires more than providing decent wages and benefits, stability, training, and opportunities for success and growth. Companies pursuing it also need to think carefully about their offering of products and services, their work design, their staffing, the allocation of work among employees, and how employees will actively engage in improvement.

Companies that pursue the good jobs strategy achieve something that others do not: They satisfy employees, customers, and investors all at the same time. Even if we look at no more than their financial performance, these companies perform better than their competitors do. And, as we saw in the last chapter, the benefits of the good jobs strategy go beyond great performance. These companies enjoy two strategic advantages that allow them to stay competitive over time: They are better at adapting quickly to changes in the marketplace and more able to differentiate themselves from their competitors by creating relationships with their customers and giving them reasons to shop there.

But the good jobs strategy is no easy ride. Circumstances will often push companies in the opposite direction. Remember Howard

Schultz's investor advising him that with the economy in crisis, it was the right time for Starbucks to get rid of some of those expensive employee benefits? When faced with pressure to sacrifice employees or customers for the sake of the bottom line, clearly defined values — and the constraints that are imposed by them — help companies sustain the good jobs strategy.

The Temptation to Cheat on the Good Jobs Strategy

Companies that pursue the good jobs strategy strongly believe in the alignment of interests among different stakeholders. They believe that it is not only possible but highly profitable to take care of employees, customers, and investors all at the same time. What is more, they believe that taking care of employees and customers is not something extra but rather key to delivering long-term performance.

But they also know that while the interests of employees, customers, and investors are aligned in the long term, they are not always aligned in the short term. Freeing up some of the unusually large amount of money these companies invest in labor and in customer service could certainly deliver an impressive increase in short-term profits. When the business — or the sector or the whole economy — hits a bump, it can be very tempting to do that. It might even seem necessary if the company is in serious trouble.

For companies that are publicly held, resisting short-term performance pressure is not easy. Costco, for example, went through quarters in which, for various reasons — ranging from volatile gasoline costs to changes in consumer spending — it did not meet Wall Street's earnings expectations. Each miss was an opportunity for Wall Street to remind the company's executives that Costco did not *have* to miss earnings targets. Analysts urged the company to take a look at its expenses — especially employee expenses — and find a way to reduce those in order to meet its earnings expectations. Or the company could find a way to increase prices.

Costco did not listen and saw significant drops in its stock whenever it missed its earnings targets. Its cofounder Jim Sinegal, who was CEO until 2012, did not seem to mind the drop in the stock price. "On

Wall Street, they're in the business of making money between now and next Thursday," he remarked. "I don't say that with any bitterness, but we can't take that view. We want to build a company that will still be here 50 and 60 years from now."[1]

You can hear the same logic from other CEOs who lead public companies and invest in their people. Jim Kelly, the chairman and CEO of UPS from 1997 to 2001, said:

> We think our share owners should get treated well and should get a fair return, but we're not as concerned with whether they're going to get a fair return tomorrow or a year from now or five years from now. We've always thought that the long term was the important thing. If we were to start dancing for the folks on Wall Street because they expect something in the quarter, it would be counterproductive.[2]

Public companies are not the only businesses that face performance pressures, and the pressure is not always for cost-cutting. QuikTrip's investors would be perfectly happy in the short term with a company that did *not* grow. Why? QuikTrip stores generate great returns. But growth — especially in new markets — is very expensive for QuikTrip. The company not only has higher fixed costs than its competitors do, but when it enters a new market, it typically invests in a new distribution network. Moreover, to maintain its culture and high standards, it staffs 50 percent of its new stores with employees from existing markets and pays their relocation costs.

When QuikTrip enters a new market, it takes a long time for the stores to become profitable. Although new stores in existing markets break even a year and a half after opening and reach peak performance in eight to twelve years, stores in new markets often take seven years just to break even. In every new market QuikTrip enters, it loses millions of dollars per month for the first several years. Growth like this may not warm investors' hearts.

For QuikTrip, expansion into new markets is necessary to satisfy its *employees*. The company's stated purpose is to provide its employees with opportunities for growth and success. Those are not empty words. Providing employees with opportunities for growth and success means you have to be able to promote them. You can't keep doing that if you're not growing, so QuikTrip is obliged to grow. Once QuikTrip saturates an existing market, it has to go into a new market — and lose a pile of money for a while — in order to continue growing and providing opportunities for its employees. Investors make out fine as long as they are patient.

The long-term outlook for success is what earns these companies the respect of their employees, customers, and investors — at least, the investors oriented toward the long term. Charlie Munger, the vice chairman of Berkshire Hathaway and a legendary investor, publicly says that his favorite company outside of Berkshire is Costco. Munger mentions that Costco has a "frantic desire to serve customers a little better every year. When other companies find ways to save money, they turn it into profit. [Costco CEO] Sinegal passes it on to customers. It's almost a religious duty. He's sacrificing short-term profits for long-term success."[3]

This is all nice, but when the hard times come, how do these companies and their managers consistently resist the temptation to make — or at least save — a quick buck in the short term?

The secret lies in values-based constraints. To reduce the temptation to make such trade-offs, these companies have clear values that guide all decisions. For some of the companies, such as Mercadona, these values were deliberately developed in order to change the company's culture and create long-term success. For most of the others, these guiding values come from the founders and become so ingrained in the culture that they stay in the company even after the founders leave.

Universal Values

Apart from thinking long term, companies that pursue the good jobs strategy tend to have the following values in common:

1. They take care of their people.
2. They take care of their customers.
3. They choose excellence over mediocrity in everything they do.

QuikTrip, for example, did not hesitate to spend $12 million over three years to renovate its bathrooms, because it knew that this short-term investment would provide long-term benefits by making customers and employees happier. The company is even willing to take on longer-term losses for the long-term good of its employees. CEO Chet Cadieux told me:

> When I became the CEO, I realized that there were hundreds of employees who had been working for us for many years and who were working until midnight many days of the week. That made it very difficult to have a normal life with a family. The only way to change that was to add a full-time person in every store. It cost us $10 million a year for the rest of the company's history. I believe that it reduced turnover.

You may recall from chapter 4 that in 2007 Mercadona opened a fully automated distribution center that cost twice as much to build as a conventional center would have. The reason for building this distribution center was not related to economics. Rather, it was to improve working conditions, sparing employees from lifting heavy cases all day.

Most companies say they have similar values. No company would say, at least publicly, that it does not believe in taking care of employees or customers. No company would say publicly that it pursues mediocrity rather than excellence. But too often, the values written in the company values statement are not the values followed by the people who actually make decisions. Decision-makers can be anyone, from the CEO making huge decisions to the cashier with a long line deciding to speed things up a bit by ringing up two different types of soda as the same kind since they have the same price.

In some companies, employees do not even know the official values. In others, they know what they've been told, but they don't believe it because the company's actions and their managers' actions tell them what the real values are.

Take Mari, who works for a retailer with thousands of stores. She told me how she learned about the company's values during orientation. She said the values included "Service to customers, strive for excellence, and, oh God, what's the third one? Can't remember the third one." She soon saw that when it came down to it, cost-cutting typically won out over customer service and over excellence. Sometimes when a customer asked where something was, Mari didn't have time to take the person there; she could only point the way, although she knew that wasn't good customer service. Another employee of the same retailer at a different store told me a similar story. One day there was no toilet paper in the bathroom for the customers. Having learned during orientation that service to customers was a priority, he took a roll off the shelf—that is, a roll that had been for sale—and put it in the bathroom. His manager got mad at him and told him not to do that again.

One Hundred Percent Commitment to Values

A company's values have a very challenging all-or-nothing quality. Once a company betrays its values for short-term gain and its employees know it, those employees just won't believe in those values anymore. Sustaining the good jobs strategy requires sticking to values 100 percent of the time.

This is not as simple as saying "We will always adhere to this value." Running a business is always a matter of choosing among various options. One would think that top executives would want to do things that increase their options, but adhering to a set of values has — at first glance — the effect of severely limiting the options. The company has had a bad quarter, investors are unhappy, and right off the bat there is a whole list of things that your 100 percent commitment to your values *won't* let you do. What kind of strategy is that?

First, it is a long-term strategy. A 100 percent commitment saves you from being blown off course, which can so easily happen. Second, it is an innovation strategy. You can't do the obvious thing, so you have to think of something else. As a company that follows the good jobs strategy, you have customer knowledge, operational capacity, and workforce adaptability that other companies don't have. A 100 percent commitment to company values will force you to make full use of those strengths.

Think about it this way: Imagine that one of the problems in your life is that you work too much and don't spend enough time with your family. You know that this is bad for you and your family's long-term happiness. So you decide that during the next year, you will spend your weekends with your family.

Now it's Friday, you have an important project due Monday, and the fact is that you are way behind. Will you make an exception? I bet that without a 100 percent commitment, most of us would make this exception. Then there would be further exceptions. There would be valuable short-term wins, but we would end up working most weekends like we always did and lose out in the long term, regretting the time lost with our children.

If we can be tempted to give in to short-term pressures at the expense of our own families, imagine how easy it is to give in to them at work, where they always seem to be for the good of the company or one's career.

If we *know* that we will spend every weekend with our family — no exceptions — our "work time" will definitely be constrained. That doesn't automatically mean we must resign ourselves to accomplishing less. We will be challenged to become more productive during those five workdays. We will gradually eliminate time-wasting activities — surfing the Web and hanging out in other people's offices for long chats. We will be more careful to prioritize and to do the high-priority things first. We might actually become *more* productive. Even if we don't, we will be doing a better job of living our whole multifaceted lives.

Values Create Constraints

Southwest is a great example of a corporation that has pursued the good jobs strategy for more than forty years. Herb Kelleher, the founder and former CEO, said:

> I don't want you to yawn when I say this. But I've always thought that having a simple set of values for a company was also a very

efficient and expedient way to go. And I'll tell you why. Because if somebody makes a proposal and it infringes on those values, you don't study it for two years. You just say, "No, we don't do that." And you go on quickly. So I think that contributes to efficiency.

One of Southwest's values is job stability. Employees at Southwest know that their jobs are safe as long as their own performance is good. In fact, Southwest has never had to furlough or lay off employees. This value was severely put to the test after the September 11, 2001, terrorist attacks. No industry was hit as hard as the airline industry after those attacks. The federal government closed airports. Thousands of flights were canceled. Even after the airports reopened, people were afraid to fly. Demand went *way* down.

Most airlines responded by laying off employees. The average airline laid off around 16 percent of its workforce after September 11.[4] Southwest, hit just as hard as the others, reportedly lost millions of dollars a day in the weeks immediately following the attacks.[5] But it didn't lay people off. The company kept its commitment to its employees. How did it do after September 11? Better than any other airline. While most other airlines lost money in 2001, Southwest still made money, achieving its twenty-ninth consecutive year of profitability.

Kelleher explained why they avoided layoffs:

> We've never had a furlough. We could have made more money if we'd furloughed people during numerous events over the last 40 years, but we never have. We didn't think it was the right thing to do. And you know, one of the disciplines is not furloughing. I didn't realize this at first, by the way, so it came as somewhat of an insight to me. You know, suddenly a little synapse clicked, and I said, "You know, not furloughing is really a great discipline with respect to hiring."[6]

In 2011, Southwest acquired AirTran. The two firms did not immediately integrate their operations, but in time we will see if Southwest can continue its commitment to its values and sustain its good jobs strategy, which is so dependent on operations.

One of QuikTrip's stated values is to "do the right thing," which can be very constraining. In line with this value, the company does not sell drug paraphernalia, rolling papers, or pornographic magazines. All of these are profitable items for the convenience stores that sell them, but QuikTrip forgoes those potential earnings because in its view, selling those things is not the right thing to do.

Explicit Prioritization of Stakeholders

One powerful and practical way to create constraints based on values is to explicitly prioritize employees and customers ahead of investors.[7] This prioritization is especially important in services, where cutting labor costs or customer service is far too easy.

For example, Amazon, the world's largest online retailer, has a customer-first philosophy. Jeff Bezos, the founder and CEO, makes it clear to Wall Street that the company will always adhere to this philosophy even when it may mean poor short-term performance. "When things get complicated, we simplify by asking what's the best for the customer," Bezos says.[8] Examples of this philosophy in action include allowing reviews by customers in order to improve the customer experience, even if some of those reviews mean lost sales for Amazon; offering Amazon Marketplace, even if customers' being able to buy products elsewhere cannibalizes Amazon's own sales; and keeping prices low even when increasing them would be more profitable.[9]

Costco and Mercadona both explicitly put customers and employees ahead of their shareholders. Costco's mission statement puts obeying the law, taking care of customers, taking care of employees, and respecting suppliers all ahead of rewarding shareholders. This prioritization is there to ensure that, even under pressure, managers will not make short-term decisions that compromise employees or customers. But, strange as it may seem, this prioritization also protects shareholders by keeping the company from making short-term decisions that would eventually destroy its long-term value.

Another advantage of clear prioritization is that, as Herb Kelleher noted, it makes decision making faster and more efficient by eliminating many options. This is something similar to our first operational choice — offering less. But instead of offering your customers fewer products or services to choose from, you are offering managers fewer choices of action.

Values-Based Constraints Drive Innovation

When values related to employees or customers create constraints, companies have to innovate within those constraints. Not laying off employees, for example, is a clear constraint at Southwest. At Costco, one of the constraints is to not mark prices up by more than 15 percent. Even if other costs rise, Costco will not charge its customers more than 15 percent over what it paid for each product. A constraining value at Affinity Plus, the credit union discussed in chapter 6, is to always put the member first. If an action is right for the organization but not for the member, Affinity Plus will not proceed.

Such restrictive constraints spur companies to innovate in ways they would never have thought of otherwise. While it may be easy for an airline to lay off employees during a recession, Southwest finds other ways to reduce costs and increase sales. After September 11, Southwest took measures to improve on-time performance and urged its employees to suggest ways of cutting costs. In the fourth quarter of 2001, Southwest employees helped reduce operating expenses by 2.5 percent despite increases in security and insurance costs (and not counting a drop in fuel prices, which certainly helped but was not Southwest's own doing).[10] In addition, Southwest seized the opportunity presented after September 11 to use its capacity to enter new geographical markets and grab more total market share. This is yet another demonstration of how companies that pursue the good jobs strategy can seize opportunities that others cannot.

Southwest's improvements clearly outlasted the circumstances that spawned them. If an airline lays off employees because demand has dropped, it has to hire them back when demand recovers. The savings are convenient for a time, but only temporary. If Southwest responds to the same drop by improving operations, it can keep that performance even when demand comes back. That's how the company has maintained its profitability forty years in a row from 1973 through 2012.

While other companies may justify increasing their prices during rough times, Costco finds ways to reduce its costs and maintain its fanatical customer base. While other banks may offset increasing costs by charging their customers hidden fees, Affinity Plus finds innovative ways to reduce its costs. By removing from consideration such obvious measures as cutting investments in employees or lowering standards for customer service, these companies are forced to be more innovative in their operational improvements. Their employees are flexible, disciplined, and motivated enough to carry out these innovations.

The idea that constraints can drive innovation is not new. Marissa Mayer, currently the CEO of Yahoo!, is famous for using constraints to drive innovation at her former company, Google, where she held many leadership positions. Mayer writes:

> When people think about creativity, they think about artistic work — unbridled, unguided effort that leads to beautiful effect. But if you look deeper, you'll find that some of the most inspiring art forms, such as haikus, sonatas, and religious paintings, are fraught with constraints. They are beautiful because creativity triumphed over the "rules." Constraints shape and focus problems and provide clear challenges to overcome. Creativity thrives best when constrained.[11]

She notes that when Google was developing its toolbar, the designers first thought about the constraints. The toolbar had to work for all users regardless of their screen resolution and it had to be fast to download. Once they had these constraints identified, the team was free to be creative.

How Values-Based Constraints Help in Difficult Times

Clear values and prioritization of key stakeholders help companies sustain a good jobs strategy during difficult times. When Juan Roig took control of Mercadona in 1990, more than a decade after the company's founding, he instilled a set of values that guided all the firm's decisions. Known throughout the company as "universal truths," these values included "reciprocity," the principle that to be satisfied, one must first satisfy others; "no one is born knowing," the principle that the customer needs to be properly informed and that employees need to be trained correctly; and "how you measure me is how I behave," the principle that if a company trains its employees to become money-making machines, they will behave as such, but if it promotes initiative, involvement, and commitment, its employees will offer customers better and better service. Roig also ensured that all decisions would be made in a way that satisfied customers, employees, suppliers, society, and investors — in that order.

Mercadona's values were sorely tested during the global financial crisis. In 2008 — for the first time in thirteen years — the company did not meet its sales targets. That had serious implications for employees because, as mentioned earlier, Mercadona has a tradition of paying its employees a bonus if the company meets its sales and profit targets and if the employees meet their local and individual targets. The bonus is one month's salary for employees who have worked there for fewer than four years and two months' salary for employees who have worked there four years or more. The bonus is all or nothing, so if the targets are not met, employees do not receive any bonus. That, by the way, goes for everybody from the CEO on down. But of course, it hits harder the lower in the organization one is.

In a typical year, most employees qualify for the bonus. Everyone in the company counted on the bonus as part of his or her salary. Like the Southwest employees, who know that their jobs are safe as long as they perform well, Mercadona employees know that their bonus is safe as long as they perform well. Indeed, 95 percent of Mercadona's employees met their individual goals in 2008, but the company's global targets were not met. It was not the store employees' failure, but, according to the company's policy, it still meant that there would be no bonus for anyone.

Mercadona had made a little over €500 million in profits that year, and paying the bonus would cost the company €190 million. For most companies, that would be a no-brainer. How can you pay out 38 percent of the year's earnings in employee bonuses? But it was obvious for the management committee at Mercadona that they *would* pay the full bonus to the 95 percent of employees who had met their individual goals.

It was obvious because it was the clear consequence of Mercadona's values and its prioritization of employees before investors. With those constraints, holding back on the bonuses — however sound the business case for doing so — simply wasn't an option. In fact, the economic disaster that, for others, would have justified withholding the bonus was, for Mercadona, a strong reason for paying it. For one thing, it was a way for Mercadona to reinforce its commitment to its values. For employees, values become real when they are tested under performance pressure. When a company sticks to its values during difficult times, employees believe those values. When a company doesn't, as we saw with Mari, employees know that its official values are not its real values. For another thing, Mercadona's store employees would really need their bonuses during such hard times. Finally, management knew that the following years would be even worse for Spain and for Mercadona's customers. The company knew it was going to need its employees' commitment more than ever. The principle of reciprocity mattered here: To be satisfied, one must first satisfy others.

Since the economy was still slow and earnings were lower, Mercadona had to look for other ways to cut costs and simultaneously increase sales. Under this constraint, Mercadona innovated in many ways to do exactly that. As we saw in the last chapter, these innovations ranged from small things such as reducing and eliminating duplicate labels on bottles of wine and oil (which saved €900,000 a year) to larger changes such as eliminating packaging for fruit and vegetables (which saved around €175 million a year) and reducing product variety. And as we saw, improvements such as these allowed Mercadona to cut prices by an astounding 10 percent in 2009, saving the average household €720 per year in grocery spending. At the same time as Mercadona cut prices, it increased its sales by 1 percent. At the end of 2009, the second year of the crisis, employees received €200 million in bonuses.

For Spain, things did indeed get worse in the following years. The country's gross domestic product continued shrinking until 2011 and then grew by only 0.7 percent that year.[12] During this period, Spain recorded the highest rate of unemployment in the European

Union — over 20 percent in 2011. Yet, during this same period, Mercadona kept growing and kept increasing its investment in its labor force.

At the end of 2010, Roig warned Mercadona's shareholders that 2011 was going to be another tough year, but by no means a year in which to back down from the company's investment in employees. Mercadona's investment in its employees is not only extraordinary by most standards but also continually growing. Wasn't it reasonable for the company to at least slow down or level off, if not actually cut back? Not in Roig's view. "Now more than ever," he explained in Mercadona's 2010 annual report, "we have to realize that the future of Spain is going to depend on the decisions we make and on how far we are willing to go to make good on our commitment. That is why our obligation as a company is to continue improving our productivity, to invest as much as necessary in our people so that we can have employees who lead and who make decisions and take risks in keeping with our business paradigm."

He meant it. In 2011, Mercadona opened 60 stores, created 6,500 new jobs in Spain, and gave €223 million in bonuses to its employees. These were not sacrifices of profit for the social good. Sales per square foot grew by 4 percent that year and overall sales grew by 8 percent. Mercadona continued capturing more market share from its competitors. The company made a €474 million profit (after taking out the bonuses) from sales of €17.8 billion. The employees had been the center of that success and had earned their bonuses.

In Mercadona's 2011 annual report, Roig stressed the importance of contributing to society *by improving productivity*:

> We believe that we must continue moving forward in our commitments as a company and that we have to contribute to generating wealth and employment. We have to do so by avoiding any hint of waste and concentrating on productivity, which must be the driving force behind the social and economic development of our country.

In his own terms, Roig was making it clear that operations are the backbone of the good jobs strategy.

Social Costs of the Bad Jobs Strategy

Juan Roig truly understands that excellence produced by combining investment in employees with smart operational decisions — the good jobs strategy — is not just good for Mercadona's employees, customers, and investors. It also contributes to the well-being of society.

Companies that choose the bad jobs strategy, on the other hand, not only make life hard for their employees, frustrate their customers, and miss out on a lot of money that could have gone to their investors, but they also contribute to a lot of unnecessary suffering in society.

When we as customers interact with other people who are not at their best and who are disengaged, it can bring us down or provoke us to be insensitive or hostile. I was recently with someone who was complaining about day care teachers. Because their work is so important, she expected much better of the teachers. She was shocked when I told her that an average day care teacher's pay is below the poverty threshold and that even the best-paid day care teachers generally make less than $30,000 a year.

And we all, whether or not we are customers of any particular business, pay a very tangible price. Many employees with low wages require government assistance, so we taxpayers are subsidizing the cost of bad jobs. When wages are so low and benefits are almost nonexistent, people rarely go to the doctor until it is too late. The results are expensive emergency room visits, bankruptcies brought on by seeking necessary treatment no matter what the cost, and illness and even death from untreated or insufficiently treated conditions.

Beyond all this, bad jobs are damaging to communities. Think about the effect of unpredictable schedules on families. It is hard for parents to find proper care for their young children or to get involved in their education when work schedules are erratic. The effect on an entire generation of kids who are not well parented can be disastrous. When a child's education gets off to a bad start, it can be very difficult or impossible for him or her to recover from that disadvantage. All this social harm comes back to bite business, as it becomes harder to find good employees, harder to find good customers, and harder to compete with companies in less socially damaged areas or in other countries.

Keep in mind that bad jobs are found well beyond the retail industry, so the harmful effects I am describing can be quite widespread.

Spreading the Good Jobs Strategy

Society as a whole would clearly benefit if more companies pursued the good jobs strategy. But the benefit to society is just the icing on the cake. Throughout this book, we have seen how companies, their customers, and their investors benefit from the good jobs strategy. In the right circumstances, it is a more profitable, more productive, and more innovative way to run a business.

I have described the key ingredients of the good jobs strategy so that more companies can adopt it. My focus was solely on what *companies* can — and should — do. That's what I've researched; that's what I teach. But the good jobs strategy would likely be pursued by more companies if the overall business environment did more to promote it and less to hinder it.

Investors, for instance, should have a better understanding of the interdependencies among operations, investment in employees, and long-term financial performance. Perhaps then they wouldn't take such a short-term view and influence managers to do things that are not in the firm's best long-term interests. Constraints forced by either governments or unions in the form of higher wages, better schedules, more training, and better working conditions could force companies to innovate operationally and encourage them to pursue the good jobs strategy. Customers, for their part, can vote with their feet.

Colleges and universities — particularly business schools — have a chance to contribute to an environment that supports and promotes the good jobs strategy. We can teach future leaders not just the tools and techniques of business but also how to use them in a way that does well by employees, customers, and investors at the same time. We can highlight the dangers of focusing on short-term profit maximization and encourage our students, both those who will run companies and those who will invest in them, to focus on creating long-term value.

We all have it in our power to help spread the good jobs strategy — as citizens, as businesspeople, as investors, as union leaders and union members, as customers, as academics, and as employees. In return, companies can increase their profits and growth in ways that create good jobs for more people. The good jobs strategy is difficult, but it is possible, profitable, and very much worth the effort.

Acknowledgments

THIS BOOK IS the product of over ten years of research. Much of it was conducted in the field working with companies, observing their processes, and collecting quantitative and qualitative data. During this period I interviewed hundreds of people — employees, managers, and executives — whose tales and insights showed me something so valuable that I had to write a book about it. All these people had many demands on their time, so I deeply appreciate their willingness to talk with me — and to speak so honestly. I am grateful, too, to all the companies and organizations that participated in my research and gave me access to their employees, members, and data.

Most of this research took place while I was a doctoral student and then an assistant professor at Harvard Business School. What amazing colleagues I had there! They taught me how to ask interesting research questions, conduct field research, and teach by the case method. In particular, I would like to thank Mike Beer, Kent Bowen, Jan Hammond, Bob Hayes, Tom Piper, Walter Salmon, Roy Shapiro, and Steve Wheelwright for the profound impact they had on my development as a scholar and teacher. Jan and Roy, an extra special thanks to you for being amazing mentors, always believing in the significance of my research, and pushing me to do better work every day. I would also like to thank Nitin Nohria for encouraging me to write this book. Finally, I had the opportunity at Harvard to work with the kind, talented, and capable Evgenia (Jenya) Eliseeva, who not only supported my teaching and research but also gets the credit for taking the photo for this book. Thank you, Jenya!

I wrote this book while working at MIT Sloan. From the start, I was excited about working with world-class researchers in my field. But I had no idea how generous and supportive those colleagues would be. In particular, I would like to thank Charlie Fine, Tom Kochan, Georgia Perakis, Don Rosenfield, and David Simchi-Levi for making MIT Sloan such a wonderful place for me. I feel blessed to work at an institution that gives me the opportunity to work part-time so that I can continue to do the work I love and at the same time enjoy my family. It is also great to work with colleagues who deeply respect and support that choice.

Writing this book proved to be more challenging than any other project I have worked on. I couldn't have done it without the help of two people: Barbara Feinberg and John Elder. I remember sitting at Barbara's dining room table two years ago, staring at all the papers and case studies I had written and wondering how I could ever tie it all together in a compelling way. Barbara not only helped me do that, but also was a constant source of motivation and enthusiasm. Whenever I felt stuck, I knew I could call her for help. Thank you, Barbara, for the key role you played in helping me "put the ducks in a row," tighten the argument in each chapter, and stay on track. And thank you for believing so much in the importance of the message that I wanted to convey and for reminding me of that when I sometimes wondered what I had gotten myself into.

John Elder tirelessly and patiently read and edited various drafts of this manuscript. I have been working with John for eight years and all I can say is that he's a masterful editor, a rare talent. He gets the big picture and helps communicate ideas clearly. At the same time, he attends to the smallest details, making each sentence tighter. John deeply understood where I wanted to go with this book and helped me get there as effectively as possible. Thank you, John, for your beautiful editing and for putting your heart into this project.

A great team at Amazon Publishing brought this book to market.

I especially want to thank David Moldawer for acquiring this book and Katie Salisbury for her editing, support, and patience throughout the process. Thank you, Katie, for the great ideas you gave me and for being so responsive to my preferences. It was truly a pleasure to work with you. I am also grateful to my literary agent, Carol Franco, who went above and beyond her duties as an agent and offered her help every step of the way. Thank you, Carol, for being so generous with your time. I benefitted greatly from your experience, thoughtfulness, and genuine interest in the topic. Thank you, my great friend Andrew McAfee, for introducing me to Carol and for guiding me through the publishing process.

When I finished the first draft, I shared it with several colleagues and executives in the field. José Alvarez, Chet Cadieux, Marshall Fisher, Jan Hammond, Tom Kochan, Rajiv Lal, and Doug Rauch all read the book within a few weeks and offered me feedback. These reviewers helped me frame some of the ideas better, pointed me to literature and examples that supported the points I was making, and asked great clarifying questions. The manuscripts I got back from José and Jan had almost every page marked with encouraging comments or opportunities for improvement. I am truly humbled by how generous they all have been with their time and thank them for helping make this book much better. I also want to thank Dennis Campbell. Chapter 10 was built up from many conversations with him about values-driven constraints.

I thank my MBA and executive education students at Harvard Business School and MIT Sloan. The ideas in this book were first tested in the classroom. My students pushed back when necessary, which helped me refine my thoughts and conclusions. My MBA students are a constant inspiration to me. I go to work every day knowing that I will spend time with people who will improve the world. I am confident that the companies they will someday lead will try harder to deliver value to their employees, customers, and investors all at the same time.

On a more personal note, I started working on this book when my husband and I were expecting our third child and finished writing it about two weeks before the birth of our fourth child. My family and close friends helped tremendously during this period. I feel incredibly lucky to live near David Ager, Andy Zelleke, and Dina Zelleke. We started as friends in graduate school but I now consider them my family in Boston. I am so grateful for their unwavering support and love. Apart from all this, these friends proved to be diligent and insightful readers who gave me wonderful feedback and were a great help to me in improving this book.

My in-laws and parents were also always there to help. Thank you, Mary Ellen and José Ignacio Gonzalez, for the amazing love you show for our family and for being the best in-laws I could ever have asked for. My parents, despite the thousands of miles between us, always make me feel like they are only a phone call away. My mom came and helped when our babies were born and my dad has patiently stayed with us several months for each of the last several years, helping us with the children during my busy teaching semesters. The values my parents instilled in me influence not only how I live my life and raise my children, but also how I conduct my research and teach. The voice in this book is the voice of Handan and Necmi Ton's daughter.

My parents also taught me the joy of sharing your work with your family. When I was growing up, my father coached basketball and my mother, my brother Ali, and I hardly ever missed his games. When our team won, we all celebrated, and when we lost, we were all sad together. It made us all closer. Being a professor is certainly not as cool as being a coach and doesn't lend itself to that type of sharing. But my older children, Ali (seven and a half) and Hakan (six), have both been to my classes and spoken in front of my students. I bet they know more about retail operations than any other kids their age. During the last two years, our bedtime conversations involved this book more than a few times. They even offered their help. When they saw me struggling to come up with a title, they came up with some titles of their own. Their favorite was *Throw Out the Bad Jobs and Throw In the Good Jobs*. You would have bought that book, wouldn't you? And they have been good students. They can certainly tell you which stores treat their employees well and which ones do not.

Ali, Hakan, their little sister Ela (16 months), and newborn brother Kerem make my life more meaningful and inspire me to help create a world where everyone is treated with respect and dignity.

Finally, I would like to thank the love of my life, my husband, Carlos. Writing a book eats up a lot of time, and time is scarce enough when you have small children. Carlos and I both knew that writing this book would come at the expense of our time together. Still, he not only encouraged me to write the book but also gave me support all through the process, discussing the content of every chapter, reading and offering feedback on each draft, saving me from a few mistakes, and giving me advice on how to get my message across to a nonacademic audience.

More importantly, Carlos has been the most wonderful husband. He's the type of person who makes life simpler, more joyous, and more interesting for people around him without even trying. Exactly fifteen years ago, when he came to Turkey to meet my family, my late grandmother (nene) said to me, "If he asks you to marry him, you make sure to answer 'yes.'" My nene did not even speak a common language with Carlos. Yet, like everyone else who meets him, she was immediately taken by his charm, kindness, and his sheer comfort in his own skin. Thank you, nenecim, for the advice. Marrying Carlos was the best thing that ever happened to me!

Notes

1. An Unnecessary Sacrifice

1. Paul Osterman and Beth Shulman, *Good Jobs America: Making Work Better for Everyone* (New York: Russell Sage Foundation, 2011). Working adults are those aged twenty-five to sixty-four.
2. Bureau of Labor and Statistics, Occupational Employment Statistics, 2012 and U.S. Census Bureau Poverty Thresholds, 2011.
3. Macro data on part-time employees come from research by Francis Carré of the University of Massachusetts, Boston, and Chris Tilly and Lauren D. Applebaum of UCLA, which was published by the UCLA Institute for Research on Labor and Employment, www.employmentpolicy.org/topic/23/research/competitive-strategies-and-worker-outcomes-us-retail-industry-1.
4. Arindrajit Dube and Ken Jacobs, "Hidden Cost of Wal-Mart Jobs: Use of Safety Net Programs by Wal-Mart Workers in California," UC Berkeley Institute for Research on Labor and Employment, Center for Labor Research and Education, August 2004, laborcenter.berkeley.edu/publiccosts/.
5. Democratic Staff of the U.S. House Committee on Education and the Workforce, "The Low-Wage Drag on Our Economy: Wal-Mart's Low Wages and Their Effect on Taxpayers and Economic Growth," United States House of Representatives, May 2013, democrats.edworkforce.house.gov/sites/democrats.edworkforce.house.gov/files/documents/WalMartReport-May2013.pdf.
6. A survey of 436 retail employees in New York City, for example, found that only 17 percent of them had set schedules and 70 percent of them knew their schedule only one week in advance. Luce Stephanie and Naoki Fujita, "Discounted Jobs: How Retailers Sell Workers Short," Retail Action Project, 2012, retailactionproject.org/wp-content/uploads/2012/01/FINAL_RAP.pdf.
7. The survey of New York City employees showed that over 40 percent of them had to be available sometimes, often, or always for on-call shifts; they were expected to call the store the morning of the shift or the night before to know if they were scheduled that day or the next.

8. Bureau and Labor Statistics, Current Population Survey, 2012.

9. Sarah Cassidy, "Supermarket staff live 'in poverty,'" *Independent* (London), January 19, 2012, www.independent.co.uk/news/business/news/supermarket-staff-live-in-poverty-6291599.html.

10. Osterman and Shulman, *Good Jobs America*. The statistics are from 2010.

11. Steven Greenhouse and Stephanie Rosenbloom, "Wal-Mart Settles 63 Lawsuits over Wages," *New York Times*, December 23, 2008, www.nytimes.com/2008/12/24/business/24walmart.html?_r=1&adxnnl=1&ref=stevengreenhouse&adxnnlx=1347116541-SBhg/tATyDyI8NIZCcTvAA.

12. Arindrajit Dube, T. William Lester, and Barry Eidlin, "Firm Entry and Wages: The Impact of Wal-Mart Growth on Earnings Throughout the Retail Sector," University of California, Berkeley Institute for Research on Labor and Employment, 2007. David Neumark, Junfu Zhang, and Stephen Ciccarella, "The Effects of Wal-Mart on Local Labor Markets" (Working Paper 11982, National Bureau of Economic Research, 2005).

13. A better comparison would have been with Sam's Club, but Sam's Club is part of Walmart.

14. Adi Ignatius, "We Had to Own the Mistakes, An Interview with Howard Schultz," *Harvard Business Review* 88, no. 7–8 (2010): 108–115.

15. This transformation is described in Paul Adler, "The 'Learning Bureaucracy': New United Motor Manufacturing," Draft 3.1, School of Business Administration, University of Southern California Los Angeles Working Paper, April 1992. The NUMMI plant operated successfully for more than two decades but ended up closing in 2010 after GM pulled out of the partnership with Toyota.

16. Researchers before me have observed the dependency between operations and investment in employees in other settings. I describe some of this research in chapter 2.

2. Great Operations Need Great People

1. Jose B. Alvarez, Zeynep Ton, and Ryan Johnson, "Home Depot and Interconnected Retail," Harvard Business School Case No. 9-512–036, March 2012.

2. Ibid.

3. Bernie Marcus and Arthur Blank, *Built from Scratch: How a Couple of Regular Guys Grew the Home Depot from Nothing to $30 Billion* (New York: Crown Business, 2001), 104.

4. Marcus and Blank, *Built from Scratch*, 115.

5. Alvarez, Ton, and Johnson, "Home Depot and Interconnected Retail."

6. Craig A. Shutt, "Safety Is No Accident at Home Depot," *Building Supply Home Centers* 158, no. 4 (April 1, 1990): 62. "OSHA Fines Home Depot for Violations in Employee Death," *National Home Center News*, August 22, 1994.

7. Alvarez, Ton, and Johnson, "Home Depot and Interconnected Retail."

8. At Walmart, for example, around 4 percent of the employees were reported to have a military background in 2006. Brian Grow, Diane Brady, and Michael Arndt, "Renovating Home Depot; Skip the Touchy-Feely Stuff," *BusinessWeek,* March 6, 2006.

9. Ibid.

10. The Toyota Production System has been studied by many researchers, including John Krafcik, John Paul MacDuffie, Jeffrey Liker, Steven Spear, and H. Kent Bowen.

11. Steven Spear and H. Kent Bowen, "Decoding the DNA of the Toyota Production System," *Harvard Business Review* 77, no. 5 (1999): 96–106.

12. Michael Dertouzos, Richard K. Lester, and Robert M. Solow, *Made in America: Regaining the Productive Edge* (New York: Harper Perennial, 1990).

13. C. Ichniowski, K. Shaw, and G. Prennushi, "The Effects of Human Resource Practices on Manufacturing Performance: A Study of Steel Finishing Lines," *American Economic Review* 87: 291–313.

14. J. P. MacDuffie, "Human Resource Bundles and Manufacturing Performance: Organizational Logic and Flexible Production Systems in the World Auto Industry," *Industrial and Labor Relations Review* 48, no. 2 (1995): 173–88.

15. R. Batt, "Work Design, Technology and Performance in Customer Service and Sales," *Industrial and Labor Relations Review* 52, no. 4 (1999): 539–64.

16. J. H. Gittell, *The Southwest Airlines Way: Using the Power of Relationships to Achieve High Performance* (New York: McGraw-Hill, 2001).

17. O. C. Richard and N. B. Johnson, "High Performance Work Practices and Human Resource Management Effectiveness: Substitutes or Complements?" *Journal of Business Strategy* 21, no. 2 (2004): 133–48.

18. J. H. Gittell, R. Seidner, and J. Wimbush, "A Relational Model of How High Performance Work Systems Work," *Organization Science* 21, no. 2 (2010): 490–506.

19. Thomas Bailey and Annette Bernhardt, "In Search of the High Road in a Low-Wage Industry," *Politics and Society* 25, no. 2 (1997): 179–201. Bureau of Labor Statistics, Occupational Employment Statistics, 2011.

20. Bureau of Labor Statistics Occupational Employment and Wages, May 2012, www.bls .gov/news.release/ocwage.htm.

3. The Penalties of Going Cheap on Retail Labor

1. Marshall Fisher, Jayanth Krishnan, and Serguei Netessine, "Retail Store Execution: An Empirical Study," The Wharton School, University of Pennsylvania Working Paper, 2006.

2. IBM/A. T. Kearney for the Grocery Manufacturers of America, "A Balanced Perspective: EPC/RFID Implementation in the CPG Industry," p. 14, http://www.globalscorecard .net/live/download/BalancedPerspective.pdf.

3. Renee Dudley, "Wal-Mart Customers Complain Bare Shelves are Widespread," Bloomberg.com, April 2, 2013, www.bloomberg.com/news/2013-04-02/wal-mart-customers-complain-bare-shelves-are-widespread.html.

4. "Best and Worst Supermarkets," *Consumer Reports Magazine*, May 2012, www.consumer reports.org/cro/magazine/2012/04/best-worst-supermarkets/index.htm#ratings.

5. Zeynep Ton, "The Role of Store Execution in Managing Product Availability" (DBA dissertation, Harvard Business School, 2002).

6. James Tenser, "In-Store Implementation: Current Status and Future Solutions" (ISI Sharegroup Working Paper, April 14, 2008).

7. B. Hardgrave, M. Waller, and R. Miller, "Does RFID Reduce Out of Stocks? A Preliminary Analysis" (white paper, Information Technology Research Institute, Sam M. Walton College of Business, University of Arkansas, 2005).

8. See, for example, Erik Brynjolfsson and Lorin M. Hitt, "Computing Productivity: Firm-

Level Evidence" (MIT Sloan Working Paper No. 4210-01, 2003); Adam S. Litwin, "Technological Change at Work: The Impact of Employee Involvement on the Effectiveness of Health Information Technology," *Industrial and Labor Relations Review* 64, no. 5 (2011): 863–88.

9. Rob Garf and Fenella Sirkisoon, "Bridging the Merchandising Store Operations Divide," AMR Research, Retail Strategies Report, December 2007. http://www.cisco.com/web/strategy/docs/retail/AMR_Bridging_Merchandising_Store_Ops.pdf.

10. DeHoratius's findings are reported in Ananth Raman, Nicole DeHoratius, and Zeynep Ton, "Execution: The Missing Link in Retail Operations," *California Management Review* 43, no. 3 (2001): 136–52.

11. This anecdotal evidence is taken from: Nicole DeHoratius and Zeynep Ton, "The Role of Execution in Managing Product Availability," in *Retail Supply Chain Management*, ed. Narendra Agrawal and Stephen Smith, International Series in Operations Research and Management (Springer, 2008).

12. Clara Xiaoling Chen and Tatiana Sandino, "Can Wages Buy Honesty? The Relationship Between Relative Wages and Employee Theft," *Journal of Accounting Research* 50, no. 4 (2012): 967–1000.

13. Marshall Fisher and Ananth Raman, *The New Science of Retailing: How Analytics are Transforming the Supply Chain and Improving Performance* (Boston: Harvard Business Press, 2010), 159.

14. An expert report by the MIT Sloan management scholar Thomas Kochan, "Evaluation of Wal-Mart's Performance Management, Incentive, and Control Systems and Their Relation to Unpaid Work Of Hourly Associates," which concerns the lawsuit brought by "Nancy Hall, on behalf of herself and all others similarly situated v. Wal-Mart Stores Inc. and Sam's West, Inc.," highlights how the combination of performance management systems that encourage managers to cut labor costs and a lack of similar systems for compliance with employment policies and regulations contributes to off-the-clock work at Walmart stores.

4. Model Retailers: Who Knew It Could Be This Good?

1. "The Future of Fast Fashion," *The Economist*, June 16, 2005.

2. "Entrevista: Juan Roig," *Instituto de la Empresa Familiar Magazine*, no. 26 (Second Quarter, 2006).

3. According to the Ministry of Employment and Social Security in Spain, in 2012 the minimum wage in Spain was €7,696 per year. http://www.empleo.gob.es/es/informacion/smi/contenidos/evolucion.htm.

4. This policy was put to the test in 2008, the first year of the global financial crisis and the first time in thirteen years that Mercadona had not reached its sales targets. We'll see in chapter 10 how the company met this challenge.

5. Mercadona 2012 Annual Report.

6. Let me make it clear that not every employee working at these chains makes enough to support a family. For high school or college students who cannot work full-time, and for those looking for a supplemental income, these retailers provide just that: part-time jobs and supplemental income.

7. Brad Stone, "Costco CEO Craig Jelinek Leads the Cheapest, Happiest Company in

the World," *Bloomberg Businessweek,* June 6, 2013, www.businessweek.com/articles/2013-06-06/costco-ceo-craig-jelinek-leads-the-cheapest-happiest-company-in-the-world.

8. The exact hours may differ from store to store.

9. The information in this paragraph was collected through interviews with current and former Trader Joe's employees. Salary data gathered through interviews are consistent with data from Glassdoor, a popular online community in which people anonymously provide information about their jobs.

10. Michelle V. Rafter, "Welcome to the Club," *Workforce Management* 84, no. 4 (2005).

11. These data were reported in glassdoor.com on August 28, 2012. The number of employees who responded from each store was 480 from Costco, 76 from QuikTrip, and 199 from Trader Joe's.

12. Cheapism.com found that while Costco was 3.6 percent cheaper for groceries, there were other categories, such as office products, for which Sam's club was cheaper (www.cheapism.com/sams-or-costco).

13. "Retail, Where to Find Cheaper Prices in Spain," *Green Med Journal,* June 1, 2010, www.greenmed.eu/news-353.html.

14. See, for example, www.themadhapa.com/2012/04/is-trader-joes-cheaper-or-more.html.

15. Angel Abcede and Melissa Vonder Haar, "What Mystery Shoppers Think," *CSP Magazine,* August 2012, pp. 53–62, http://www.cspnet.com/sites/default/files/magazine/article/pdf/CoverStory2_CSP_0812.pdf.

16. "Best and Worst Supermarkets," *Consumer Reports Magazine,* May 2012, www.consumerreports.org/cro/magazine/2012/04/best-worst-supermarkets/index.htm#ratings.

17. Wegmans is not, however, a model retailer in this book's terms because it is not strictly a low-cost retailer. Its stores carry a mix of low-priced items — especially those products that are used the most by families — and premium products such as the restaurant-quality entrées at its Market Cafés and the French pastries at its Patisseries.

18. As mentioned in chapter 1, a better comparison would have been with Sam's Club, but Sam's Club is part of Walmart. Costco's other major competitor, BJ's, is now owned by private equity firms.

19. These data are calculated from Costco's and Wal-Mart's 2010 annual reports. Costco's sales were $76.2 billion and its total operating space was 77.3 million square feet, leading to $986 of sales per square feet. Sam's Club's sales were $46.7 billion and its total space was 79.4 million square feet, leading to $588 of sales per square feet.

20. Wayne F. Cascio, "Decency Means More than 'Always Low Prices': A Comparison of Costco to Wal-Mart's Sam's Club," *Academy of Management Perspectives* 20, no. 3 (2006): 26–37.

21. Costco's and Walmart's inventory turnover performance was calculated using the companies' financial statements. Inventory turnover for the industry is from Vishal Gaur, Marshall Fisher, and Ananth Raman, "An Econometric Analysis of Inventory Turnover Performance in Retail Stores," *Management Science* 51, no. 2 (2005): 181–94.

22. Data for U.S. supermarkets come from the Food Marketing Institute (www.fmi.org/facts_figs/?fuseaction=superfact). Data for Trader Joe's come from a speech by Trader Joe's former CEO John Shields at California Lutheran University on November 9, 2010, for the Corporate Leaders Breakfast Series. (The speech may be found online at www.youtube.com/watch?v=roOy8NsRyUM), and Beth Kowitt, "Inside the Secret World of Trader Joe's," *Fortune,* August 23, 2010, money.cnn.com/2010/08/20/news/companies/

inside_trader_joes_full_version.fortune/index.htm. Data for Mercadona come from Zeynep Ton and Simon Harrow, "Mercadona," Harvard Business School Case No. 610089, 2010.

23. The data for QuikTrip come from Zeynep Ton, "QuikTrip," Harvard Business School Case No. 611045, 2011.

24. Checkpoint, "The Global Retail Theft Barometer 2010. The Worldwide Shrinkage Survey," Centre for Retail Research, 2010, http://www.globalretailtheftbarometer.com/pdf/GRTB_2010.pdf.

25. http://www.workforce.com/articles/welcome-to-the-club.

5. Offer Less

1. Steve Martinez, *The U.S. Food Marketing System: Recent Developments 1997–2006.* (Washington, DC: Economic Research Service, U.S. Department of Agriculture, ERR-42, 2007).

2. Daniel Cortsen, Thomas Gruen, and Sundar Bharadwaj, "Retail Out-of-Stocks: A Worldwide Examination of Extent, Causes, and Consumer Responses" (research study conducted at Emory University, Goizueta Business School; University of St. Gallen, Institute of Technology Management; and College of Business and Administration, University of Colorado at Colorado Springs 2002.

3. Ibid.

4. Dana Gunders, "Wasted: How America Is Losing Up to 40 Percent of Its Food from Farm to Fork to Landfill," Natural Resources Defense Council 2012.

5. Jean C. Buzby, Jeffrey Hyman, Hayden Stewart, and Hodan F. Wells, "The Value of Retail- and Consumer-Level Fruit and Vegetable Losses in the United States," *Journal of Consumer Affairs,* Fall 2011, 492–515.

6. Ellen Byron, "Whitens, Brightens and Confuses" *Wall Street Journal,* February 23, 2011, D1.

7. Zeynep Ton and Ananth Raman, "The Effect of Product Variety and Inventory Levels on Sales: A Longitudinal Study," *Production and Operations Management* 19, no. 5 (2010): 546–60.

8. See, for example, J. P. MacDuffie, K. Sethuraman, and M. L. Fisher, "Product Variety and Manufacturing Performance: Evidence from the International Automotive Assembly Plant Study," *Management Science* 42, no. 3 (1996): 350–69; and M. L. Fisher and C. D. Ittner, "The Impact of Product Variety on Automobile Assembly Operations: Empirical Evidence and Simulation Analysis," *Management Science* 45, no. 6 (1999): 771–86.

9. Sandelman & Associates, Inc. consistently places In-N-Out in its Fast Foods Awards of Excellence. The awards are based on surveys from users. In 2012, for example, In-N-Out ranked third in a survey that gathered information about 1.4 million fast-food visits by more than 110,000 customers in over 90 U.S. media markets.

10. In 2013, In-N-Out was ranked ninth in Glassdoor's best-place-to-work awards, just two rankings below Google. The wages, starting at $10 per hour, are among the highest in its industry. In-N-Out offers benefits to full-time and part-time employees and extensive training. All store managers are promoted from within.

11. Mark Gottfredson and Keith Aspinal, "Innovation Versus Complexity: What Is Too

Much of a Good Thing?," *Harvard Business Review* 83, no. 11 (2005): 62–73.

12. Tom Searcy and Henry DeVries, "In-N-Out Burger Suitors Need to Take Fear Off the Table," *Forbes Online*, February 19, 2013, www.forbes.com/sites/dealmakers/2013/02/19/in-n-out-burger-suitors-need-to-take-fear-off-the-table/.

13. Ton and Raman, "The Effect of Product Variety and Inventory Levels on Sales."

14. Cortsen, Gruen, and Bharadwaj, "Retail Out-of-Stocks."

15. Trader Joe's website: http://www.traderjoes.com/about/general-faq.asp, accessed January 12, 2013.

16. I thank my students Alexander Chang, Nicholas Holda, Allison Katz-Mayfield, Jit Hin Tan, and Mandy Yeung for sharing this script with me.

17. Inventory turnover for food stores is reported in Vishal Gaur, Marshall Fisher, and Ananth Raman, "An Econometric Analysis of Inventory Turnover Performance in Retail Stores," *Management Science* 51, no. 2 (2005): 181–94. Inventory turnover for Trader Joe's comes from a speech by John Shields, former CEO of Trader Joe's, at California Lutheran University on November 9, 2010, for the Corporate Leaders Breakfast Series, www.youtube.com/watch?v=r0Oy8NsRyUM.

18. Ilan Brat, Ellen Byron, and Ann Zimmerman, "Retailers Cut Back on Variety, Once the Spice of Marketing," *Wall Street Journal*, June 26, 2009, A1, http://online.wsj.com/article/SB124597382334357329.html.

19. Gogoi Pallavi, "Walmart's 'Project Impact' Craters Sales, but the Retailer Persists," *Daily Finance*, March 31, 2010, www.dailyfinance.com/2010/03/31/walmarts-project-impact-leaves-a-crater-in-sales-but-the-ret/.

20. James Lardner, "Building a Customer-Centric Company," *Business 2.0*, July 10, 2001, 55–59.

21. J. P. MacDuffie, "Human Resource Bundles and Manufacturing Performance: Organizational Logic and Flexible Production Systems in the World Auto Industry," *Industrial and Labor Relations Review* 48: 173–88.

6. Standardize and Empower

1. Timothy Walch, *Uncommon Americans: The Lives and Legacies of Herbert and Lou Henry Hoover* (Westport, CT: Praeger, 2003), 251.

2. Frederick Winslow Taylor, *The Principles of Scientific Management* (Atlanta: Engineering and Management Press, 1998 [1911]), 5.

3. As Wallace Hopp and Mark L. Spearman describe in *Factory Physics* (second edition, New York: McGraw Hill, 2001, 31–32), Taylor's scientific management has been criticized as being far from scientific and merely an advocacy. His work-measurement studies were thought to be carelessly done and there was little evidence of using any scientific criteria for selecting workers.

4. Theodore Levitt, "Production-Line Approach to Aervices," *Harvard Business Review* 50, no. 4 (1972): 41–52.

5. John H. Fleming and Jim Asplund, *Human Sigma: Managing the Employee-Customer Encounter* (New York: Gallup Press, 2007), 189.

6. Knowledge@Wharton, "Call Centers: How to Reduce Burnout, Increase Efficiency," June 16, 2004, http://knowledge.wharton.upenn.edu/article.cfm?articleid=997.

7. Fleming and Asplund, *Human Sigma*, 46.

8. Tony Hsieh, *Delivering Happiness: A Path to Profits, Passion, and Purpose* (New York: Business Plus, 2010), 145.

9. Content on Affinity Plus is based on Dennis Campbell, "Employee Selection as a Control System," *Journal of Accounting Research* 50, no. 4 (2012): 931–66; and Dennis Campbell and Peter Tufano, "Affinity Plus (A)," Harvard Business School Case No. 9-209-026, 2012.

10. Zeynep Ton and Robert S. Huckman, "Managing the Impact of Employee Turnover on Performance: The Role of Process Conformance," *Organization Science* 19, no. 1 (2008): 56–68.

11. Bowen and Lawler, for example, argue that businesses that have (a) a high-volume, low-cost strategy, (b) a predictable environment, (c) a transactional tie to the customer, (d) routine, simple technology, and (e) employees with weak interpersonal skills and little need for growth should use standardization. They call this the production-line approach. See Bowen and Lawler, "The Empowerment of Service Workers: What, Why, How, and When," *Sloan Management Review* 33, no. 3 (Spring 1992): 31–39.

12. Roger Hallowell, David Bowen, and Carin-Isabel Knoop, "Four Seasons Goes to Paris: 53 Properties, 24 Countries, 1 Philosophy," Harvard Business School Case No. 9-803-069, 2003.

13. Alex Frankel, *Punching In: The Unauthorized Adventures of a Frontline Employee* (New York: Collins, 2007), 205.

14. Chester Cadieux, *From Lucky to Smart: Leadership Lessons from QuikTrip* (Tulsa: Mullerhaus, 2008), 87.

15. Campbell, "Employee Selection as a Control System."

16. J. L. Heskett, T. O. Jones, G. W. Loveman, W. Earl Sasser, and L. A. Schlesinger, "Putting the Service-Profit Chain to Work," *Harvard Business Review* 72, no. 2 (1994): 164–174. R. M. Fernandez, E. Castilla, and P. Moore, "Social Capital at Work: Networks and Employment at a Phone Center," *American Journal of Sociology* 105, no. 5 (2000): 1288–1356.

7. Cross-Train

1. Earl Sasser, "Match Supply and Demand in Service Industries," *Harvard Business Review* 54, no. 6 (1976): 132–38.

2. Frances Frei and Anne Morris's book *Uncommon Service: How to Win by Putting Customers at the Core of Your Business* (Boston: Harvard Business Review Press, 2012) offers an excellent discussion of how companies can use customers as operators in service operations.

3. Anika Anand, "Major Grocer Getting Rid of Self-Checkout Lanes," NBC News, July 20, 2011, www.msnbc.msn.com/id/43687085/ns/business-retail/t/major-grocer-getting-rid-self-checkout-lanes#.UPnKFegtqtc.

4. Kris Maher, "Wal-Mart Seeks New Flexibility in Worker Shifts," *Wall Street Journal*, January 3, 2007, A1.

5. David Simchi-Levi's book *Operations Rules: Delivering Customer Value through Flexible Operations* (Boston: MIT Press, 2010) offers a great discussion of the benefits of cross-training in manufacturing.

6. Richard J. Hackman and Greg R. Oldham, *Work Redesign* (Reading, MA: Addison-Wesley, 1980).

7. The content of this paragraph is based on James L. Heskett, "Southwest Airlines 2002: An Industry Under Siege," Harvard Business School Case No. 9-803-133, 2003, 9.

8. Operate with Slack

1. The logic I am using here is the same logic used for managing inventory of products that last for only a specific period, that have uncertain demand, and for which there is only one opportunity to decide how many units to order for a particular period. This problem is called the "newsvendor problem."
2. Marshall Fisher, "Retail Rage," HBR Blog Network, http://blogs.hbr.org/cs/2012/01/retail_rage.html.
3. Ananth Raman and Zeynep Ton, "Operational Execution at Arrow Electronics," Harvard Business School Case No. 603–127, 2003.
4. That's not to say that QuikTrip never fires anyone. The CEO told me that the company never hesitates to fire people if it is convinced that they are not performing well enough for QuikTrip. What the company *does not* do is lay people off to reduce head count.
5. Paul Adler, "The 'Learning Bureaucracy': New United Motor Manufacturing," Draft 3.1, School of Business Administration, University of Southern California Los Angeles Working Paper, April 1992, 16.
6. Mark Graban describes this approach in his LeanBlog with a post titled "To Layoff or Not To Layoff—That Really Is a Question," on December 12, 2008: www.leanblog.org/2008/12/to-layoff-or-not-to-layoff-that-really/.

9. Seizing Strategic Opportunities

1. John Shields described this in a talk he gave at California Lutheran University on November 9, 2010, for the Corporate Leaders Breakfast Series (www.youtube.com/watch?v=roOy8NsRyUM).
2. Mike Brewster and Frederick Dalzell, *Driving Change, the UPS Approach to Business* (New York: Hyperion, 2007), 21.
3. http://www.ups.com/content/us/en/about/facts/worldwide.html, accessed May 1, 2013.
4. The material on Frito-Lay comes from Janice Hammond, "Frito-Lay: The Backhaul Decision," Harvard Business School Case No. 9-688-104, September 25, 1992.
5. Deborah Ball and Ilan Brat, "Spanish Supermarket Chain Finds Recipe," *Wall Street Journal,* October 23 2012, http://online.wsj.com/article/SB10000872396390444592704578066803363005258.html.
6. Reader response to Sophie Quinton, "The Trader Joe's Lesson: How to Pay a Living Wage and Still Make Money in Retail," *The Atlantic*, March 25, 2013, www.theatlantic.com/business/archive/2013/03/the-trader-joes-lesson-how-to-pay-a-living-wage-and-still-make-money-in-retail/274322/.
7. The story here is based on Barbara Glance's description: http://lets-inspire.blogspot.com/2009/03/johnny-bagger-written-by-ken-blanchard.html.

10. Values and Constraints

1. Steven Greenhouse, "How Costco Became the Anti-Wal-Mart," *New York Times,* July 17, 2005, www.nytimes.com/2005/07/17/business/yourmoney/17costco.html?pagewanted= all&_r=0, accessed April 4, 2013.

2. Julia Kirby, "Reinvention with Respect: An Interview with Jim Kelly of UPS," *Harvard Business Review* (2001): 116–123.

3. Morgan Housel, "Charlie Munger's Love Affair with Costco," MSN Money, July 7, 2011, http://money.msn.com/investment-advice/article.aspx?post=7f0e084a-3473-41cc-b7e9-f4353e0deeb3&ucsort=3.

4. Jody Hoffer Gittell, Kim Cameron, Sandy Lim, and Victor Rivas, "Relationships, Layoffs, and Organizational Resilience: Airline Industry Responses to September 11," *Journal of Behavioral Science* 42, no. 3 (2006): 300–329.

5. Melanie Trottman, "Southwest Airlines Considers Cutbacks, Halts Delivery of Planes From Boeing," *Wall Street Journal,* September 21, 2001, A4.

6. Jennifer Reingold, "Southwest's Herb Kelleher: Still Crazy After All These Years," *Fortune,* January 14, 2013.

7. Note that the key stakeholders can vary from company to company. Apart from employees, customers, and investors, key stakeholders could include suppliers, the community, the environment, the government (and possibly foreign governments), researchers, and others.

8. Adi Ignatius and Jeff Bezos, "Jeff Bezos on Leading for the Long-Term at Amazon," *HBR IdeaCast,* January 3, 2013, http://blogs.hbr.org/ideacast/2013/01/jeff-bezos-on-leading-for-the.html.

9. Ibid.

10. Southwest 2001 annual report.

11. Marissa Ann Mayer, "Creativity Loves Constraints," *BusinessWeek,* February 12, 2006, 102.

12. World Bank: http://data.worldbank.org/indicator/NY.GDP.MKTP.KD.ZG.

Index

Page numbers for figures are in italic type

About the Author

Zeynep Ton is an adjunct associate professor at the MIT Sloan School of Management. Previously, she was on the faculty of the Harvard Business School. She has received a number of awards for teaching excellence from both schools, and her research has been featured widely in the media, including the *Atlantic*, *The New Yorker*, the *Washington Post*, Bloomberg TV, and MSNBC. She lives in Cambridge, Massachusetts, with her husband and four children.